Aug 12, 2000

Joe Buchanan —

May we never forget
the War Dog of Vietnam.

Dog Tags of Courage

The Turmoil of War and the Rewards of Companionship

John C. Burnam

LOST~~~
COAST
Fort Bragg
California

Lost Coast Press
155 Cypress Street
Fort Bragg, CA 95437
(707) 964-9520

Contact the author at http://www.dogtagsofcourage.com

Burnam, John C.
    Dog tags of courage : the turmoil of war and
the rewards of companionship / John C. Burnam.
    p. cm.
    LCCN 99-73668
    ISBN 1-882897-42-0

    1. Burnam, John C. 2. Vietnamese Conflict,
1961-1975--Personal narratives, American. 3. Dogs
--War use. 4. German shepherd dog. I. Title.

DS559.5.B67 2000   959.704'3'092
                QBI99-1671

Cover design by Christian Musson

Book production by Cypress House
http://www.cypresshouse.com

Printed in the United States of America
First edition
10 9 8 7 6 5 4 3 2

Dedication

This book is dedicated to the exceptionally brave and loyal war dogs and their handlers and to all the men and women who lost their lives in Vietnam; to every military servicemen who was wounded in action, but found the strength to carry on; and to every dog lover who shares in my grief over those war dogs we were forced to abandon in the Republic of Vietnam.

Let us not forget our servicemen still missing in action (MIA) or prisoners of war (POW).

Acknowledgments

I could not have written this book without the support, advice, and friendship of many people. I would like to express my gratitude to Mark Hart and his family for locating my Vietnam friend, Kenneth L. Mook, after twenty five years; to Kenneth L. Mook whose reunion with me inspired this book; to Dan Scott, Oliver Whetstone, and Michael McClellen, former German shepherd scout dog handlers of the 44th Scout Dog Platoon in Vietnam, whose advice and friendship gave me guidance and the determination to see this project through; to my editors, Beth Berry and Linda Anderson, who helped me to become a better writer; and finally to my daughter, Jennifer, who needed a clearer understanding of what life was like for me when I was nineteen years old.

FOREWORD

W e celebrate the heroes of World War I and World War II, but Vietnam also produced numerous heroes. More than 50,000 American lives were lost in Vietnam, there were thousands of POWs and MIAs, and countless thousands wounded in action. But, make no mistake about it, thousands more would have been wounded and killed, or become imprisoned and lost had it not been for the use of German shepherds for scouting, sentry, and patrolling, and Labrador retrievers for tracking.

The primary dog breed used during the Vietnam conflict was the German shepherd. Their natural abilities made them the breed of choice for the difficult and dangerous job of jungle warfare. Because of their uncanny abilities, German shepherd war dogs were able to detect the scent in the wind blowing over land mines, trip-wired booby traps, the slightest movement of an enemy sniper hundreds of yards away, and even the body odors of the enemy hiding in underground tunnels.

John Burnam's unforgettable account of his intrepid experiences as a nineteen-year-old combat infantryman who served as rifleman with the 1st Air Cavalry Division and as scout dog handler with the 44th Scout Dog Platoon is a gripping and powerful saga. *Dog Tags of Courage* is a superbly written testimonial to the strength and courage of America's teenage soldiers and the heroics of the war dog teams during the Vietnam Conflict, one of the most unpopular wars of the twentieth century.

Are these young American men and their war dogs heroes? Yes, they are! The tragedy is that America classified these animals as equipment and ordered their handlers to abandon them when they pulled out of Vietnam. Their recognition is long overdue, but now the Vietnam War Dogs' story is out.

Whether you are a war veteran, a family member of a military service person, a military historian, a college student, or just a plain old dog lover, you will discover the true meaning of brotherhood and the power of canine companionship in this must-read book.

The members of the United Shutzhund Cubs of America are carrying on the hundred-year-old historical legacy of the great German shepherd working dogs.

Michael A. Hamilton, President,
United Shutzhund Clubs of America
July, 1999

Table of Contents

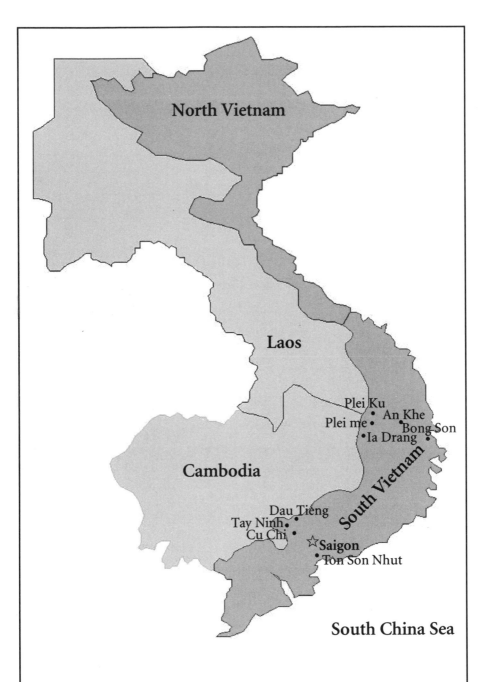

North Vietnam

Laos

Plei Ku
An Khe
Plei me
Bong Son
Ia Drang

Cambodia

South Vietnam

Dau Tieng
Tay Ninh
Cu Chi
Saigon
Ton Son Nhut

South China Sea

This map depicts the primary locations where the author performed combat missions as an infantryman and German shepherd scout dog handler in South Vietnam, 1966–1968.

Preface

I am proud to have served my country in Vietnam from March 1966 to March 1968. As a nineteen-year-old, I went on my first Vietnam tour with other young combat infantrymen. My life depended on a combination of basic military training, streetwise instincts, luck, and the men around me. At times, I begged for heaven, while my jungle boots ground me into hell. In that war, I learned the significance of the word *brotherhood*.

Before my second tour in Vietnam, I trained and patrolled with a German shepherd sentry dog named Hans. When I arrived in Vietnam for the second time, I served as a German shepherd scout dog handler. I led combat infantry patrols from behind the leash of magnificent scout dogs named Timber and Clipper. My life depended on how effectively I read the dog's natural reactions and alerts to danger. I came to know the truth of the saying: *A dog is man's best friend.*

Because of my U.S. Army military service, I received a Combat Infantry Badge, Paratrooper Wings, a Purple Heart Medal, a Bronze Star Medal, an Air Medal, a Vietnamese Cross of Gallantry Ribbon, a Legion of Merit Medal, two Meritorious Service Medals, an Army Achievement Medal, and a personal Letter of Appreciation from the former President of United States, Jimmy Carter.

Approximately 10,000 war dog handlers and 4,000 war dogs served in Vietnam. They were an important segment of the several million American and allied men and women, who rotated in and out of that country between 1965-1975.

German shepherds became the dogs of choice for military scouting and sentry duty. Labrador retrievers were selected for tracking. These two breeds, well-suited because of their accommodating dispositions, displayed an ability to work with multiple handlers. They train easily, and adapt to variable climates, terrains, and environments.

Each war dog's ear was branded with a four-character, alpha-numeric service number to make the dogs identifiable and to account for their whereabouts. The dogs had official military service and medical records established and maintained for them. These military records followed the dogs, as they progressed through training and service in the United States military.

We gained a grudging respect for our enemy, the Viet Cong, or Charlie, as we called these fierce and savvy warriors. They constantly surprised us with their hit-and-run tactics. During the Vietnam war, the Viet Cong (VC) inflicted thousands of casualties on American and allied soldiers. They destroyed tons of war equipment worth billions of dollars. The VC, adept at hiding invisibly under cover of neatly camouflaged positions and base camps, were exceptionally difficult to find or surprise.

Courageous, well-trained war dog teams were called on to counteract the success of the hit-and-run tactics of the enemy. Their deployment in Vietnam dramatically improved the infantrymen's ability to search, locate, engage, and eradicate enemy forces. War dogs saved thousands of lives and significantly reduced the enemies capacity to surprise and inflict casualties, or destroy equipment. Due to the extraordinary success of the war dog teams walking point, tracking, or guarding, the Viet Cong placed price tags on their heads and used a variety of methods to try to eliminate them.

The following are the various types of K-9 units that supported the Army, Air Force, Navy, and Marine Corps in South Vietnam:

1. *Infantry Platoon Scout Dogs (IPSD):* A handler and a German shepherd teamed together with the mission of leading combat patrols and providing early silent warnings. They were the "pointman," the most vulnerable and dangerous position of a tactical combat formation. Scout dogs detected enemy movement, booby traps, land mines, base camps,

and searched tunnels. The U.S. Army had the highest number of scout dog units deployed throughout South Vietnam and consequently suffered the most casualties. Fort Benning and Fort Gordon, Georgia were the primary training centers. Upon graduation, entire classes were formed into K-9 units, fully equipped, and shipped to Vietnam for service. Veterinarian technicians were also assigned to K-9 units for medical support.

2. *Combat Tracker Teams (CTT):* Labrador retrievers tracked the enemy's scent or blood trails after contact had been broken. A combat tracker team consisted of a dog handler, cover man, visual tracker, and a team leader. The dog handler concentrated on the tracker dog for signs of danger. The Labrador's naturally heightened ground-scent instincts could be relied upon. The team was equipped with a radio for communication and support. Combat Tracker Teams were highly effective in locating of the enemy, including wounded and dead American soldiers in all types of weather and terrain conditions. Combat Tracker Teams received most of their training in Malaysia at the British Jungle Warfare School(JWS).

3. *Sentry Dog Teams:* German shepherds were very effective in defending aircraft, airfields, supply depots, ammunition dumps, defensive perimeters, and many other strategic military facilities throughout South Vietnam. Sentry dog teams were usually deployed as the first line of defense and patrolled mostly at night. Sentry dog handlers received their initial training at Lackland Air Force base in San Antonio, Texas.

4. *Patrol Dog Teams:* A handler and his German shepherd dog were deployed to patrol and protect air bases. The patrol team normally operated along the perimeter and many times outside the wire. Patrol teams were trained to track, search buildings, and attack. Often times, they rode in jeeps with law enforcement officers and assisted as required. The patrol dog teams proved to be very effective in Vietnam.

5. *Mine, Booby trap and Tunnel Dog Teams:* A German shepherd and his handler were generally deployed with infantry and combat engineering units. They were trained to detect mines, boobytraps, search enemy

tunnel complexes, and search Vietnamese hamlets and other populated communities for hidden enemy caches of arms, ammunition, and other war supplies. Their deployment successfully reduced the enemy supply of hidden war material.

6. *Water Dog Team:* The Navy successfully used war dogs on patrol boats to track the scent of enemy divers underwater throughout the waterways of South Vietnam. They proved to be quite successful in saving lives and equipment as well as reducing the enemies ability to conduct underwater operations.

If a war dog handler was killed, wounded, injured, or lucky enough to complete his twelve-month tour of duty in Vietnam, his dog was reassigned to another handler. In what turned out to be a tragic decision, the U. S. Defense Department designated war dogs as military surplus equipment. Their mission was to serve in Vietnam, until they died in combat, were overcome by disease, or became the victims of some other unfortunate circumstance. They weren't expected to die of old age. When men had to say good-bye to their dogs and best friends, this parting brought on deeply felt emotions and tears.

When the military ground forces pulled out of Vietnam, the K-9 units were instructed, despite the heated protests of the dog handlers, to abandon several thousand heroic four-footed soldiers. Official military records show that fewer than 200 war dogs reached American soil after the war in Vietnam. No one knows how many war dogs, if any, may have been smuggled out of Vietnam by their handlers. The rest of these brave animals were either euthanized or turned over to the South Vietnamese Army, which meant that most likely, according to Vietnamese cultural practices, the dogs could be slaughtered for food.

When Hans, Timber, Clipper, and the rest of their special breed died in Vietnam, no one held a twenty-one-gun salute, no military burial ceremony was performed, no white cross marked their grave sites, and to this day, the U.S. government has not given them any special recognition in honor of their courageous military service.

While writing this book, I often became tearful when I touched upon deeply-rooted emotions as I recalled vivid details about life, truth, death, and the shear bloody horror of the combat situations I'd encountered in Vietnam. In the pages that follow, I've tried to describe my experiences from an infantryman's viewpoint, an ant's-eye view, and not from a command, strategic, or politically motivated perspective.

I've made my story as historically accurate as I could, but it's based on my own perspective from personal notes, recollections, letters home, military documents, paraphernalia, tactical military maps, war citations, photographs, and interviews and discussions with the men I served with in Vietnam.

Soldiers wear dog tags for identification, to make sure that they're accounted for on the battlefield, remembered, and honored properly. It's my goal that *Dog Tags of Courage* will help to secure a place in history for the Vietnam war dogs who earned their *dog tags* through courageous service.

Chapter 1

Where Is the War?

Iboard a commercial passenger jetliner for a nonstop 12,000 mile, twenty-four hour trip from San Francisco to Saigon. The pilots and crew are civilians, but American soldiers sit in every seat. Female attendants serve food and drink throughout the flight, though no alcohol is permitted. Many of the guys can't wait to talk to the pretty airline attendants. As far as I'm concerned, there's too much competition for their attention. Sitting, standing, and going to the restroom is about all the physical activity I get during this flight. Sleeping in a sitting position is difficult, so I catnap most of the way.

The pilot announces our arrival in Saigon. It's daylight outside, and we all look out from the aircraft portholes. I strain my neck and eyes for my first glimpse of this foreign land. Everyone buckles up before the aircraft's wheels touch down on the runway. I heave a sigh of relief at the familiar sound of screeching rubber on pavement. The long ride is over, and I will be able to get off the plane at last.

As we exit the aircraft the flight attendants wish each soldier good luck.

Immediately upon our arrival in Vietnam, military policemen ushered us aboard military buses with bars and thick wire mesh in place of windows. For the first time, I saw a sentry dog and his handler in combat gear standing a short distance from the aircraft.

I thought, *Wow! I didn't know they had dogs over here.* Little did I know

1

then that this quick sighting of a Vietnam war dog was a glimpse into my future.

The driver told us that the wire mesh over the windows was installed to protect us from being hit by grenades that might be hurled at the bus, while we traveled through the crowded city of Saigon. I smelled the hot, sticky air with its peculiar odor of stale fish. Being from Littleton, Colorado, a Denver suburb, I'd never experienced a climate like this. Back home, the air was dry and clear, and the land a mile above sea level.

As the bus slowly maneuvered through the crowded streets, I stared at the foreign cars, bicycle riders, and pedestrians. Most wore black or white pajamas, straw hats, and flip-flop sandals. I was happy to notice plenty of beautiful girls. During the thirty-minute ride I didn't hear any shooting, witness explosions, or see buildings on fire. In fact, I didn't see anything in the city of Saigon but Vietnamese civilians and soldiers. Despite the noisy streets, everyone appeared to go about his or her business peacefully.

I thought, *Where's the war?*

The bus drove a short distance through the busy streets and stopped at the front gate of Camp Alpha, the U.S. Army replacement center. A military policeman looked us over and then motioned the bus driver through the gate. After the bus stopped, armed guards quickly herded us into a large wooden building, where the Army processed incoming replacements for assignment to organizations throughout South Vietnam. After I handed over my Vietnam assignment orders to the military personnel clerk, I was directed to another part of the building. We were told that our luggage—one duffel bag each—would be delivered to Camp Alpha later that day. For easy identification, each duffel bag was clearly marked in large block letters with our names and service numbers. No one talked much. I began to feel like a robot following orders: "Stop! Wait here! Follow me! That's far enough!"

Our entire group gathered in a large room and the camp commander gave a mandatory "Welcome to Vietnam" orientation. He briefed us on the Vietnamese culture and why we were fighting in this foreign country. I surmised, from what he said that I was serving in Vietnam to help stop the spread of Communism from North to South Vietnam. He declared that our presence was no more than a "police action," because the United States had not declared war on North Vietnam.

2

Where Is the War?

I whispered to the soldier next to me, "What the hell is the difference between a *declared war* and a *police action,* if both sides are killing each other?"

He didn't respond, so I shut up and continued to listen. Fresh out of high school with only a few months of military service and training, it looked to me as if I was now at war. But what did I know?

After the briefing and in-processing, I was told I'd be staying at Camp Alpha until my assignment came through. This could take from a day to a week. I was surprised at not being processed as quickly as possible. After all, I'd come here to fight a war, or rather a "police action," not to waste time hanging around in a replacement center.

Camp Alpha consisted of long rows of wooden buildings that had screens for windows. It reminded me of the infantry training centers in Fort Leonardwood, Fort Ord, and Fort Benning.

I was assigned to a numbered building and issued bedding. On concrete slab floors, several rows of metal bunk beds with thin mattresses lined the inside walls. Each building accommodated about fifty men and had electric lights but no air conditioning. I doubted that I'd ever adjust to the heat, humidity, or the persistent smell of stale fish in the air.

Most of the replacements were teenagers like me, fresh out of training, wearing new fatigues, with no hair on top of our heads, and no service experience other than our initial training. We felt completely confused by the sight of armed guards and sentry dogs, patrolling the guard towers and roaming everywhere within the tall, barbed wire fences which surrounded the compound. Watching them made me feel as if I was living in a small prison.

I lived only with male enlisted men at Camp Alpha. No American women soldiers were housed there, and I didn't see any American female troops during my entire stay. Because the Army didn't mix officers with the enlisted troops, military officers were assigned to a separate compound within the camp.

Camp Alpha had a small store, where we could buy soft drinks, candy, cigarettes, toothpaste, and other sundries. A small club featured live American music and a Vietnamese rock and roll band. I thought it was hilarious that the musicians couldn't speak English but could sing all the words to the Rolling Stones' and Beatles' songs. The club, always crowded, sticky hot, and filled with cigarette smoke, served alcoholic beverages and soft drinks. There was nowhere else to unwind. Offering an alternative to the club, Camp Alpha housed a small chapel that posted notices that it conducted services for any religious denomination.

I spent most of my time walking around inside the compound. Everyone was restricted to staying there and we were accounted for by having our names called three or four times daily. A loudspeaker system managed the entire population. Several times a day, the cadre blared out instructions for us to report and stand single file behind assigned numbered poles in a staging area that resembled a small parade ground. There we received instructions, were assigned details, and then were released. We repeated this activity several times during the day. Well-organized and managed, Camp Alpha hustled hundreds of soldiers in and out every day.

Being a gregarious person by nature, I usually started conversations by asking a soldier where he was from or what was his Military Occupational Specialty (MOS). Each soldier had been trained in a specific MOS at various military training centers in the states. While at Camp Alpha, I met guys from almost every state in the U. S. They were truck drivers, hospital medics, helicopter and vehicle mechanics, personnel and supply clerks, military police, cooks, and construction engineers. Most of them had trained for jobs other than the infantry.

I'd heard that it took more than ten trained support personnel to keep one infantryman in the field, but I had no idea what that meant. When I told anyone I was an infantry paratrooper, they typically responded, "Good luck!" They were all glad to be trained to do something other than carry a gun for a living.

I met Kenny Mook the same way I met everyone else. Kenny had been in Camp Alpha for several days before I'd arrived. I was five-feet-six inches and weighed 130 pounds. Born in Denver, I'd finished high school in the nearby suburb of Littleton, Colorado. Kenny, then a twenty-one-year old who hailed from Saegertown, Pennsylvania, was five-feet-nine inches and weighed 175 pounds. I'd volunteered for the service and had a service number that started with the letters RA, which meant Regular Army. Kenny had been drafted. His service number began with US, which designated him as a draftee. I grew up in the city. Kenny was a farm boy. I tended to talk; Kenny liked to listen. But when Kenny spoke, I listened because, after all, I respected my elders.

Both Kenny and I were in excellent health and physical condition. Before joining the Army, I'd played varsity football as a starting linebacker and was on the varsity baseball team at Littleton High School. I'd also placed first in several conferences and invitational wrestling tournaments in the 122-pound class. Kenny wasn't an athlete but he was strong from farming in northern Pennsylvania.

In spite of all the differences in our backgrounds, we immediately felt a certain kind of chemistry between us and became instant friends. Besides, as infantrymen, we were both destined to fight in the jungle and defend a base camp. We'd protect supply roads, airfields, motor pools, hospitals, and all noncombatant men and women. Although our mission was a little scary, we liked to talk about how important our jobs would be. Anticipating our common tasks, Kenny and I began spending time together in Camp Alpha while we awaited our assignments.

Kenny and I had no idea where we'd be assigned. Kenny was what paratroopers call a *Leg*—a nickname for infantrymen who didn't jump out of planes.

I said, "I didn't go to three weeks of jump school hell to be assigned to an infantry Leg unit. I'm sure the Army will assign me to an elite paratrooper outfit."

Kenny replied, "The only things that fall out of the sky are bird shit and fools. Besides, after you land, you're a Leg, too."

Throughout our infantry marksmanship training, Kenny and I had both trained on the M14 rifle. We didn't know what the standard issue M16 rifles looked like until we saw camp guards carrying them. I asked one of the sergeants, who ran the camp, if I'd be issued one. The sergeant looked at me with a smile on his face and said, "No!" He told me that Camp Alpha was well-protected, and I'd get an M16 when I arrived at my final destination.

As replacements, we were all unarmed and vulnerable to enemy attacks on Camp Alpha. I knew that by the time I was issued weapons and ammunition during an attack, assuming there were enough to go around, I'd be dead. A lot of frightening thoughts like this ran through my mind, while I waited there for my assignment.

A week had passed in Camp Alpha when I finally heard my name called over the loud speaker for assignment instructions. When I reported to the office, Kenny was already there. With a stroke of good luck, Kenny and I had both been assigned to the 1st Cavalry Division in the central highlands about 250 miles northwest of Saigon. I learned that this division had one battalion of paratroopers, so I felt hopeful that I'd soon join them. We were told that we'd receive further instructions when we got to the division replacement center.

Kenny and I were sick of replacement centers and always happy to leave them. We knew their routine all too well: "Hurry up and wait." I'd been waiting since September 1965 to get to an assigned unit. Now, by late March 1966, my training was over; the travel had ended; and replacement centers were about to be history. I liked the prospect that I stood only one step away from fighting in real combat as an elite paratrooper.

At last, Kenny and I were heading for our first infantry assignment in the mountains of South Vietnam. Although Kenny and I were becoming good friends, back then I had no idea that what we were about to experience together would change our lives and cement our friendship for a lifetime.

Chapter 2

We Meet Gary Owen

Early in the morning, with our duffel bags packed, Kenny and I waited at the entrance gate of Camp Alpha with a bunch of other soldiers. As soon as it was daylight, we boarded a military bus to Tan Son Nhut airfield. From there, we climbed the ramp of a C130 military transport plane that soon filled with troops and supplies. The aircraft wasted little time getting into the sky. For the first time since I'd arrived in Vietnam, I felt cool air.

With the ride making the inside of the plane incredibly noisy, it was almost impossible to carry on a conversation. The aircraft flew north of Saigon for several hours before the pilot banked the plane left and began his descent. As I peered through the small window, I saw an airstrip and rows of green military tents and equipment near it. Camp Radcliff, home of the 1st Cavalry Division, was directly below us. Kenny pointed out a large yellow and black 1st Cavalry Division shoulder patch, painted on the mountainside above the camp.

I thrilled at the thought that we'd soon be wearing that patch.

The circular base camp was surrounded by dense jungle. I saw mountains rising up everywhere and that the small Vietnamese village of An Khe rested near the camp's outer perimeter. Trucks, jeeps, and troops moved along the dirt roads inside the base camp. Helicopters sat idle in neat rows along the airstrip, which was called *The Golf Course*, because it was so enormous. The 1st Cavalry Division (Air Mobile), nicknamed *The First Team*, had more helicopters than any other division in Vietnam.

From the air, the camp appeared well-fortified. With the vegetation bull-

7

dozed away, a wide buffer protected the perimeter from the surrounding jungle. Three or four heavily fortified bunkers were evenly spaced between lookout towers. Strategically positioned artillery pieces and tanks dotted the perimeter.

After the plane landed, we went to the division's personnel and administration building. A clerk collected our individual personnel, finance, and medical records to process us into the division. He checked to ensure that we had our metal dog tags hanging from chains around our necks. If a soldier was killed, his dog tag would be used to properly identify him. One dog tag would be taken from his body, and the other would be stuck between the dead man's teeth.

The personnel clerk congratulated us as he handed over a set of orders officially promoting all of us from Private to Private First Class. The Army's policy at the time was to promote a Private to Private First Class, effective on his arrival in South Vietnam. That meant at least a monthly pay increase of $50. We also got another $60 per month in combat pay. At the time, I made $300 a month and didn't have to pay taxes on that amount. If I was assigned to a paratrooper outfit, I'd get an additional $55 monthly. An infantry division's organizational structure is layered in the shape of a pyramid. At the top of the pyramid, with ultimate power and authority, is the division commander. The rest of the pyramid is layered sequentially in power and authority from brigade commander, battalion commander, company commander, platoon leader, squad leader, fire team leader to rifleman. Kenny and I were assigned to be riflemen—peons with no authority.

The personnel clerk told us that we were to join Company B, 1ˢᵗ Battalion, 7ᵗʰ Cavalry Regiment. George Armstrong Custer at Little Bighorn had commanded the 7ᵗʰ Cavalry Regiment in 1876. Now we were told that, whenever we passed an officer outside cover of a building, the 7ᵗʰ Cavalry tradition was to say, "Gary Owen," as we saluted. "Gary Owen" was the title of General Custer's favorite Irish marching song that he liked to have the 7ᵗʰ Regiment band play at parades and other festive military functions. I found it quite interesting that this historical tradition had continued to be observed through the years.

After in-processing, we followed the company clerk down a dirt path, separating two rows of tents. Our new home was to be a skimpy old green canvas tent, surrounded by sandbags stacked waist-high and held up by two wooden center poles and wooden tie-down-stakes. Several empty canvas cots stood on a dirt-packed floor inside. I couldn't believe that this dark and misty tent would be my home for the next twelve months.

Kenny said, "Well, Johnny, we're finally here."

"Yeah, but I wonder where the platoon is? All I saw when we flew in were mountains and very little civilization."

"We're not in Saigon anymore," Kenny said. "We're in a war zone. The platoon is probably out in the jungle hunting for the enemy."

When we went to the mess hall, we found it to be a big wooden building with screens for windows and a concrete floor. Just outside it were large green canvas bags full of drinking water. We ate from metal trays and sat on picnic tables, but we hadn't realized that we'd need to bring our own canteen cups, if we wanted something to drink. Breakfast consisted of powdered eggs, powdered milk, fresh baked bread, and bitter coffee. We were soon to discover that neither lunch or dinner were anything to write home about.

After we ate breakfast and were on the way back to our tent, we passed an officer, saluted him, and said, "Gary Owen, Sir!"

The officer returned the salute and replied, "All the way!"

After the officer had passed, Kenny and I looked at each other and chuckled. We thought it was really cool to say, "Gary Owen!" instead of "good morning" or "good afternoon, Sir!"

Later that day, Kenny and I were introduced to the company supply sergeant. He lived in a tent where every inch was packed and stacked high with supplies. The supply sergeant told us that he had everything we'd ever need for fighting a war. He issued us backpacks, water canteens, ammunition pouches, medical field dressings, a plastic poncho, a nylon poncho liner, a helmet (steel pot), a helmet liner, an entrenching tool (field shovel), and a bayonet. The supply sergeant also gave us several division patches like the one we saw on the mountainside when we flew into the base. This pleased us because the cloth insignia meant that we were no longer trainees in transit without a unit.

9

The supply sergeant told us we'd get weapons, ammunition, grenades, claymores (mines), trip flares, and other goodies after the platoon returned from the its mission in the field. He advised us that our new platoon sergeant would decide when we'd be ready to go on S and Ds.

I asked, "What are S and Ds?"

The supply sergeant smiled and shook his head. "Search and destroy missions," he said. "That's what we do for a living around here, young trooper!"

Kenny and I wondered what it would be like to meet the other members of the 2nd Platoon. After several days, we heard that the platoon would be arriving back at our base camp within the hour, and helicopters would land on the road nearby. I felt nervous and eager to see real combat infantrymen for the first time. *Would the other soldiers accept us?* I wondered. Kenny appeared to be calm, but his eyes showed that he too was concerned.

I heard the sounds of helicopters outside the tent and ran to look. In the distance, fifteen or twenty ships drifted into view. They flew in groups of three or four. As they came closer, the helicopters strung out and slowly descended. Fully equipped soldiers clutched their weapons and sat inside the open doors of the choppers. Between their legs, the door gunners held M60 machine gun that were mounted on posts.

Dirt kicked up on the field, as the first group of ships touched down about one hundred feet away from us. Air from the helicopters' rotating blades rippled our fatigues and almost whipped the caps off our heads. Dust flew everywhere. I watched with excitement, as the ships landed. Four or five men climbed out of each chopper and slowly walked in our direction. The door gunners stayed aboard, when the empty ships lifted off the road and flew away.

I watched, awestruck, while the men walked past me as if I was invisible. Under their steel helmets, I could see the soldiers' tired faces and eyes. Their dirty fatigues and boots looked as if they hadn't been polished since they were new. The men carried various types of shoulder weapons, some of which I'd never seen before. They wore backpacks filled with items that

I couldn't see. As the men walked by, I noticed that they looked and smelled as if they hadn't taken a bath in a month.

I strained to listen to what they were saying to each other. Some of the men entered the tent where Kenny and I lived. I was too nervous to follow them so I stayed outside the tent and wondered about what this soldiers' mission had been. Finally, I gathered up enough courage, went to my cot, sat like a little kid, and silently watched the soldiers unpack their gear. Kenny sat on his cot, too, and quietly observed everyone. The men looked friendly. A few said, "Hello!" But they were busy unpacking, laughing, and talking among themselves. It was easy to see that they were happy to be back in base camp.

A short time later, two men walked into the tent and called our names: "PFC Kenneth L. Mook and PFC John C. Burnam."

We jumped to our feet and answered, "Here!"

The men approached us, stopped, and looked us over in silence. We remained standing to show respect as we'd been taught during training. The men looked at one another, smiled, and told us to sit down and relax. I figured that they weren't used to this type of behavior or maybe, they were amused because we looked so inexperienced. One man introduced himself as Sergeant Savage of the 2nd Platoon. He was five-feet-seven inches, about twenty-three-years old, and huskily built; he had a hardened darkly tanned face. Sergeant Savage introduced Sergeant Doreman to us as our new squad leader; then he excused himself.

Sergeant Doreman smiled and said, "I'm your squad leader. Welcome to the 4th Squad, better known as the *weapons squad*."

Sergeant Doreman was a thin, twenty-two-year-old man, five-feet-eight inches tall with bright blue eyes, dirty brown hair, and a deep tan. Even though he hadn't cleaned up yet, Sergeant Doreman had the appearance and presence of a leader who spoke with confidence. He reached into his left breast pocket and took out a little green note pad. He began to ask us for our full names, ranks, ages, service numbers, types of training we'd had, hometowns, next of kin, and the dates we'd arrived in Vietnam. He recorded our answers in his notebook.

Sergeant Doreman explained that a weapons squad had two five-man machine gun teams. Each machine gun team had one M60 machine gun.

11

Each team consisted of one gunner, an assistant gunner, and three riflemen/ammunition bearers.

He said, "That's an ideal, fully manned squad. The problem is that I only have two M60 machine gunners and one assistant M60 machine gunner. The weapons squad is critically under combat strength. You men are a sight for sore eyes.

"Forget whatever you were taught in the States about machine gun deployment," he continued. "Even though a weapons squad might be undermanned, it's still the primary firepower of the platoon. When the shit hits the fan, and we're under enemy attack, there's nothing better than the M60 machine gun. Counting you two, we now have three men on the Number two machine gun and two men on the Number one machine gun."

From what Sergeant Doreman was saying, I understood that the Number one gun provided firepower to the front. The Number two gun provided firepower and security at the rear of the platoon.

Later, Sergeant Doreman introduced us to the two fire team leaders of the weapons squad. We met Specialist Four (SP4) Engles, the number one gunner, and Private Wildman his assistant gunner. They smiled, as we were introduced, and then went on about the business of cleaning their weapons. SP4 Bob Dunn was introduced as the number two gunner. Sergeant Doreman appointed Kenny as Bob's assistant gunner; I was assigned to be the ammunition bearer. Before he left, Sergeant Doreman said, "Bob, you now have a team. Take care of them!"

Bob Dunn was five-foot-seven inches tall, weighed 170 pounds, and had blond hair and blue eyes. A New Yorker, with a crusty mustache and heavy accent, he'd been in Vietnam since early January 1966. I asked Bob where the platoon had been. He said that they'd searched the jungle for a week but had made no contact with the Gooks.

I said, "You mean, the enemy?"

Bob translated some new terminology for me.

VC meant Viet Cong. *NVA* was the North Vietnamese Army. *PAVN* meant the Peoples Army of Vietnam. *Cong, Dinks, Charlie* were all terms used for talking about the enemy. Bob said that the NVA were the toughest enemies to fight.

Bob explained the importance of keeping the M60 machine gun clean and oiled at all times. Out in the jungle, he told us, the gun got dirty quickly. The rain and humidity caused any part, that wasn't oiled, to rust and possibly malfunction.

SP4 Dunn explained what our jobs would be. He said, "We get an operations order for a mission. We pack up and leave base camp for a week or so. We hunt and kill some Gooks. After that, we come home for a few days to shower, rest, and get some hot food. Then it starts all over again. Believe me, you guys will get your share of the action and then some."

When Bob Dunn gave me my first M16 rifle, I acted like a little kid with a new Christmas toy. Kenny and I test-fired the M16s. Bob taught us how to tear them apart, put them together, and showed us where to put the most oil on the rifles.

My previous training had taught me how to maintain sight alignment, control breathing, and squeeze the trigger. I was surprised that the M16 had little or no kick. Military rifles and pistols were designed for right-handed people. When the guns are fired, hot brass casings eject to the right and away from the right-handed shooter. Because I was left-handed, the hot brass casings ejected across my face and body. Not a big problem, but on a rare occasion, I'd get a hot casing blown down my collar.

During training in the States, Kenny and I had been awarded Expert Rifle badges because we consistently scored hits in the center of targets with M14 rifles. The targets, positioned at various ranges, had been both pop-up and stationary. Shooting positions also varied based on target range. Kenny had also scored Expert with the M60 machine gun. This is probably why he got to be Bob's assistant machine gunner. The different qualification levels of marksmanship were, from lowest to highest ranking: Expert, Sharp Shooter, and Marksman.

SP4 Dunn gave us some pointers on how to conserve ammunition. He said, "Never switch to full-automatic, unless there's no other choice. Always carry your own supply of ammunition. The quicker you use it up, the less you'll have when you need it most."

The training sessions boosted my self-confidence. As each day passed, Kenny and I felt more like members of the platoon team. We'd need this camaraderie because soon we'd be meeting Charlie face-to-face for the first time.

Chapter 3

My First Mission — The Ia Drang Valley

A few days before my first mission, Sergeant Doreman told a story to Kenny and me to fill us in on the history of our new platoon. It was about a mission that happened in the middle of November 1965. The 1st Battalion, 7th Cavalry, had gone looking for a fight and flew into the Ia Drang valley—a remote area in the northern highlands of South Vietnam, at the base of the Chu Pong mountain, close to the Cambodian border. Lieutenant Colonel Moore, the Battalion Commander, had led the battalion into the valley with the 2nd Platoon, making it one of the first on the ground. Immediately, the landing zone, (LZ) XRAY, had been saturated with artillery.

Sergeant Doreman held us spellbound as he recounted the events of that day:

> When our platoon landed, we rushed into the woods with our guns firing. Lt. Colonel Moore directed our leader to move the 2nd Platoon about one hundred meters and set up a new position. The platoon fanned out and ran forward toward the base of Chu Pong mountain. We spotted two or three enemy soldiers moving across our front, and the platoon leader ordered us to chase and capture them. We pursued the enemy for fifty meters and ran into 150 NVA soldiers, dressed in khaki uniforms, wearing pith helmets, and coming down off the mountain shooting at us.
>
> These were hard-core troops from North Vietnam, not your ordi-

nary black pajama, part time soldier/farmer. When they attacked us, we took casualties before we could hit the dirt and return their fire. We tried to get behind anything that would provide cover, but we were pinned down by heavy fire and cut off from the rest of the company.

The platoon spread out. We took cover behind clumps of bushes and trees. Communication was nearly impossible above the noise of blazing machine guns, rifle fire, and grenade explosions. Totally outnumbered, we fought for our lives.

We were overwhelmed. Many of our men were wounded or dead. The Gooks screamed at the top of their lungs while they came at us, shooting. A few missions before Ia Drang, a member of the 2nd Platoon had died after drowning in a river. The men in the platoon had blamed our platoon leader for the man's death, but he hadn't been relieved of his command. It was no secret that many of us had lost our respect for him. In this battle, during one of the enemy's human wave attacks, our platoon leader was badly wounded and died bravely, fighting alongside his men.

The weapons squad suffered so many casualties that the squad leader took over one of the M60s. He fired it until he was overrun and killed. Then the Gooks turned our M60 machine gun on us. We had several more casualties before we took it back. Low on ammunition and grenades, we gathered what we could from our own dead.

I don't know how we made it after losing our platoon leader, platoon sergeant, and squad leaders. Sergeant Savage was the only sergeant left, so he took over the platoon. He got on the radio and found cover behind a log while he called for artillery strikes. We fought, on and off, all day and into the night. Sergeant Savage continued to send periodic situation reports over the radio. We received radio reports that the entire battalion was under heavy ground attack by the NVA. Hundreds of enemy soldiers were storming down from the mountain to join the fight. We were too far out for any immediate rescue attempts. Our orders were to hold our ground, until help arrived the next day.

It was very dark that first night, but none of us slept. We kept quiet and tried to comfort the wounded as we waited to be attacked again. During that night, I heard a bugle call coming from the mountain, and then all hell broke loose again. We withstood several attacks and survived until sky troopers from a sister company rescued us in the afternoon of the second day. The *2nd Platoon became known as the* Lost Platoon *because we'd been the only platoon outside the battalion lines of defense.*

The battle raged for a third day. B52 bombers dropped tons of bombs on Chu Pong mountain and the surrounding area. When the fighting was over, our battalion had taken heavy casualties; our company had forty men left out of 115. The North Vietnamese Army had lost over a thousand men. At the time, I was a rifleman in the 2nd Squad of the 2nd Platoon. I don't know how I survived without getting killed. There were bodies all over the place. The Gooks and Americans were lying dead next to each other. That was how close the fighting had become.

Our battered troops were relieved by a sister battalion—2nd Battalion, 7th Cavalry. We were flown out by helicopter for much-needed rest. The 2nd Battalion, 7th Cavalry moved on foot a mile or so away to LZ Albany. They marched in columns, strung out through the woods. We figured the fight and cleanup was over, but the North Vietnamese Army had other plans. They had fresh battalions in reserve—men who were waiting to join the action and kill Americans. The enemy paralleled the American movement until they were in a position to do the most damage. In a matter of several hours, they cut to ribbons and wiped out an entire American battalion of several hundred men.

Most of our battalion had been in-country for a little over two months before that battle during which hundreds of them were wounded or killed in Ia Drang valley. Afterwards, I was promoted to sergeant and became the weapons squad leader.

After losing so many men, the replacements we needed in the weapons squad didn't arrive until January. First, SP4 Engles, SP4 Dunn, and PVT Wildman arrived. You and Kenny are the second set of replacements. It's now the first week of April and my weapons squad is still short-handed.

I only have to make it a few more months before I go home in August. We haven't been back to Ia Drang since November. I hope that I never have to see the place again.

After he told his stories, Sergeant Doreman had tears in his eyes as he got up, excused himself, and left immediately. I was wide-eyed and astounded. I didn't know what to think or say to someone like him. I felt honored and humbled to know this brave man who had such an extraordinary story. I'd been in Uncle Sam's Army for about a month at the time of the Ia Drang valley battle. Now I was assigned to a platoon that had been almost wiped out there.

Would I be brave in the face of the enemy or too scared to fight? Would I be killed instantly, severely wounded, or survive like Sergeant Doreman? I wondered. I found it difficult to sleep that night. Instead, I stayed awake, thinking about the Lost Platoon.

A few days later, Sergeant Doreman came into our tent and said, "Wake up and listen up. After you get some chow, meet me here for an operations order."

I got out of my cot, grabbed my shaving gear, and slipped on my *rice-paddy-racers* (our nickname for rubber flip-flops). I headed for the showers, which consisted of several green fifty-gallon drums welded together, sitting on top of a wood frame with canvas siding. Flat wooden pallets underneath the shower heads provided a place to stand above the moldy, wet, mosquito-infested ground beneath. A trench was dug around the wooden pallets for water drainage. Towels and clothes hung on nails, hammered into the posts holding the shower frame together. A faucet, attached to a pipe, controlled the flow of cold water. There was no hot water. We took quick showers to conserve water for others and shaved outside the shower, using our steel helmets as sinks. Water tankers filled the shower water containers daily, when the troops were in from the field.

After showers and shaves, it was time for breakfast. Kenny and I sat at a picnic table with our new team leader, Bob Dunn. He couldn't tell us anything more about our upcoming mission or operations order. I ate fast and returned to my tent. A few minutes later, everyone in the weapons squad came back from breakfast.

Sergeant Doreman arrived and gathered us together. He took out his green notebook, glanced at his notes, and began to talk in a serious tone.

"We are going back to Ia Drang Valley," he said.

From the story he'd told us only a few days before, Kenny and I knew how Sergeant Doreman must have felt about returning to the site of so much carnage, but he didn't betray his emotions. Instead, he put his military field map down and pointed to a grid that he knew all too well. The terrain appeared wooded and flat until it reached the base of Chu Pong mountain. Inside the wooded area, near the base of the mountain, LX XRAY was clearly marked on the map in grease pencil. The Cambodian border was within walking distance from the LZ. The entire area was completely isolated from man-made objects such as roads and villages.

Sergeant Doreman said, "S2 battalion intelligence reported small concentrations of enemy troops operating in this area. Our mission is to engage the enemy but not pursue them across the Cambodian border.

"We'll link up with the rest of the company, when we get to LZ XRAY, and set up in a company-sized perimeter. Our objective is to check out the area, hike up Chu Pong mountain, and look for enemy base camps. Then we'll sweep the Ia Drang valley, southeast to LZ Victor, spend the night there, and come back home the next day. We'll be supported by field artillery, gun ships, and jet fighters, if necessary.

"Pack a basic load and enough food for three days. We'll be re-supplied in the field. Be ready to move out to the road for pickup in an hour. Are there any questions?"

Sergeant Doreman looked at Kenny and me and said, "You two are about to get your cherries busted." With those words, we knew that, as two raw recruits, who had never seen combat, we were going to lose our innocence on this mission.

Bob Dunn turned to Kenny and said, "Don't forget to pick up the M60 machine gun spare parts bag from my tent."

The spare parts bag contained one extra gun barrel, an asbestos glove, used to grab and change the barrel when it got too hot, cleaning rods, metal chamber, bore brushes, small oil cans, and cleaning cloths. It had a shoulder strap and weighed about twelve pounds.

I grabbed my pack and filled it with several pairs of socks, underwear, and T-shirts. I checked my shaving kit to make sure I had a toothbrush, shaving cream, soap dish with a new bar of soap, a bottle of aftershave lotion, a hand towel, and a razor. I decided to pack writing paper and envelopes in case I had time to write letters home. With my small green canvas pack already full, Bob directed me to go with Kenny to the supply tent to pick up a basic load of M16 rifle ammunition — 300 rounds, two grenades, two trip flares, one claymore mine, and eight 100-round belts of M60 machine gun ammunition.

I frowned, *Damn! That's a hell of a lot of extra shit to carry.*

When I got back with everything, I had twenty M16 magazines and twenty boxes of ammunition. I loaded each magazine and discarded the empty cartons, inserted several clips in a bandoleer with a shoulder strap, and crammed the rest of the M16 clips into my pack. I rolled my poncho as small and tight as I could and strapped it underneath the pack.

The M60 machine gun ammunition was issued in a 100-round belt per box. Every fifth round was a red tracer, which lit up when it left the barrel. Tracers were used to help zero in on a target and for night firing. Each box came with a green cloth bag and a strap so it could be carried slung from the shoulder.

Kenny put two boxes of M60 machine gun ammunition in the spare parts bag. He set the other two boxes aside to be carried over his shoulder. I brought two 100-round boxes and Bob attached a 100-round belt to the feeding mechanism of the M60 machine gun. My pistol belt held two canteens of water, two ammunition pouches, two grenades, one bayonet, and a field shovel. We attached adjustable shoulder straps to the backpack and pistol belt to help distribute the weight more evenly between the small of the back and shoulders. Medical field bandages, attached to metal D-rings, were sewn to the shoulder harness. We placed a plastic bottle of mosquito repellent inside the elastic headband on top of the steel pot.

I lifted the pack onto my back. When I bent over to pick up my M16 rifle and steel pot, the weight shifted forward. I nearly fell on my face. At that time, soaking wet, I may have weighed 130 pounds. The pack added at least fifty pounds. My feet pressed heavily into the soles of my boots. I didn't know how I was going to carry all that stuff for any great distance, let alone climb Chu Pong mountain with it. Kenny looked as if he was also surprised at the weight of his load.

When I thought I had everything packed, Bob told me to put my gear down and get three days of C-rations. Each soldier was issued a case of C-rations that contained twelve meals. A case of C-rations was a little larger than a case of beer and about as heavy. When I got back to the tent, there was little time, before I had to be at the road for pickup.

I complained, "How am I going to carry nine meals when my pack is full and I have all this other stuff to carry?"

Bob looked at my gear and asked, "What the hell did you pack?"

"Extra clothes, shaving gear, and ammunition," I replied.

Bob laughed. "Take the extra clothes out and use the room to pack essentials. Put cans of food in your long green socks and tie them to your shoulder harness. By the way, John, I know your pack is heavy. Mine is too. Pack only the bare necessities and as much ammunition as you can carry. Also, take only what you think you'll eat for three days and leave the rest here."

Although I felt like a complete moron, I did everything Bob said. It was my first mission, so what the hell did I know?

Sergeant Doreman cried out, "Saddle up!"

I looked awkward in my new gear. When I walked, it sounded as if I was carrying pots and pans. Kenny seemed a little uncomfortable, too. The other soldiers in the platoon looked at us, like the new recruits we were, but didn't say a word. When we reached the road, we joined the other members of the weapons squad. We sat and waited for the choppers in the hot morning sun.

Sergeant Doreman briefed the squad on the loading plan. The squad was split into machine gun teams—one on each side of the road. When the choppers landed, soldiers were to simultaneously board from both sides of the ship.

The first group of choppers landed and SP4 Engles and PFC Wildman climbed aboard with members of another squad. The ships quickly took off and another group of slicks landed. Sergeant Doreman signaled Bob's machine gun team to board the closest ship. When it touched down, I ran a short distance and climbed aboard. I sat down against the inside wall away from the open door. I felt a little uncomfortable, because the doors remained open during flight.

As the ship lifted off the ground, I felt the metal floor underneath vibrate and rattle. I braced myself. I thought I'd slide across the vibrating metal floor and out of the open door. My stomach got butterflies. I felt as if I was getting ready to go down the first steep drop of a roller coaster ride. As the aircraft gained altitude, it joined a column formation of other ships. I was still a little tense, when the helicopter reached cruising altitude a few thousand feet up. As I looked down, I watched the base camp slowly disappearing. Several gun ships flew escort at a lower altitude barely above the treetops.

At least thirty ships were in the air. I could see men, sitting inside the helicopters, flying alongside us. I thought that riding inside a fully armed formation of flying warships was an awesome thing.

The cool air felt good against my face. As I looked around, I noticed that no one talked. Everyone stared out the open doors of the ship. The door gunners had their machine guns loaded and tilted down. They wore green flight crew helmets with intercoms so they could communicate with the two pilots. The formation of ships traveled for about an hour before descending. Then the treetops seemed to be coming closer and closer.

Green smoke swirled up from the ground of LZ XRAY in the Ia Drang valley. That meant the LZ was cleared for landing. The gun ships buzzed around the LZ as the choppers approached the landing area. In the near distance, Chu Pong mountain stuck out like a pyramid, covered up in tropical vegetation. When the chopper got ready to land, I noticed soldiers scooting closer to the open doors. As soon as the landing gear touched the earth, everyone quickly jumped out. Kenny and I followed Bob and we created a small perimeter around the ship until it lifted away.

Sergeant Doreman barked, "Bob, get your gun over to those trees and cover our asses."

Bob ran. Kenny and I followed to a tree line about fifty yards out. My adrenaline spiked. My eyes were wide open and scanning for anything unusual. Bob put the gun down on its bipod. He loaded the chamber for firing. He told me to move to my left and link up with the next man in the platoon. I reacted without saying a word. About twenty yards away, I spotted another member of the platoon. After we made eye contact, I dropped down on one knee and faced out.

The helicopters kept landing with more troops. Bob and Kenny manned the M60 machine gun stationed ten yards away from me. Knee-high grass, dried by the hot sun, surrounded the trees. I nervously tapped the bottom

21

of the magazine, inserted into the M16 rifle. I loaded a round into the chamber and made sure the selector switch was on safe. Everyone lay quietly in a prone position on the hard dry grass. I scanned my front, trying to see and listen for anything resembling enemy movement. Minutes passed. Nothing happened. Sergeant Doreman was busy going from man to man, checking that each of us was present and in correct position.

Sergeant Doreman ordered Bob to follow him to a better location. Kenny and I briskly moved behind them in a crouched position. As I walked, my helmet felt loose on my head and kept moving in front of my eyes. When we finally stopped, Sergeant Doreman pointed where he wanted the M60 machine gun set up. The position he picked faced Chu Pong mountain.

He instructed Bob, "Before you dig in, check in front of your position about thirty yards to make sure you know there's nothing out there."

Bob took Kenny with him but ordered me to stay back to cover them. They slowly walked around with the machine gun at the ready and returned with nothing to report.

More than a hundred men were on the ground by then. The gun ships still buzzed around but weren't firing. Gun ships didn't have door gunners but were heavily armed with machine guns and aerial rocket artillery, controlled by the pilots. I felt safe but still didn't know what I was doing or what to expect.

The order was given to dig in. Bob stood guard behind the M60, while Kenny and I dug a three-man foxhole. Sergeant Doreman said he normally didn't put three men in one position, but since we were new, he wanted Bob to teach us how to set up a machine gun position.

After we dug the foxhole, Bob showed Kenny and me how to set up a claymore mine. He said, "The first thing to remember is that the claymore has FRONT printed in large letters on one side. Be sure to point this in the direction of the enemy. Claymores are real easy to set up, but if you don't do it right, Charlie will turn the mines around and place them closer to your foxhole. When it's time to squeeze the trigger, you'll blow up your own ass. Remember, surprise is important. Camouflage the mine without disturbing the natural look of the surrounding vegetation. A claymore mine has a fifty-foot wire. One end has the blasting cap attached. It screws inside a well in the claymore. The other end has the trigger mechanism. There's also a circuit tester to make sure it's armed.

"Don't set trip flares out during the day. Do it before dark. Trip flares are a little touchy, but you want them that way. When the enemy trips the wire, the pin should easily pop out and ignite the flair. To keep Charlie from tampering, attach a second trip wire to the bottom of the claymore. Charlie will be caught by surprise like a deer in headlights. Then we'll kill him."

Patrols were scheduled for the next morning to search the area and climb Chu Pong mountain. The sun was setting. I went out with Bob to assemble the claymores and trip flares while Kenny watched from behind the machine gun. When we got back, I boasted to Kenny with a big smile and said, "It's a cinch!"

Kenny replied, "Good; then you can do it all the time."

Bob laughed and said, "Kenny, tomorrow it's your turn."

Sergeant Doreman came by to remind us to keep alert and to make sure someone manned the M60 machine gun at all times. He also gave us the password for the night. We would use the password, which changed daily, to get back through friendly lines if people got split up during a fire fight at night.

Bob scheduled two-hour guard shifts. Everyone ate canned C-rations for supper before the first watch. I used a tiny can opener, called a P38, to open a warm can of beefsteak and potatoes. It tasted terrible, but I ate every bit of it.

Each box of C-rations had a dark brown plastic bag full of goodies — a plastic spoon, a tiny roll of toilet paper, a sample-size box of four cigarettes; little packets of sugar, creamer, salt, and pepper; one book of matches and a packet of instant coffee.

To cover our exposed skin, we used mosquito repellent. It was powerful enough to keep the bugs from biting us at night. Each man carried a green plastic poncho to sleep on. By then, I'd concluded that sleeping in a foxhole was like sleeping in a grave.

At first light, everyone awoke. We used water from canteens to brush our teeth, wash up, and mix powdered coffee. We were required to have a clean-shaven face, even though no one but the Army cared what we looked like. When I finished shaving, I slapped on some Mennen Skin Bracer. My face burned from the cuts and scratches I made using the razor.

To my surprise, Bob blurted, "Who the hell has the aftershave on?"

I confessed, and Bob ripped into me. He said, "You can't go on patrol smelling like a whore. Charlie will smell you a mile away. Charlie has instincts like a fucking animal. He lives out here for crying out loud. What the hell is wrong with you? You don't need to fucking help him out."

I was stunned and so embarrassed that I didn't say a word. I also knew the smell would take time to wear off. I quietly dug a hole and buried that bottle of Mennen Skin Bracer and wiped my face with dirt, trying to get rid of the smell. When Sergeant Doreman found out what I did, he couldn't stop howling. Before long, I was the topic of conversation throughout the platoon. They called me "The Mennen Boy."

What a way to start my first full day in the field with a bunch of combat veterans!

Bob and Kenny went to retrieve the trip flares and claymores. Our orders were to hike to Chu Pong mountain and scout for enemy base camps. Sergeant Doreman directed the number two machine gun to bring up the rear of the platoon. He ordered the number one machine gun team to get behind the pointman. The platoon spread out and traveled in a column formation. Flank guards were placed on each side of the column about twenty-five yards out. With a flat terrain, visibility was good. We walked slowly and cautiously through the trees and knee-high brown grass while avoiding large termite mounds. My gear was still awkward to carry and I made clanging noises every step I took.

I was close to the last man in the formation. We traveled at a slow pace through a clearing. I stepped over a branch and crushed two huge millipedes crawling near my boot. Red ants, called fire ants, covered the trees. When they bit, it stung like hell, so I quickly learned to avoid them.

The patrol halted before reaching the base of the mountain. Nearby, I spotted a helmet on the ground a short distance away. I picked it up. It had a large bullet hole in the front. I examined the inside and saw a piece of dried scalp stuck to the back of the helmet liner. The name on the headband read, "Sgt. Bernard." I put it down and wondered about the man who had worn it, feeling sorry that an American had been killed in the middle of nowhere. I looked around and noticed that other soldiers were finding remnants of a battle that had previously taken place there.

Shallow foxholes, overgrown with grass, appeared everywhere. Military web gear from a backpack stuck out from a mound of dirt. Tarnished brass from all types of spent shells littered the area around the shallow foxholes. The positions of everything indicated that the fighting had been fierce, possibly hand-to-hand combat.

Kenny located a human skull with a bullet hole in it and a splintered human jawbone. Near me, the rains had partly washed away the dirt and exposed what appeared to be human bones. Bob told me that these weren't American remains, because we don't leave our men behind. I wondered how this had all happened. Never in my nineteen years had I seen this amount of devastation.

The patrol moved out again, and we eventually reached the base of the mountain that was rugged, dense with vegetation, and dark. The pointman used a machete to cut a path. The sunlight barely penetrated to the jungle floor, as we started to climb at a snail's pace up the mountain. My pack snagged on vines every step of the way.

We didn't travel far, before someone at the head of the platoon spotted a huge enemy base camp. A few soldiers checked for and found no booby traps before we entered the camp. The entire platoon slowly moved inside the base camp that had been built inside a huge bamboo forest. The sunlight reflected off the bamboo, creating a yellow glow. We were warned to watch out for snakes, especially bamboo vipers. I shuddered because I'd always hated the sight of snakes.

We set up a defensive position inside the enemy base camp. Half the platoon spread out and searched the camp, but it was empty. However, we uncovered a huge cache of ammunition, mortars, and rockets, hidden in camouflaged holes in the ground. We found cooking utensils, a meeting area, and a small hospital with a few medical supplies. Bunkers and tiny one-man foxholes dotted the area. Small piles of grenades, with wooden handles and strings dangling from them, were scattered throughout the camp that looked as if it could have held several hundred North Vietnamese soldiers.

I thought *this had to be one of the base camps that the enemy used to launch attacks on our company.*

Sergeant Doreman couldn't believe the B52 bombers had missed this place, although it couldn't be seen from the air. There wasn't a crater anywhere inside the base camp. The platoon leader got on the radio to speak with the company commander. They decided to set charges and blow up the enemy munitions.

When we returned to the foxholes that evening, we were dirty and tired. I had to take a shit real bad, so I asked Kenny, "Where do you think I should go?"

"Out in the woods, I guess. I haven't had to go yet."

Bob overheard us and said, "We'll cover your ass!"

He and Kenny broke into laughter. It would have been terrible for the enemy to catch me by surprise with my pants down, so I put up with the sarcasm and accepted their protection.

At a creek beside the mountain and about 150 yards from my foxhole, we set up an ambush that night. Sergeant Doreman teamed me with SP4 Johnson, a twenty-five-year-old black soldier and a survivor of the battle of Ia Drang. He spoke in a tense and nervous voice about not being very happy to be in this place again. After we talked for a few minutes, he set up the trip flares and claymores in front of our foxhole.

That night, while on guard duty in the foxhole, I heard rifle and machine gun fire coming from the direction of the creek. Johnson woke up and jumped in the foxhole with me. We pointed our weapons into the darkness and listened and waited to be attacked.

Johnson blurted out, "I hope them Gooks trip the flair, so I can blow their asses to hell with the claymore."

He instructed me to put my ammunition in front of me, so I could reload as fast as possible. The firing in the distance lasted about a half minute. Then, total silence. Nothing else happened the rest of the night.

The next morning, Sergeant Doreman told us that the first platoon had killed two enemy soldiers at the creek. He said that the company commander was pissed because someone had sprung the ambush too soon, and the main element had gotten away. The two kills were NVA who had been armed with AK 47 rifles.

Later that morning, the entire company swept the valley to LZ Victor a few miles southeast of LZ XRAY. Our route followed the east side of Chu Pong mountain parallel to the Cambodian border. I walked next to Kenny. It seemed to get hotter and hotter, as we pushed in the direction of LZ Victor. The water inside my canteen was so hot from the sun that it was unbearable to drink, but I forced it down anyway. The temperature must have been over 115 degrees. My fatigue jacket was soaked with sweat.

Almost out of water, my legs weakening under the heavy load on my back, I kept walking as Kenny pointed out the bomb craters. Helicopters flew around to cover our advance through the lightly wooded area. After the platoon stopped for a break, Kenny saw that I was slowing down. Determined not to give in to the heat, I wanted to make it to LZ Victor on my own.

When the platoon stopped again, I drank the last of my water, but was unable to stand. I felt dizzy and went down on one knee. I stayed in that position for a moment. Then struggling to stand, I felt a hand on my shoulder and heard a voice ask, "Are you okay, trooper?"

Without looking up, I replied, "I feel a little dizzy and weak."

"How long have you been in-country?"

I finally looked up and recognized Lieutenant Colonel Moore, the battalion commander who had led the battle of Ia Drang valley, which Sergeant Doreman had told us about before we'd left.

I tried to steady my legs, but fell against the tree. LTC Moore grabbed me under the arm and held me up. I thanked him and confessed that this was my first mission.

He gave me some water from his canteen and said, "Where are you from, trooper?"

"Littleton, Colorado, Sir."

"It's going to take you a while to get used to this type of heat and humidity, but it's an unusually hot day."

LTC Moore didn't have a pack on, only a belt with a 45-caliber pistol and two canteens of water. He looked fresh, as if he'd just arrived, and he'd hardly broken a sweat. He instructed me to take off the pack.

27

"Now you'll cool down faster. Grab your rifle and follow me."

LTC Moore picked up my pack and carried it. We walked at a brisk pace, and I finally cooled down. When we got to LZ Victor, I followed my commander to his command post. He gave me my pack and ordered one of his men to fill my canteens and have the medic check me out.

LTC Moore turned and began to walk away, so I said, "Gary Owen, Sir!"

He turned and smiled, "All the way, Sky Trooper!"

I made it back to my platoon area and didn't see LTC Moore there again, but I knew that I'd be forever grateful for this act of kindness from my commander.

Our mission to Ia Drang valley was over. The helicopters lifted us off LZ Victor and we headed home to An Khe. My first mission had taught me valuable lessons about going on missions, even though I hadn't fired a shot.

Later, I'd learn the value of having a scout dog lead me through the jungles and valleys of Vietnam. But my next mission would teach me that combat was nothing like I'd imagined it to be.

Chapter 4

My First Close Encounter with the Enemy

By the last week of April 1966, we'd been running patrols every day and had been out in the field for seventeen days guarding Highway 19, a major supply road to An Khe. Although we were making no enemy contact, Kenny and I were learning important lessons about tactical deployment, field artillery capability, and jungle infantry maneuvers. Each soldier had a specific task to do in this on-the-job training and we were beginning to understand the ways that our team members depended on one another.

I now considered living in a tent to be luxury compared to how we had to live, eat, sleep, and hunt in the heat, rain, and mud of the Vietnam countryside. It wasn't easy to make friends in Vietnam. Other than Kenny and Bob, I hardly knew the guys who shared my tent. When we moved in a tactical formation, the men maintained distance from one another. Riding in helicopters made it hard to talk. At night, when on missions, platoon members teamed up in foxholes strategically spaced apart. Visiting between them was prohibited, so the only men we got to know were the ones with whom we shared a foxhole. I began to realize that getting to know others and making lots of friends wasn't encouraged in a combat zone. The men, we befriended one day, might be killed in the next battle, so friendships often ended in pain and loss.

I could see, though, that some of the veterans were attached to one another like brothers, especially if they shared the same foxhole. For example,

29

two men named Tom were close friends. Tom Knutson carried an M79 grenade launcher that he could use to blow a coconut out of a tree 200 yards away. Tom was five-feet-eight inches tall and weighed 150 pounds. His close friend, Tom Bible, had short brown hair, was six feet tall, wore glasses, had a slender build, and carried an M16 rifle. Bible and Knutson were in the same squad and teamed up in a foxhole, whenever we humped through the jungle.

Although I didn't think of him as my friend, I liked Sergeant Doreman and thought he was the ultimate sergeant. He commanded respect from every member of the platoon and his fellow squad leaders. Sergeant Doreman always smiled and asked how Kenny and I were getting along. He teased me for being a *cherry jumper*. This term described a paratrooper who had recently graduated from jump school, but hadn't made a parachute jump since then. I'd earned my parachute wings by going through a physically rigorous, three-week course at Fort Benning, Georgia where the dropout rate had been very high. There were three levels of paratrooper qualification: basic, senior, and master jumper. Although I'd placed at the bottom, I felt proud to be a paratrooper.

Sergeant Doreman told Kenny and me that soon we'd be eligible to earn a Combat Infantry Badge (CIB) which was awarded only to infantrymen. To qualify for a CIB, a soldier had to have been officially schooled as an infantryman and awarded an 11B Military Occupational Specialty. Ultimately, a soldier had to serve in a combat infantry unit for at least thirty days during wartime. The CIB was considered the badge of courage. Only a small percentage of soldiers in the entire Army were authorized to wear a CIB. When a soldier earned it, he wore it with pride.

The CIB, about three inches long and an inch wide, was designed with a long silver rifle inlaid in a small, rectangular, blue-enameled background. An oval silver wreath surrounded the inlaid rifle. The CIB was worn above the left breast pocket and above all other service medals, ribbons, and badges. Sergeant Doreman once said, "A CIB is only for men with enough guts to be infantrymen and the balls to hunt Charlie for a living." Sergeant Doreman had already earned his CIB in the battle of Ia Drang valley. His combat awards included a Purple Heart for wounds, Bronze Star for valor, and an Air Medal for making combat air assaults from Huey helicopters into enemy-held jungle territory while under fire.

Kenny and I met two men in our squad with whom we didn't want to make friends. One of the men had a chip on his shoulder and enjoyed pulling pranks. He seemed to relish getting guys agitated. Ever since I'd seen him break a young Vietnamese girl's soft drink bottle for no good reason, sleep on guard duty, and throw a dummy grenade at me, I had no respect for him as a man or a soldier. I suppose every platoon had a guy like him. It's strange how the Army threw men together and hoped for the best. I worried that this guy would cause someone to get hurt or killed. This man and his buddy got along okay and shared the same tent. I didn't have much contact with them in the field and wanted to keep it that way.

Rodrigues (Rod) was a guy Kenny and I got to know the day he showed us how to mix and spice up C-rations. A large man of Hispanic descent, Rod was well-liked by everyone. He carried himself with the confidence and experience of a veteran combat soldier. Rod was being considered for the next available promotion to squad leader.

Doc, the platoon medic, was not an infantryman but was a highly trained combat medical specialist whose job was to take care of casualties, save lives, and issue survival basics such as malaria and salt pills. His field gear consisted of a large green shoulder bag, containing field medical supplies. His weapon was a .45 caliber pistol, which he carried in a holster, secured to the belt of his web gear. Doc was a stocky black man with the biggest smile in the platoon. In the field, he spent most of his time near the platoon leader and radio/telephone operator. He wasn't eligible for a CIB. Instead, he had earned a Combat Medical Badge that very few soldiers in the medical field received. Like the CIB, the CMB could only be earned during combat. When in base camp, Doc's quarters were with the battalion medical staff.

By the first week of May 1966, we'd been back in base camp for only a few days, when Sergeant Doreman gathered the squad to brief us on a new operations order. He told us we were going to Bong Son plains. In this mission, dubbed *Operation Davy Crockett*, our entire battalion was to sweep Bong Son from the mountains to the South China Sea.

Sergeant Doreman put his map down on a cot, so we could see, and pointed out the location of Bong Son plains. The valley started at the base of a mountain range, appeared to be several miles wide, and ended on the shores of the South China Sea. The map showed hundreds of rice paddies dotted with hamlets. The 2nd Platoon would be settling on top of the mountain range for the night. Choppers would pick us up in the morning and fly us into the valley.

The intelligence report from battalion S-2 indicated that Bong Son was a major North Vietnamese army stronghold. For years, Charlie had used the protection of the heavily populated villages as safe havens. It was reported that several thousand heavily armed North Vietnamese army regulars were operating in small groups throughout the area of operation. We were told it was *hot,* meaning that some firefights were already underway between the enemy and our battalion's advance forces.

The entire 1st Battalion, 7th Cavalry was to air assault and clear Bong Son of the NVA. A truck convoy would be used to transport the battalion from An Khe to Bong Son and deploy before nightfall. Everyone had to pack supplies and ammunition for three days. After that, we'd be re-supplied. Sergeant Doreman told the 2nd platoon that when we reached the beach, our reward would be swimming in the ocean and eating hot food.

After Sergeant Doreman left the tent, we prepared to go. I turned to Kenny and said, "Did you hear him say fighting is already going on?"

"Yes, I did."

"Well, I guess this is it, Kenny. We're finally going to see combat."

For a few seconds, Kenny and I stared at one another. Neither of us said a word.

Then I said, "Kenny, if anything happens to me, please write my family and tell them how it happened. I want them to know from you."

"Johnny," he said, "if anything happens to me, you write my folks." We exchanged addresses and stuffed them into our packs.

Shortly afterwards, I asked Kenny, "Hey, buddy, how do you feel?

Kenny turned and looked at me with a smile and simply replied, "Fine!"

Having never experienced combat before, I hoped that all the missions leading to this would help me to be brave, when I actually faced the enemy.

My First Close Encounter with the Enemy

While I packed my basic load, Bob Dunn came by and asked me how many more belts of M60 ammunition I could carry. Between Bob, Kenny, and me, we had ten belts amounting to 1000 rounds. I told Bob that I'd add two more 100-round belts to my load. I also packed several grenades. When I finished packing, my total load was at least seventy pounds. I decided not to lighten the load and risk being sorry about my decision later.

A few more new men had been assigned to the platoon, after we'd returned from our last mission on Route 19. I figured that the new men probably felt the same way Kenny and I had, when we prepared for our first mission, wondering if they'd be accepted by their elders. Now the 2nd Platoon had at least twenty-five men and our morale was high. We talked and joked while we waited to move to the pickup point on the road.

Out of nowhere, a loud voice yelled, "Saddle up!"

We lifted gear up and onto our shoulders and headed toward the waiting trucks. When we arrived, I saw a long column of trucks lining the road, bumper to bumper, as far as the eye could see. Each two-and-one-half-ton truck was stripped of its canvas top, except for the cab area. The drivers stood behind the dropped tailgates of their trucks. One-by-one, soldiers climbed into the backs of the trucks and sat on foldout wooden bench seats. The trucks' floors were a solid sheet of steel. The squad leader accounted for each of his men before he climbed into a cab with a driver.

One at a time, like a long train, each truck slowly rolled down the dirt road. As the convoy moved, more trucks linked up from other roads that led out of An Khe. The distance between the trucks increased as they drove off the base camp.

On top of its cab, each truck had an M60 machine gun, resting on a bipod. Every other man, sitting in the back, faced out with weapons at the ready. Overhead, gunships and helicopters flew escort. If Charlie were to attack, the battalion could retaliate with troops, gunships, artillery, and fighter jets. It was quite an impressive sight to see so much military power assembled for combat.

The convoy motored ahead, winding through the mountains and thick vegetation on each side of the road. Several men catnapped, while others watched the trees and road for signs of danger. Riding in the back of an open truck made us easy targets. If Charlie wanted to snipe, fire a rocket, or spring an ambush, he could easily cause a lot of casualties and bring the convoy to a halt in an instant.

The ride was long, as day became night. The drivers turned on the special night-lights and slowed their pace as the convoy tightened up. Kenny kept poking the driver of our truck, because he'd veer left and then right. I wondered if these drivers, unlike infantrymen, weren't used to going many hours without sleep.

Early the next morning, the vehicles stopped on a huge mountain plateau, covered with short vegetation and dense jungle, where we dismounted and moved away from the convoy. The 2nd platoon secured the edge of the mountain that was high above the Bong Son plains.

The sun shone early that morning as the 2nd platoon overlooked the mountain into rice paddies below. The steep cliff, thick with vegetation, made the mountain appear impossible to climb. Except for the road we'd come in on, there were no visible signs of roads or paths leading down into the Bong Son plains from where we were. Water on the rice paddies reflected the sun like tiny rectangular mirrors. Bong Son, a giant checkerboard of colorful rice paddies dotted with small villages all the way to the South China Sea, was a beautiful sight.

To the left of our platoon, a steep ravine separated two mountains. Another company of the 1st Battalion, 7th Cavalry Regiment occupied the other side. After we settled in, I accompanied a patrol to check out the ravine between the mountains. When the patrol got there, we looked down and had a breathtaking view. At the bottom of the ravine, terraced with rice paddies, a river of water wound its way into the mouth of the plains. It must have taken hundreds of years to carve this mountainside into giant terraced rice paddies. However, we saw no Vietnamese civilians working in the area. The other side of the ravine was nothing but a green dense jungle wall.

Kenny quipped, "It looks like a picture straight out of *National Geographic.*"

In spite of all this beauty, war raged in the valley below. Almost directly to the 2nd platoon's front, I pointed out several Navy warships in the waters off the coast of the South China Sea. From my vantage point, the tiny vessels appeared to be firing their deck guns inland. Puffs of smoke blew from the stationary ships. Seconds later, flashes of light and a billow of smoke from the exploding rounds appeared on the ground below.

To the right, Air Force jet fighters dropped bombs and fired their twenty millimeter cannons which can only fire on full-automatic and expend 2000 rounds per minute. When the pilot presses the trigger, the air is filled with a long burping sound that lasts several seconds. One twenty millimeter bullet is about five inches long and is as big around as a large man's thumb. I could imagine what was happening, when those huge bullets hit their targets.

Above the valley floor, I could hear helicopter gunships, firing M60 machine guns and launching rockets at the trees and rice paddies. On and off during that night, I saw bright flares in the sky above the valley and fire flashes from explosions. The whole situation was unlike anything I'd seen in Vietnam.

I commented to no one in particular, "There must be a hell of a lot of enemy troops down there to get the Navy, Air Force, and the Calvary involved."

Bob replied, "The reason for all the fireworks is to prepare the valley for our air-assault tomorrow morning."

Kenny and I didn't get much sleep that night, knowing that in the morning we'd be going into the valley.

Everyone stirred, when the sun came up in a blue sky, clear of rain clouds. I wiped the morning dew from my weapon, gave it a quick mechanical check, and oiled the exposed metal parts. Breakfast was C-rations and water. Within minutes, everyone in the 2nd platoon was prepared to move at a moment's notice.

Soon, a long stream of choppers flew in and landed not far behind our position. Every chopper was empty except for two pilots and two door gunners. With doors locked in the open position, the rotors turned at an idle speed. The first load of infantrymen from another platoon climbed into the slicks, lifted off, and headed into the valley.

A familiar voice called, "Saddle up!" and brought the 2nd platoon to their feet. A few minutes later, twenty choppers roared to a landing. Following

Bob and Kenny, I ran to our designated chopper. As soon as everyone was aboard, it swiftly lifted off and flew fifteen feet above the ground. When our chopper reached the ravine, the pilot made a sharp right banking maneuver. I thought I was going to fall out. I instantly sucked a huge amount of air into my lungs as the open doors faced the ground, directly. When the chopper leveled out, I let it out in one big sigh of relief. The pilot then dove straight down the ravine at high speed. The air escaped from my lungs as I held on for dear life. The chopper swooped so close to the treetops. I could almost reach out and touch them.

We flew into the valley like a swarm of bees above the rice paddies. This was the fastest helicopter ride I'd ever had. The chopper suddenly slowed down to land in a huge, dry rice paddy a mile or so away from the mountain we'd left behind.

A stream of red smoke—not a good sign—marked the landing area for the pilots. The red smoke meant that enemy contact was imminent. As the choppers prepared to land, they slightly lifted the noses of the ships and briefly touched down. Everyone exited and rushed for cover. I looked around and saw more and more choppers dropping men into the dry paddies. Eventually, the entire battalion of several hundred men would join together in the sweep to the South China Sea.

Bob and Kenny were ahead of me on the ground in prone position, behind their M60. Suddenly, a loud voice bellowed, "Move out!"

I rose to my feet and felt the extra-heavy weight of my pack pulling me down and cutting deep into my shoulders. Rice paddies surrounded us in every direction. Each man spread out about fifteen to twenty feet apart, as the platoon began to cautiously step forward. I kept my eyes on the uneven ground in front of me and tried to keep my footing.

Other American soldiers, on the left and right of the 2nd platoon, slowly faded into the distance. After a while, the 2nd platoon was moving alone. The valley seemed a lot bigger and much different from how it had looked from the mountain top. I couldn't see the ocean or the Navy ships anymore. The mountain we'd left was at least a mile behind.

A shot rang out overhead and broke the silence. We hit the ground at once. The shot sounded as though it had come from the tree line to the front. We waited a minute, but nothing more happened, so we were ordered to move out. One-by-one, we got up, then crouched, and carefully advanced toward the tree line from where we'd heard the shot.

As the 2nd platoon continued its sweep, I was positioned close to the rear. Someone spotted two enemy soldiers in the distance, running across the front. The platoon leader ordered us not to shoot or pursue, because the soldiers were too far out of our range. He didn't want a repeat of the situation, which had trapped the 2nd platoon in the Ia Drang valley, after they'd chased a few fleeing enemy soldiers.

We didn't encounter any resistance, as the platoon continued to move through the tree line from where the shot had originated.

By late afternoon, the platoon had pushed deep into the Bong Son plains. We eventually halted inside a lightly treed area, surrounded by rice paddies. The platoon leader decided to set up a perimeter around it and partly encompass a nearby dry rice paddy. Bob found a good spot to set up the M60 machine gun.

After the platoon sergeant was satisfied with the perimeter and each platoon member's defensive positions, he ordered us to dig foxholes for the evening. I had excellent visibility to the front of my position and clear lanes of fire on flat ground. I could easily see and communicate with adjacent fighting positions. Bob and Kenny placed their machine gun in a defensive position.

Before dark, I was about twenty-five yards away from my position and setting up the claymore mines and trip flares when a loud explosion filled the air, no more than one hundred feet behind me. I reacted by sprawling into the dirt and looked in the direction of the sound. I saw a small billow of white smoke.

Someone yelled, "Incoming!"

Seconds later, a second explosion ripped through the same spot.

I quickly crawled on my belly back to the foxhole. Kenny and Bob were already inside and preparing for the worst. From the direction of the explosions, I heard men repeatedly crying, "Medic!" In total silence, we waited for the enemy to attack. Several minutes passed. Nothing happened. Not one bullet was fired. Except for the commotion behind us, where someone had been hit, a strange quiet hung in the air.

Bob said that mortars were attacking the platoon. The first round had been white phosphorous or, as we called it, a *Willy Peter*. The second round had been a high explosive, or *H.E.* Bob told me that Charlie didn't use Willy Peter. Americans used Willy Peters as spotter rounds to mark targets with smoke before firing a volley of high-explosive rounds.

This led us to suspect that the mortars had been launched accidentally by an American platoon from another company that didn't know friendly troops were operating in their target area. The platoon leader, platoon sergeant, a squad leader, and two riflemen had been wounded. All of them had been standing in the center of the command post (CP), when the two small mortar rounds had exploded nearby. They suffered from severe lower torso and leg wounds, but no one had been killed. Several hundred American troops were operating in platoon-sized elements all over the valley. Now someone had become careless, and their *friendly fire* had made the 2nd platoon lose five men.

Later on, a medical evacuation chopper landed and lifted the wounded to a field hospital. Although the 2nd platoon now had only nineteen men, we still had to carry out our mission. Sergeant Doreman took over as platoon leader.

Nothing else happened the rest of that night.

Early the next morning on May 6, 1966, the sun was very bright and the sky clear blue. A chopper landed in the rice paddy nearby. Two men helped another member of the 2nd platoon aboard. During the attack of friendly fire, Tom Bible had been hit by shrapnel but he'd refused to evacuate because we were already shorthanded. Today, he was leaving as another wounded veteran of an Ia Drang valley battle.

I went out to disarm and retrieve the claymore mines and trip flares. We packed our gear and buried the trash from the food we'd eaten. It was time to continue the mission of sweeping on foot to the South China Sea. As the platoon moved out, the men began to put some distance between each other. Bob's M60 machine gun team joined the rear of the formation.

As the last man in the platoon formation, my job was to keep an eye on the rear. As we moved across the rice paddies, I spotted the flank guards about fifty yards to the left and right of the column. I visually searched my surroundings and saw no other friendly units.

The platoon crossed several large rice paddies before pausing at a dike. I knelt on one knee and heard jet aircraft in the distance. Soon the jets were flying about two hundred feet directly over our heads. Their engines screamed as they flashed by and headed toward the trees in front us. Bombs released from their wings exploded with tremendous force in the wood line ahead. If they'd dropped the bombs one hundred yards closer, they'd have exploded on top of us. Someone had called in those air strikes, and I assumed it must have been Sergeant Doreman.

Gunships suddenly appeared and fired aerial rocket artillery into the trees ahead. After the air strikes, I visually searched for signs of the enemy but saw nothing.

The platoon sergeant organized the platoon in a circular defensive position. We were told to keep looking for the enemy. Each rice paddy had dikes, roughly two feet high on all four sides, which held in the water for the Vietnamese who rotated their rice crops by manual water irrigation. The platoon happened to be set up in a dry rice paddy, although there were many wet ones in the area. These dikes presented excellent cover from the exploding bombs' shrapnel.

In the distance, other American troops halted and took cover from the air strikes. Our front was clear of obstacles all the way to the tree line that was less than one hundred yards away. The platoon held tight until the Air Force's and the cavalry's gunships stopped their strafing runs.

Kenny and Bob positioned the M60 machine gun on the corner of the dike and aimed at the trees ahead. I set up a short distance to their right side. I pointed my M16 rifle toward inside the perimeter. A jet screamed from behind us, a few hundred feet above the ground, and released two bombs from its wings, simultaneously. The bombs fell into the trees and made an earth-shattering explosion. The ground underneath my feet shook violently. At that very instant, I had my finger on the trigger of my M16 rifle. As the bombs exploded, I flinched and jerked the trigger back. My M16 rifle was on full-automatic and fired a long burst of rounds into the center of the perimeter. I watched with fright as the bullets kicked up clumps of dirt and soldiers scrambled for cover. As my finger released the trigger,

I realized instantly what I'd done, but it was too late. Everything had happened in a few seconds.

Someone yelled, "Where the hell did that come from?"

Sergeant Doreman rushed over in a crouched position and asked where the shots came from. Kenny and Bob looked at him and said nothing. I confessed that it was my fault and tried to explain what had happened.

Sergeant Doreman interrupted and screamed, "Are you fucking nuts? Do you have any fucking idea what you did? You just about fucking killed me and the other squad leaders!"

I froze while looking into the rage of Sergeant Doreman's eyes.

"Next time you check your fucking weapon and always keep it pointed out and away from anyone. Do I make myself clear?"

"Yes, Sergeant!"

Sergeant Doreman turned and stomped away cursing and shaking his head. I'd almost killed someone by mistake. I'd never felt so humiliated and embarrassed in all my life. I told Kenny and Bob that I must have left the selector switch on the *auto* setting after I'd oiled my M16 that morning. Kenny saw that I was completely dejected by the whole event. He put his arm around my shoulder and said, "Hey, buddy, it's okay. Besides, this could have happened to anyone. Shake it off!"

I reflected back to the aftershave lotion incident in the Ia Drang valley and thought, "Man, am I prone to make mistakes, or what?"

After the bombing stopped, the platoon ended up not going in that direction anyway. Instead, we headed back the way we'd come and circled to the left toward what appeared to be a village in the distance. We spread out and walked very cautiously, looking into the trees and on the ground in front of us. My load kept shifting. This made it difficult to walk on the uneven ground.

I kept watching the ground and thinking about what had happened back at the rice paddy. Then I felt something blunt hit my helmet, and a voice said, "Keep your head and eyes up; Charlie's not in the dirt." I looked up and recognized one of the other squad leaders. It really was an art to learn to walk on uneven soil with a heavy load and keep your head up with your eyes constantly scanning around for signs of danger. I was beginning to realize that my months of intensive stateside infantry training hadn't adequately prepared me for the real thing. I was experiencing the mistakes of war that new guys usually make and it scared me. I knew I had to stay focused as I learned to be a combat soldier on the job.

Our platoon, now somewhere in the middle of the Bong Son plains with mountains behind us, was about to enter a Vietnamese village. The front of the formation stopped. Everyone dropped to one knee. A squad of men was signaled to enter the village first. The men separated from the platoon and went forward with their weapons at the ready. Bob lay behind his M60 machine gun with Kenny at his side. I held my position at the tail end of the platoon and faced the rear.

The squad entered the village and checked out the straw huts inside it, while the rest of the platoon waited nearby. From a distance, the village appeared to be deserted. Not long into the search, someone uncovered several Vietnamese hiding inside spider holes and bunkers. Then the rest of our platoon quickly moved into the village and provided security.

We trained our weapons on the Vietnamese and ordered them to move into a group as we rounded up ten old unarmed women and some young children. They wore black pajamas and no shoes. They squatted and huddled nervously. It was easy to see the fear in their eyes and on their faces. An older woman cradled her crying infant. The babies didn't have a stitch of clothing covering them.

An American soldier spoke in Vietnamese, saying that we wouldn't harm them. He asked where the Viet Cong were hiding. An elderly woman cried out over and over again, "No VC! No VC!" Several men continued the search and uncovered nothing else.

At noon a decision was made for us to stay in the village and have lunch. This village, completely surrounded by rice paddies, impressed me with how clean and well-maintained it was. Palm, coconut, and several banana trees bore fruit. The occupants appeared to be simple peasant farmers.

I wondered where all the men and boys were. I speculated that maybe these captives were families of Viet Cong soldiers. Bob surmised that we hadn't found young men, women, and boys, because the Vietnamese thought we'd take the young men as prisoners, rape the woman, and kill the boys. Bob went on to say that the men and boys were probably hiding

41

somewhere nearby. When the platoon left, they'd return to their families—a typical maneuver when American troops invaded a village.

We eventually sent the Vietnamese back to their homes. After their release, several women hospitably brought the troops fresh coconut and bananas. The soldiers accepted their gifts and thanked them. I felt safe and didn't think Charlie was anywhere near the village. The platoon relaxed in the shade of the trees for an hour or so.

Some of the guys started to horse around by chasing chickens through the village. The Vietnamese children laughed at these crazy grunts. After we ate and rested, it was time to move again. There was a constant noise of helicopters overhead nearby, but I heard no sounds of gunfire. When the platoon departed the village, an older Vietnamese woman bowed as each soldier passed.

The 2nd platoon headed across another rice paddy to continue our mission of sweeping to the South China Sea. As we approached another village, we saw gunships ahead. They were firing rockets and machine guns into a treed area. Our platoon continued to move forward across the rice paddy. As we came closer to the village, I heard a machine gun. It was shooting back at the gunship but didn't sound like an M60 or anything I'd heard before. It had a slower, thudding, firing rhythm. Bob quickly pointed out that this was the sound of an NVA heavy machine gun firing up at the aircraft.

Because Bob had been in firefights with Charlie before, I valued his knowledge and combat experience. This was his second time in Bong Son. The first time he'd served had been in February—a month before Kenny and I had arrived in Vietnam.

My mind filled with crazy thoughts of how I could sneak up with a grenade and knock out that enemy machine gun. I wanted to make up for my earlier mistakes and regain the respect that I thought I'd lost from my squad members. My fantasy quickly disappeared when we were ordered to move to the far right of the enemy machine gun nest.

Another apparently deserted village lay ahead. The platoon entered it much as we had the previous one. As the first squad approached the vil-

42

lage, nothing happened. The rest of platoon moved forward in three-man fire teams. One team crouched and rushed about fifty feet and knelt down. The other team moved in the same manner. The advance alternated, until we were all inside cover of the village. Engles' machine gun provided protection for the few men who searched the straw huts. The platoon checked for hiding places outside and underneath or wherever might provide a hiding place.

As the platoon poked around outside, they were completely surprised when several Vietnamese men, with hands held high over their heads, came running out of an underground hiding place. Some of the Vietnamese wore black pajamas, while others were dressed in khaki shirts and trousers. American weapons quickly trained on the unarmed men. One of the Vietnamese repeated loudly, "Chieu Hoi! Chieu Hoi!" He was referring to the open arms program, promising clemency and financial aid to Viet Cong and North Vietnamese soldiers and cadres who stopped fighting and returned to South Vietnamese authority.

In short, it meant, "I surrender."

The one man in our platoon, who could speak some Vietnamese, made the men lay face down on the ground, so they could be searched. The soldiers found no weapons or documents that anyone could interpret. The prisoners' hands were tied together behind their backs with rope. Bob, Kenny and I guarded them. After a short while, we captured several other Vietnamese men who were hiding in the village. Our platoon now had eight male Vietnamese prisoners. After a short interrogation, they confessed to being deserters from a battalion of North Vietnamese Army regulars who had been operating in that area.

For the first time, Kenny and I were seeing the enemy close up. I wasn't afraid to guard them. The men didn't appear to be afraid of me, either. They stared at me and probably wondered what I was going to do with them. The platoon stayed in the village for about an hour but didn't find anything else. We linked the prisoners together with a rope that kept them separated by a few feet. A squad leader positioned the prisoners near the center of our formation.

I asked, "What if they try to escape?"

Sergeant Doreman replied, "Shoot first and ask questions later."

The platoon headed out of the village to the edge of a clearing. The prisoners had to be evacuated as soon as possible. The platoon sergeant used the radio to call for a chopper and to make contact with the company commander. Since I was in the center of the platoon, I heard what was going on over the radio and could see the pointman leading the formation. We spotted a chopper nearby. Sergeant Doreman popped green smoke in the air to mark a landing site. The chopper, already crammed with gear, took all but two of the prisoners after the crew chief used a knife to cut them loose. As the chopper lifted away, we left the area.

I now had full responsibility for watching the remaining two prisoners. I walked behind them as they followed Kenny and Bob. Not long into the journey, across a clearing, a sniper fired several shots at the platoon. We hit the ground and got into a prone position. The front of the platoon quickly returned fire. Engles's M60 machine gun let go several short bursts. I didn't fire my weapon. Instead, I watched the prisoners to make sure they remained tied up and didn't try to escape. I wasn't going to make another mistake. If they ran, I'd shoot them, as ordered.

The sniper had shot the platoon's pointman. Walking point was the most dangerous position in a tactical formation. The squad leaders would ensure that no man walked point more than his share. Doc assisted the wounded pointman, while Sergeant Doreman radioed for a dust-off. With the platoon, still in the middle of a rice paddy, we crawled on our bellies to form a hasty perimeter. A few minutes later, a dust-off (medical evacuation chopper) hovered overhead. We popped red smoke and the dust-off descended close to the ground with its nose up.

An enemy machine gun fired at the dust-off. The chopper must have gotten hit because it took off before the wounded man could be loaded. As soon as it was airborne, the enemy stopped firing. Sergeant Doreman thought that the platoon's counterfire had silenced the enemy's machine gun. It was quiet for a while, so we radioed the dust-off to return. As soon as it started to touch down, the enemy opened fire again. This time, Charlie fired intensively at the chopper with a machine gun. No one could believe what we were witnessing. Here was an unarmed medical evacuation helicopter with easily visible bright red crosses painted on a white background on each side door. Charlie was determined to knock it out with complete disregard for the rules of the Geneva Convention. The medical evacuation helicopter had to take off again and leave our wounded comrade behind.

The front of the platoon opened fire again to try to silence the enemy in the trees. A short time later, two Air Force jets appeared directly overhead. I checked my M16 to ensure I'd secured the safety. I didn't want to repeat my earlier mistake. One jet dove down, no more than a few hundred feet above our heads, and released two silver-colored canisters. The aircraft was so close, that we could see the pilot in the cockpit.

Kenny and I watched in absolute amazement as those canisters tumbled over our heads. When they hit the trees, they exploded into a huge wall of orange and red flames. Bob told me that this was Napalm—a jelly-like substance mixed with fuel that sticks to and burns everything it touches. I could feel the intense heat fifty yards away. A few seconds later, the second jet zoomed over and fired twenty-mm cannons, shattering tree limbs and kicking up dirt everywhere. I thought nothing living could have survived it.

After the blaze died down, the enemy didn't shoot during the platoon's advance across the clearing. The wounded pointman was placed in the center of the formation with Doc. He had one arm in a sling. A bloody bandage was tightly wrapped around his shoulder and he carried a rifle in his other hand. He appeared to be in pain but was able to travel without assistance.

It wasn't long before we made it across the clearing and moved inside what was left of a tree line. Smoke billowed everywhere with small fires burning all around. The men carefully stepped through the area. I kept my weapon trained on the two prisoners. They appeared to be emotionally shaken and remained silent as they moved forward.

As I passed a burning hut, directly in front of me, a dark figure came walking out of the smoke. I froze dead in my tracks and yelled, "Oh, my God, it's a woman!" Her clothes had been burned off and her body was charred and smoking; her face was badly burned and bleeding. She raised her hands and cupped them to her mouth, as if asking for water or help. She stood in front of me and spoke softly in Vietnamese. I knew she was going to die, and there was nothing I could do to stop it. I actually thought for a brief second that I should shoot her to put her out of her misery. She took a few steps past me and fell to the ground. I did nothing but look at her smoking, charred body lying motionless, face down on the ground.

Seeing the burning woman had briefly caused me to forget what I'd been doing. When I realized where I was, I looked for the prisoners. They hadn't moved and appeared to be as terrified as me, but they hadn't tried to escape. I quickly composed myself. The incident had happened in less than a minute, but everyone else had gone on ahead. I moved the prisoners away from the scene and didn't turn back to look at it.

When I caught up with Kenny and Bob, Kenny asked me if I'd shot the woman. I told him that I'd thought about it but hadn't. What Kenny had thought was gun fire was actually the sounds of crackling wood from the fire. Kenny asked what had happened to her, and I told him that she'd fallen down and died. Kenny said that there was nothing anyone could have done for her.

The platoon slowly made its way through the burned-out village. Not too far ahead of us, the soldier who had been wounded by the sniper was still walking. I hoped we could get him on a dust-off soon.

A deep, wide ditch with muddied water halted the platoon's advance. The only way across it was to walk on a rotting board that connected to the other side. One at a time, soldiers crossed over on the board. The weight of their bodies and their loaded packs bowed the plank to its limits.

Rod stepped onto the plank. About halfway across, his 220-pound body and heavy pack cracked the rotting plank. He fell straight down into the muddy water about five feet below and sunk up to his chest, keeping his rifle above his head. He couldn't move anything but his arms and head. Rod cursed up a storm, as the rest of us laughed hysterically.

Someone found a long tree branch to help Rod, but it broke under the weight of pulling him. Then we tossed a thin rope to Rod, but it snapped under the strain. We had to radio a chopper for help. It lowered a thick rope through the burned trees. Rod grabbed the rope, tied it to his upper body, and the chopper plucked him out like a giant turnip. When he was free, two troopers grabbed Rod and pulled him to dry ground.

A few men searched and found another place where it would be safer to cross the ditch. After everyone was across, the platoon continued our trek to the South China Sea. None of us had any idea how far away it was. As the platoon spread out and moved in a tactical sweeping formation, we entered another village that was still smoking from the Napalm drop. The air filled with the smell of fuel and burning debris. My throat and lungs burned from inhaling smoke, so I drank some water.

Suddenly, the front of the platoon came under attack by automatic weapons fire. We hit the dirt and returned fire. Being close to the rear with the prisoners, I wasn't in a position to fire. Bob and Kenny covered the rear of the platoon and waited behind their M60 machine gun but they weren't in a good position to use it. Enemy bullets cracked over our heads. After a brief exchange of fire, we fired and maneuvered to the right, away from the incoming attack.

Several VC tried to flank the platoon on the left front as each squad maneuvered right. We had little protection as the bullets zipped through the air. It was a miracle that none of us were hit. A small clearing on the right led to a group of trees that had a straw hut on the other side. We crouched, ran in that direction, but stopped short of entering the clearing.

Rod led the first assault squad. He directed a team of three riflemen to provide a base of fire while he and two others crouched and darted into the open clearing. They stopped and got down into a prone firing position. Then they shot a base of fire into the direction where they were heading. The next three men charged into the clearing the same way. They followed the classic textbook leapfrog technique commonly used by the infantry.

In the distance, Charlie kept the pressure on our platoon's left side. As the first squad entered and secured the other side of the clearing, the rest of us quickly moved across in small groups of four or five troops. Bullets cracked the air very close to me. I figured that Charlie had spotted the prisoners. Kenny pointed out a huge water buffalo frantically exiting a water hole where Rod stood. Its horns appeared to scrape against Rod as he desperately tried to get out of its path. The water buffalo ran through the middle of the platoon into the clearing behind us.

When I reached the trees, a fellow soldier lay on his back in the open with his helmet off. Blood gushed in spurts from his throat. His face was full of dirt and sweat. A continuous stream of blood ran down the side of

47

his mouth. He lay on his back, bleeding and gasping for air with his eyes bulging. I stopped and knelt down beside him to see what I could do.

Sergeant Doreman screamed, "Get your ass and those prisoners under cover before you're shot."

Doc came out of nowhere and began to assist the wounded soldier. I held the rope that tied the prisoners and pulled them behind me as I rushed into the trees and jumped into the same water hole the water buffalo had left moments before. The pit was about chest deep at the edge of a row of banana and palm trees. About ten feet to my right, Kenny and Bob lay flat behind a banana tree and savagely fired the M60 machine gun. On my left, Knutson used his M79 grenade launcher to fire at targets across the rice paddy.

The platoon made a stand and fought off Charlie's onslaught. We'd set up a defensive perimeter around a small clump of trees with the remains of a burned-out straw hut in its center. We lay flat on the ground and fired up a storm. The heaviest action was on the left side of our platoon's small defensive perimeter.

Engles yelled to me from the left, "There they are! There they are!" as he fired his M60 machine gun.

VC, clad in khaki uniforms, fired back and darted from place to place across the front. Many VC fell dead from a hail of our bullets and grenades.

For the first time since I'd been in Vietnam, I aimed my M16 at the enemy and fired. The VC bobbed up and down and fired back from behind a dike fifty yards in front of me. I carefully aimed and fired many magazines of ammunition above the dike. I tried to hit the VC as they bobbed up to fire back. I hit some of them, but others held their positions and fought back hard.

On my right, Kenny loaded another 100-round belt of ammunition into the M60 while Bob maintained his aim behind the gun. Their M60 kicked up dirt and debris all over the area. Lifeless bodies of VC, some no more than thirty yards out, littered the ground in front of their position.

American voices called for a medic. The platoon had taken heavy casualties. Deadly enemy machine gun fire had strafed our small perimeter. Everyone kept reloading and firing back. I noticed that less shooting and explosions came from the right side of the perimeter.

A loud voice screamed, "There they are on the left! On the left!" This was the direction of the village the platoon had vacated minutes earlier.

Gunships swarmed overhead, firing rockets that exploded almost on top of our platoon. I flinched, as shrapnel whizzed through the air, splintered the trees, and kicked up the dirt around me. The noise was intense. Charlie fought from well-fortified defensive positions in the rice paddies' dikes. He kept shooting back fast and furiously after each rocket exploded. We were all in a reaction mode, and I wasn't thinking about what could happen to us.

The extra ammunition I'd decided to carry now came in handy. I'd already used about two-hundred rounds by firing on semi-automatic.

Kenny's machine gun jammed with a bullet still in its chamber. If it cooked off, the bullet would explode inside and make the weapon useless. Kenny had little time to fix the problem. He reached back to pull his bayonet out of his pistol belt to pry the jammed bullet out of the chamber. Almost immediately, his arm smacked him in the chest; he fell over onto his side and curled up on the ground beside his gun. Kenny's helmet rolled away from his head.

He told Bob, "I'm hit!"

Bob replied, "Are you sure?"

Kenny lifted his arm to show Bob. "I guess you are!" he said.

Bob yelled for a medic and then called, "Johnny, Kenny's hit!"

I looked in Bob's direction and saw Kenny lying still in a curled up position. I was afraid he'd died. I quickly crawled over to him and left my prisoners unattended.

Kenny first words were, "You're white as a ghost!"

It was shocking for me to see my best friend lying there moaning and in severe pain with open flesh wounds that made him look as if he was bleeding to death. All I could think was, *Please, don't die. Please don't die. This is my best friend. You can't take him away from me like this!*

When the medic arrived, he couldn't work on Kenny in the open with all the lead flying around. Incoming bullets kicked dirt up and whizzed around us. We dragged Kenny a few yards into the water hole. I thought, *Thank God he's still alive!*

Kenny had been hit by a VC 30-caliber machine gun blast. He was suffering and complained of sharp stomach pains. With his fatigue shirt soaked in blood and one sleeve ripped completely off, a large part of his forearm muscle was missing and the white of the bone was exposed. He bled heavily from his wounds. The bullets had torn his arm apart. Several holes were in his stomach, but he didn't have any exit wounds in his back. I carefully removed Kenny's shoulder harness and backpack to make him more comfortable. After I got his gear off, Kenny doubled up in pain. The medic placed Kenny's good arm under his armpit to try to slow the bleeding. He dressed the wounds and gave him a shot of morphine to ease the pain. The two prisoners looked scared but remained tied together and lying on the dirt at the bottom of the hole, where I'd left them.

The medic grabbed my shirt and pulled me down into the hole. He told me that if I didn't keep my head down, I'd be killed. After Kenny's wounds were dressed, I rejoined the fighting and tried to keep an eye on him and the prisoners. Bob was still on the right firing the M60 machine gun and reloading it himself. I tossed him another 100-round belt of ammunition from Kenny's pack.

Above all the shooting and explosions, Sergeant Doreman yelled, "Grab the wounded and dead and get ready to move out!"

The enemy had surrounded our platoon on three sides and was closing in fast. We were about to be overrun, captured, or killed. As fast as I could, I untied Kenny's poncho from his pack, rolled it out, and put it under him. Charlie continued to pour it on with AK-47 rifles, machine gun fire, and grenades. The grenades all fell short and exploded outside our perimeter.

Sergeant Doreman yelled, "Hurry up. We've got to go!"

I couldn't lift and carry Kenny by myself. Bob was loaded down with equipment, M60 machine gun, and ammunition. I cut the two prisoners loose and ordered them at gun point to each grab a corner of the poncho. Bob and I held on to the other two corners. The four of us lifted Kenny and rushed in a crouched position to the far right side of the perimeter, away from the enemy. Our platoon carried out six or seven men who were lying in ponchos.

Sergeant Doreman took a quick count of his men and pointed ahead. He said, "The rest our company is waiting for us in the graveyard on the other side of this rice paddy."

The only way out was to move one hundred yards across the wide open space of a rice paddy and take the risk of being exposed to enemy fire. A three-foot dike on the left of the paddy provided our only cover. Every able-bodied man helped to carry the wounded in their ponchos. It took only a few minutes, from when Sergeant Doreman gave the order for us to grab up the wounded and dead and move into position to cross the rice paddy.

The next words I heard were, "Let's go!"

Almost at once, we started running in a crouched position as fast as our legs could go. Firing continued in front and behind us. No one stopped running, even for a short breather. As our ragged platoon came closer to the other side of the rice paddy, Americans waved us on while they covered our advance with a base of fire. When we finally reached the American lines, we were exhausted and breathing heavily. I turned over the two prisoners to soldiers who took them away at gunpoint.

Inside the American lines, other soldiers helped us to move the 2nd platoon's wounded and dead comrades to a Vietnamese graveyard. The Vietnamese build their graveyards on high dry ground above the rice paddies. Each grave is a mound of dirt about three feet high. The graves are lined up in rows. They provided a great defensive position and security for our wounded and dead.

Medics began to assist more than fifty wounded men who lay scattered on the ground in ponchos. Not far from the wounded, the bodies of twenty or thirty lifeless young men were completely covered in green plastic ponchos and lined up in rows. Only their boots exposed. I stared at them and thought how sad it was to see these men, lying in the hot sun, side-by-side, in the dirt, underneath pieces of plastic.

When I saw Kenny again, I looked at him and said, "We made it! How do you feel?"

It was difficult for Kenny to talk, but he said he was fine and that the morphine was helping to relieve much of his pain. I assured him that I'd keep my word and write to his folks to tell them what had happened to him. Kenny strained to speak and said, "Thanks for helping me, Johnny! Don't forget to tell my folks that I'm okay."

The fighting seemed to have stopped. Charlie apparently had broken contact or had been wiped out.

Sergeant Doreman, Rod, Bob, Engles, and the other survivors of the 2nd platoon came by to pay their respects to the dead and wounded. I stayed with Kenny until the medics assisted him. I helped to lift him onto a stretcher and we carried my friend to the designated lift-off area.

Several dust-off helicopters landed and the wounded were loaded aboard them. I watched as Kenny and the others lifted off safely into the sky and went on their way to a field hospital. After Kenny was gone, I felt relieved that he'd be okay but desolate at the thought of not having his company.

Would I ever see my friend again? I wondered as I walked along the perimeter.

I found Bob sitting behind his M60 and staring at the rice paddy. I took Kenny's place as Bob's assistant gunner. It was quiet except for the dust-offs and supply ships flying in and out of the graveyard.

The day was getting late and darkness settled in. Bob and I talked about how the events of the day had unfolded. Sergeant Doreman came for a visit. He told us that the platoon had five KIA (killed-in-action) and seven WIA (wounded-in-action). The figure included the men who had been wounded by our own troops' *friendly* mortar fire.

I thought, *Hell, we left An Khe with twenty-five men in our platoon, and two days later, only thirteen of us are left.*

Sergeant Doreman also told us that our sister company had made a sweep of the area. They'd counted about fifty dead North Vietnamese army soldiers around the positions our platoon had defended. Sergeant Doreman told us how proud he was of us for being brave and fighting like hell. After Sergeant Doreman left, it started to rain.

I thought, *If God is up there, this rain must be his tears.*

I felt empty inside and alone for the first time since I'd arrived in Vietnam. I felt like I'd lost my brother. I didn't know if Kenny was going to live or die before they got him to a hospital. What would I say to Kenny's family? What does anyone say to all the families of the men who have died?

I reflected on the details of my first combat experience and realized how quickly death can come. I tried to hold my tears back but I couldn't. They streamed down my face. Bob put his arm around me and assured me that it was okay to cry.

I pulled my poncho over my head and stared into the dark night, feeling sad and angry. I couldn't stop thinking about every detail that had happened that day, but these memories only pushed me deeper into depression. I promised myself that I'd never forget the men who had lost their lives that day. I hadn't known most of them, but they were Americans. That was all I cared about. Now I wanted to kill every VC, for what they'd done to Kenny and the others.

Later that night the rain stopped and the clouds cleared. Bob and I stayed alert all night, waiting for a counterattack that never came. We took turns catnapping. The fighting appeared to be over, and my first combat experience had finally ended.

The next morning I ate my C-rations, shaved, and prepared to move out. I felt better, but I was ready to get the hell out of that place. The platoon was re-supplied with more ammunition, water, and food for the rest of our journey to the South China Sea. Because we'd been reduced to a squad and a half, we were now being attached to another platoon.

No one talked much as we joined with the other platoon. My squad, led by Sergeant Doreman and his radio/telephone operator (RTO), was positioned as rear guard for the lead platoon. Bob and I walked at its end. Two radios supported us as we passed through a few more burned-out villages that showed no signs of inhabitants. We didn't even see a chicken, dog, or water buffalo. Small bomb and rocket craters pitted the ground. We didn't make contact with Charlie or get sniped at, but we did see dead bodies of the enemy as we moved forward. As I looked at the dead enemy soldiers, I didn't feel sad or get sick seeing their bullet riddled bloody bodies lying in contorted positions on the ground where they died.

To my amazement, we were within a mile of the ocean. I figured that the platoon must have covered several miles since we'd started moving a few days earlier. I could see the ocean straight ahead.

When the platoon arrived at the beach, hundreds of American soldiers were already in the water. Men spread out and relaxed in the sand all along the shoreline. I appreciated the peaceful setting even though I wasn't in the best of spirits. It was great to see the soldiers splashing in the water and having fun. I stopped for a moment and stood on the white sand listening to the waves splashing against the shore. In the distance, I spotted large gray Navy ships. I wondered if they were the ones I'd seen from the mountain, firing into the valley.

The platoon stopped in an area where we had room to spread out and set up positions. After Bob and I put our equipment down, Sergeant Doreman came by and told us to enjoy ourselves for the rest of the day. As Sergeant Doreman promised, we had hot food, relaxation, and time to go swimming.

I kept thinking about Kenny and knew that this beach time would have been something he'd enjoy. I started to feel much better as I walked on the beach. I propped my back against a palm tree and rested in the shade. After a while, I decided to go back to my gear and get some writing material. I returned to the palm tree and wrote a letter to Kenny's parents to explain what had happened to their second son. I also wrote several other letters to my family and friends back home in Littleton, Colorado.

The platoon stayed at the beach that night and got some well-deserved sleep. Another battalion pulled perimeter security guard. I slept on the beach beneath a palm tree and awoke the next morning to the sounds of sea gulls and ocean waves.

The next day, Bob and I lounged on the beach until late morning, and talked about all the things we were going to do as soon as we returned to our stomping grounds in the States. Later that day, we packed and got ready to go home to An Khe.

A bunch of slicks landed on a road not far behind the beach. I climbed aboard one of them, and we lifted off. The choppers gradually climbed to a high altitude and headed toward the mountains. I sat on the floor of the chopper and peered out the open doors. I tried to locate the positions we'd fought with Charlie, but everything below looked the same. The Bong Son plains appeared peaceful from several thousand feet up. I don't remember how long it took for us to fly home, but it was a very long ride over the mountain range.

My First Close Encounter with the Enemy

When the base camp became visible in the distance, the choppers began their descent. As we flew closer to the huge perimeter of Camp Radcliff, I could see the road, which we'd traveled on when we were in the back of the truck going to Bong Son. The choppers made a sharp left turn and landed single file on the road behind the green canvas tents of our company's living quarters. As we exited the choppers, I couldn't believe my eyes and ears. The Division Band stood on the side of the road and began to play. The sound of the music, mixed with the noise of helicopters, made me feel patriotic. *A nice welcome home touch,* I thought; *Kenny would have liked it, too.*

I slowly walked past the band and headed to my tent. When I got to my cot, I took my steel pot off and laid down my gear. I unpacked the empty magazines, ammunition, claymore mines, grenades, and trip flares. I had to check over everything for future serviceability or for possible replacement. I immediately cleaned and oiled my weapons. My M16 had become full of carbon buildup and sand.

I saw Tom Bible sitting on his cot and reading a book. He was the guy who had been wounded by friendly mortar fire the first day in Bong Son. Even though Tom had been hurt, he'd refused to evacuate until the next day because he wanted to stay with his squad. I asked Tom how he was doing and he assured me that he was okay. The mortar shrapnel had been removed from his leg and his injury had turned out to be only a flesh wound. He didn't ask me what had happened, but there was something about the way he acted and looked that told me he already knew. Back at base camp, the rear echelon had been kept informed by radio of the fight and the casualties we'd sustained.

Sergeant Doreman walked into the tent and came over to my cot. He asked me to pack Kenny's gear and take it to the company supply tent. So I stuffed all Kenny's belongings into his duffel bag that was lying on his cot. Kenny had spent only a handful of nights sleeping in that cot. His wounds were so severe that Sergeant Doreman suspected Kenny would be evacuated to a major Army field hospital in Qui Nhom near Bong Son.

It looked as if Kenny wouldn't be reporting back for duty. Neither would the soldiers who had been killed in action. They would be sent home to their families in caskets. I learned that some of those who had died had been scheduled to serve only a few more months in Vietnam, while others had recently arrived. I felt terrible about the whole situation. I watched several soldiers quietly packing the personal effects of their fallen comrades.

Kenny had spent sixty-five days in South Vietnam. Most of that time, he'd marched long distances through the heat in the jungles and rice paddies, hunting for a fight, eating C-rations, digging foxholes, carrying a sixty-pound pack, pulling guard duty every night, and catnapping in the dirt, rain, and mud. I was beginning to learn and understand the true meaning of the nickname, *grunt*. Kenny Mook had definitely earned a Combat Infantry Badge and a Purple Heart. He and all the others were the real heroes of our platoon. As darkness fell, I prayed for Kenny and those who hadn't made it back with us.

After our return, I got a second liberty pass to go to An Khe — *Sin City* — the small Vietnamese town outside base camp. I went with Sergeant Doreman and Bob Dunn. We had a great time. I bought a small mirror with a frame that was handmade from a metal beer can. The back of the mirror was a cardboard C-ration box. The Vietnamese always seemed to find uses for our discarded trash and sold back to us what we'd originally gotten for free.

Several weeks after Kenny was wounded, Sergeant Doreman called me into his tent. He asked if I'd written to Kenny's parents to tell them what had happened to their son in Bong Son. I told him that I had. He said that my letter had gotten to Kenny's folks before the Army's official telegram of notification and the Army brass was embarrassed that they hadn't written to the parents first. I told Sergeant Doreman, before we went to Bong Son, Kenny and I had promised each that we'd write to the other person's parents if anything happened to one of us. I thought that others must have made the same promises. He said to consider myself warned not to do this again. I'd only been in the Army for eight very long months and didn't know much about protocol. This was another lesson on how the Army's official channels worked.

Chapter 5

Wounded in Action

O n the morning of July 8, 1966, I ate a quick breakfast at the mess
hall and returned to the platoon area for an operations order. After breakfast, Sergeant Doreman directed the platoon to pack a
basic load of ammunition and food for one day. He showed us the map
and pointed to several mountains for a mission he called *hill jumping*.

On the map, several mountain peaks appeared to have small clearings
that were large enough for helicopters to land on them. After studying the
map, we could see that the mission wasn't far from base camp. Battalion
Intelligence had reported sighting VC. They had been operating in small
groups and possibly carrying mortars and rocket launchers. Our platoon
was to locate and destroy the enemy's capability to attack our base camp.
We didn't want Charlie to get lucky and take out the choppers parked on
our runways or blow up the ammunition dumps.

The platoon was to air-assault small squad-size elements on each hilltop. Squads were to probe into the surrounding woods and jungle for about
one hundred yards and then return to the LZ for pickup. If the LZ got hot,
we were to secure it until we got help and could be extracted. We had
gunships and a battery of artillery on standby for close-in support.

If we made no enemy contact, our squad was to air-assault into the next
LZ. The operation was to check out all selected targets and return before
darkness. Each team leader had a radio/telephone operator assigned.

Bob Dunn got his M60. I grabbed the M60 spare parts bag. I'd packed
several 100-round belts of M60 ammunition. I also checked the amount
of magazines I'd need for my M16 rifle. I packed a basic load of 300-rounds

57

in my pack and tucked away in shoulder sling bandoleers. I also hung several grenades on the webbing of my shoulder harness.

Sergeant Doreman headed the ten men in my team. Each team had a grenadier with an M79 grenade launcher. One man carried a twelve-gauge shotgun. There were several M16 riflemen, a medic, and an M60 machine gunner. Each squad had enough diversified fire power to handle any small group of VC they might run into. Three squads were alerted, packed, and ready to go.

The time came to assemble at the pickup point on the road not far from our living quarters. Since Bong Son, I had been on several missions without Kenny. Kenny had been like a brother to me, and we'd been inseparable from the day we'd met in Saigon. It felt strange not to have him around to talk with. I didn't trust anyone as I trusted Kenny. I missed him terribly and wondered, now that my best friend was gone, who would protect my back?

While we waited for the choppers to arrive, I sat on the ground and leaned against my backpack like the other veterans. Now I knew what to do and how to fight, if and when I made contact with the enemy. I didn't fear the possibility of seeing combat, I expected it.

The noisy choppers kicked up dust in our faces as we made our way to their open doors and climbed aboard. I was positioned in the first chopper with Bob and several other men. When we lifted off the ground, I noticed there were only three troop ships in our airborne formation. As we flew over the perimeter of base camp, a gunship joined the group.

The morning sun felt good with fresh air circulating inside the ship. The lush jungle canopy, covering the ground below, looked peaceful. The choppers climbed toward a small range of hills. Before long, they began their descent into a clearing on the first hilltop. As the ships got closer to touchdown, I scooted to the open door and prepared to jump out. The choppers didn't land in the clearing. Instead, they hovered a few feet off the ground only long enough for us to jump.

I jumped to the ground, ran a few feet, and crouched in a prone position, facing the trees ahead. I didn't look back but heard the sounds of choppers drifting away. When I turned around, they were gone. Our entire squad was alone on the ground. The drop-off had happened in less than a minute. The squad leader lifted his arm and pointed to where he wanted us to move. I heard birds in the trees ahead as we cautiously moved forward, still in crouched positions. The noise of a chopper was nearby, but I didn't look up. I focused on looking for danger signs.

After we were inside the woods, beyond the skirt of the small clearing, Sergeant Doreman sent two riflemen to probe the surrounding area. When they returned and reported that they'd seen nothing suspicious, the squad moved clockwise to a different spot and repeated the tactic. We continued the search, probing around the entire tree line of the clearing. We found nothing to indicate Charlie had set up mortars or rocket positions near the top of that hill. After about an hour of reconnoitering, Sergeant Doreman reported his squad's situation by radio. Minutes later, three choppers landed in the clearing and picked us up. I climbed aboard, while the door gunners on each side pointed their M60s at the trees, and the chopper almost instantly lifted off the ground.

A gunship escorted the choppers to our next drop-off point. During the short ride, I scooted on my butt to the open doors to get ready for my second jump. Tall elephant grass covered the entire clearing below. All of a sudden, bullets popped through the air and hit the metal sides of our ship. The door gunner started firing his M60 machine gun. I quickly moved into the open door and realized I was about twelve feet above the bending and weaving elephant grass below. I lowered my feet onto the landing skid and stood up. With my right hand, I held onto the side of the ship. With its nose up, the ship moved forward but didn't land. I felt exposed. Incoming bullets kept slamming into the chopper's side.

The door gunner tapped my hand as he looked down. I jumped into the tall elephant grass below and hit the ground hard. Suddenly, a sharp pain ripped through my right knee, and I fell, twisting onto my stomach. I tried to get up, but the pain in my right knee quickly drove the idea out of my head. When I looked down, I saw a yellow bamboo punji stake sticking straight through my knee. It had entered under my kneecap and exited the other side. The rest of the punji stake splintered below my leg. I tried again to move but was in severe pain and anchored to the ground.

I knew that the VC carved small bamboo spears which blended into the natural vegetation. They stuck them into the ground, leg-high, at forty-five-degree angles. When anyone walked into or fell on one of the spears, he was immediately incapacitated. Worse yet, the VC dipped the sharp end of the spear into human waste to add infection to the wounds they made. The VC also placed those sticks in man-size holes and covered them with natural vegetation. The more weight pressing against the point, the deeper the punji stake penetrated. Now I'd been wounded by one of these debilitating bamboo spears.

Although I was in pain, I prepared to defend myself. With my M16 rifle loaded and the safety off, my finger rested on the trigger. A lot of shooting and tremendous explosions shook the ground all around. Tall grass surrounded me and blocked my ability to see anything else. Over the noise, I heard Bob's M60 fire through the tall grass nearby, but I wasn't able move in his direction. As I tried to prop myself into a position to shoot, I heard American voices screaming for a medic. Unable to move, I lay in agony and tried to remain calm and silent. Soon, I heard movement in the grass nearby. Since I didn't know the source of the sound, I decided not to take any chances by calling out. I remained silent with my heart pounding.

The noise in the grass moved closer. Adrenaline rushed through my body. I pointed my M16 toward the sound and kept my finger on the trigger. A voice cried out, "Are you okay?" An American helmet broke through the grass near my feet. It was Doc. He crawled to me on his belly as the intensity of the shooting and explosions continued around us. I eased my finger off the trigger and dropped the barrel of the rifle into the grass beside me.

I felt safe with Doc. He encouraged me to lie still as he checked over me. He gave me a shot of painkiller and a drink of water. I gritted my teeth and endured the excruciating pain when Doc moved my knee and snipped away the splintered pieces of bamboo around my wound. Blood gushed out. With one hand, Doc pulled the large piece of bamboo from under my kneecap. I cried in pain. It was difficult to lie still while he bandaged the wound. I grew very dizzy, hot, and weak. Doc said that Bob had pointed to where I was, and this was how he'd found me. Doc asked me to be quiet. Then he went to help the others. I watched him crawl away into the grass and out of sight.

The whole time I lay there, I could hear VC voices through the grass but I couldn't see anyone. An hour must have passed, but I didn't fire a single shot. I couldn't believe I'd been stuck by a punji stake. While lying in the tall grass, I didn't fear being captured or overrun, but I did wonder if I'd ever be able to use my right leg again. All sorts of thoughts passed through my mind: *Hell, I was in perfect health and an athlete before I joined the Army, less than a year ago. How could this have happened to me?*

The firing and explosions eventually trickled to a stop. There was a long period of silence. I began to hear Americans moving through the tall grass saying, "Watch for the punji stakes." Then I saw Bob Dunn. He stood over me and asked if I was okay. Bob said he saw me go down before he jumped and that he was lucky not to get stuck, too. He told me that fresh punji stakes were all over the place.

I asked Bob about the rest of the squad. He told me that they had suffered four casualties—two from punji stakes and two from enemy fire. There was one American KIA who had died of multiple punji wounds. I felt fortunate to have been stuck with only one stake.

Helicopters flew low overhead like a swarm of bees. The enemy was gone. God only knows how many of them had died. Bob helped me take off my heavy pack and to stand on one foot, but I felt light-headed and dizzy. I put my arm across Bob's shoulder as he grabbed me around the waist. I hobbled on one leg to the awaiting dust-off ship. Bob went back and fetched my gear and put it beside me in the chopper that held two other wounded men. Before long, the chopper was airborne and we flew to a field hospital in Qui Nhom. After being examined by an orthopedic doctor, I was temporarily patched up until I could be evacuated to a hospital that had better facilities to perform re-constructive knee surgery.

Chapter 6

Would I Leave Vietnam Forever?

In late July 1966, I arrived at the 106th Army General hospital in Kashini Barracks, Yokohama, Japan. I felt relieved to be in a country that wasn't at war.

The hospital's concrete buildings were set up in a small Japanese army World War II installation. Tall barbed wire fence surrounded the compound. Armed military policemen, dressed in clean, starched khaki uniforms, were stationed at the entrance and exit to the base.

I was assigned to Ward D. At least thirty other men occupied its beds. The place was clean and tidy. Large fans provided air-conditioning. Covered with white sheets and green, military issue blankets, twin size metal beds lined the walls. The hospital looked much like the ones I'd seen during training at Fort Leonardwood, Missouri and Fort Benning, Georgia.

The orthopedic ward buzzed with the sounds of people talking and nurses moving about. My bed was near the entrance to the nurse's station. The fellow to my left had to lie on his stomach because of the wound in his back. The man on my right had an L-shaped cast which ran from his neck to his fingers. Other men were covered with bandages on their arms and legs.

After I got comfortable, a nurse and doctor came by to give me a complete examination. They introduced themselves as Dr. George Bogumill and Nurse Nancy Jones. Dr. Bogumill had a gentle disposition and a kind bedside manner. He told me that I was too young to be sent to war and he thought I was younger than nineteen-years-old. The doctor joked by asking if my mother had signed to get me into the Army.

62

Nurse Jones, a pretty woman in her middle twenties, had a great figure. I liked the idea that she'd been assigned to take care of me. The medical staff asked many questions about when I was injured, how it happened, and what type of treatment I'd received before arriving. I appreciated their patience and care when they removed my bandages, examined the wound, and cleaned and re-dressed my leg from thigh to ankle.

As the days turned into weeks, I became friendly with patients in the beds around me. We talked about our Vietnam War experiences. Each man told his story of how he'd been wounded. Almost everyone I spoke to came from a different infantry unit.

The man on my right, Robert Lang, had been shot in the arm while on patrol near the Mekong Delta. That was 250 miles south of where I'd been wounded. Charlie had waited for Robert's squad as they moved on foot parallel to a trail. Robert happened to be a flank guard when Charlie spotted him first. He said Charlie had been a little faster on the trigger than he was. Several bullets from an AK-47 rifle had hit Robert in his arm. The impact had spun him completely around. He'd fallen and passed out. Robert hadn't fired one round but he remembered the face of the enemy soldier who had shot him. Robert said that he often woke up at night seeing this enemy's face that wouldn't let him rest.

The bullets had shattered the bone in Robert's forearm and ripped a hole in his biceps. Robert had been healing in the hospital for several months. The doctor had told him that he'd soon get his cast off and start physical therapy. Robert was one of several men on the ward, who was able to get out of bed, eat in the mess hall, and walk around the ward.

Gary Morton was the man on my left. His platoon had been ambushed in the jungle while checking out what appeared to be a deserted VC base camp. As the Americans were leaving, the VC had ambushed them. Gary remembered getting down and not being hit by the first volley of small arms fire. He had fired back by emptying an entire clip. While he changed clips, an enemy machine gun had opened fire in front of him. Something had slammed into his upper back and rolled him instantly from his stomach to his back. Gary had felt dazed but thought he was okay. When he tried to roll back to his stomach, he realized that he had no feeling in his arms. Then he had passed out. By the time Gary awoke, he'd been moved to a field hospital.

Since Gary's back was in such bad shape, he could lie only on his stomach. A web of silver, metal wires, sewn over the open wound, kept it from splitting more. The bullets had missed his spine but had ripped about eight square inches of flesh and muscle from his shoulder. I could actually see his left shoulder blade. Although the wound was clean, it looked like fresh, raw meat. Every so often the nurse and doctor would bring small patches of skin, they'd taken from his leg, and graft them to his back. During my stay in the hospital, I noticed that Gary's skin grafts healed without much infection and the hole in his shoulder decreased. I wondered if Gary would ever have full use of his left shoulder or the left side of his back.

Even though the men in my ward had suffered wounds, as a result of combat, our morale was high. Many of the wounded knew that after they recovered they'd be medically discharged from the Army and sent home. Most had only been in the Army less than a year. Now they'd have scars for the rest of their lives. They talked about home constantly, and their hopes of soon returning there made all the difference in how they felt. My military career, however, remained in question.

Finally, the day came when I was prepped and wheeled away for a surgery that lasted several hours. When I returned to consciousness, I was in my ward bed again, feeling dry-mouthed and drowsy. I really needed to take a leak but I couldn't move because of the pain, so I called for Miss Jones to bring a bedpan to me. She placed the bedpan under the covers between my legs and stood beside me, until I used it. Talk about performance anxiety!

The operation was a success. Dr. Bogumill said that if I was to walk normally again, I'd have to work hard at physical therapy. A few days later, a physical therapist came to my bedside. He helped and encouraged me to start lifting my leg. The pain was excruciating. The guys in the beds beside me kept joking and calling me a *pussy*. This was typical verbal harassment—

a way for us to help each other to persist in whatever we had to do for healing. Even though it was painful, I lifted my right knee slowly up and down.

After I'd had some success, the therapist draped socks full of sand over my ankles. If I was going to get better, I'd have to ignore the pain and concentrate on strengthening the muscles in my leg. As my leg strengthened, the therapist added more weight and encouraged me. The guys in the beds next to me continued chanting, "More weight! More weight!" Eventually, I could sit on the edge of the bed and bend my leg slightly at the knee.

Oh man, was that a different level of pain!

The blood rushed down my leg, and I felt tears spring to my eyes. Each time I tried to sit up and hang my legs over the edge of the bed, it was the same old thing. I eventually learned to expect the pain. Over time, I got used to it.

After a month, I was able to use crutches to move around the ward, eat in the mess hall, and go to the latrine standing up. I'd gotten cocky a few times and let go of the crutches. After one step, I'd fallen flat on my face, but that hadn't stopped me from trying to walk on my own. I wasn't going to be a cripple. And that was that.

My wound seemed to be healing faster than Dr. Bogumill had expected. He eventually removed the sixty stitches that were spaced a quarter inch apart on both sides of my knee. I had an ugly ten-inch scar on the inside and an equally ugly six-inch scar on the outside of my right knee. My shaved knee had tiny hair stubs and was swollen to twice the size of my left knee. O-positive blood oozed from the puffy stitched holes. My knee looked like the face of Frankenstein's monster. Not a pretty sight.

By September 1966, my hospital stay was getting to be a bore. I saw men in the ward get well and go home. I thought about going home, too. I missed riding my motorcycle, going on dates, seeing a scary movie at the drive-in theater, eating a juicy cheeseburger with hot French fries, and hanging around with my family and friends. I craved drinking a cold bottle of Coors beer. Most of the guys, I knew, had never heard of the Coors beer slogan, "Brewed with pure Rocky Mountain spring water." I hadn't met any other men from Colorado, so no one understood the special things I missed about my home state.

As soon as a ward bed emptied, it was filled with another wounded soldier from Vietnam. The cycle of men, coming and going, never ended. The men's constant nightmares and screams in their sleep reminded me of the war.

I'd recovered well enough not to require crutches or a cane and got a liberty pass to go to Yokohama, the city right outside our compound. I had to follow the rules and return to the hospital before dark. Civilian clothes weren't authorized for patients, so I was issued a khaki military uniform, a hat, and a pair of shoes. I signed a partial-pay voucher for fifty dollars and suddenly felt rich.

No hospital patient was authorized to go off the base alone. Using the buddy system, I teamed up with another patient and we went to Yokohama. We caught a cab outside the gate. The Japanese cab driver spoke enough English to ask, "Where to?"

We replied, "Downtown."

He must have understood because he drove us to what looked like a main street near a pier full of boats and ships.

The streets of Yokohama were crowded with people, going about their usual business. The Japanese women wore colorful kimonos and the men were in street clothes and suits. This contrasted with the attire of the Vietnamese who dressed completely differently from the Japanese. We took our time, walking the streets and sidewalks and resting as much as possible. The Japanese acted as though we weren't there. They didn't stare or look at us, as if we weren't invited. I felt quite comfortable, even though we couldn't understand a word they said. There was a sense of freedom all around us—something I hadn't experienced in a long time.

We stopped in a bar and ordered a few Japanese beers but we didn't eat anything. Japanese music played on a radio. We sat, talked, and sipped beer. After a while, we left the bar and roamed the streets and market place. I wasn't much of a fish-eater, so I felt repulsed by the awful stink of the fish market with the smell and sight of fish everywhere. Not long after our walk, we found a cab to take us back to Kashini Barracks.

The day finally came when Dr. Bogumill and Nurse Jones informed me that my prognosis was good enough for me to be discharged from the hospital. I no longer used crutches or a cane to get around. My knee didn't hurt much. The muscles in my right thigh were strong again, as a result of physical therapy. I also strengthened my upper body by using weights and exercising. I even jogged a little now.

Dr. Bogumill told me that I was healthy enough to return to active duty. This wasn't what I wanted to hear.

"How about a one way trip to Littleton, Colorado, Doc?" I asked, even though my wound wasn't severe enough for me to have a medical discharge.

I sensed from Dr. Bogumill's mannerisms that he really cared about his patients. He told me to get the hell out of the infantry and find a safer job.

Since I'd joined the Army, it seemed that I was always being disappointed. First, I didn't get to go to Special Forces school to earn a Green Beret, but was sent to Vietnam instead. When I got to Vietnam, I almost killed several of my own squad by accidentally forgetting to secure my gun's safety. My best friend Kenny, after only two month's service, had almost been killed. After that, I'd been wounded. Now I couldn't get discharged from Uncle Sam's Army because I'd healed too well. I was beginning to think that it was my lot in life to be surrounded by tragedy, almost make it to safety, only to get pulled back into the soup again.

While I was in the hospital, I'd written many letters home, mentioning the possibility that I might be discharged. I'd told people to start planning my coming home party. Now I had to write home and tell everyone to put away their party hats. The Army was going to keep me on active duty in the Pacific.

The news that I'd soon be leaving the hospital made me extremely happy, even if I wasn't going home. I'd soon leave Japan for an assignment in Okinawa. What I didn't know was that my new assignment would change my life in a totally unexpected way.

I'd be meeting my first war dog.

Chapter 7

Hans, the Sentry Dog

After I left Vietnam in July 1966 and recovered from my wound, I moved from place to place and job to job. In January 1967, I was assigned to my first job in Okinawa, where I used a forklift to bust up a bunch of glass jars in a warehouse. During my second job in Okinawa, I became a truck driver and bent the hell out of a flatbed trailer stand. I knew that I was a better soldier than my record showed. It was time for me to find something I could do well.

I visited the personnel office to find a job more suited to me. There, I heard about a possible opportunity with the 267th Chemical Company. They were under their authorized manpower strength of sentry dog handlers. Hearing about this job caused me to start remembering my childhood experiences with dogs.

I'd never had a pet dog of my own while growing up, but I loved dogs. My favorites were golden retrievers, collies, German shepherds, boxers, and huskies, but I'd always had a soft spot for mixed breed mutts. I could remember being around house pets. I was totally unfamiliar with working dogs. The family dogs I'd known could perform a few tricks like fetch, sit, and come.

When I thought about being a sentry dog handler, I liked the idea of having a dog of my own for the first time. Working with a sentry dog would involve quite a learning process for me, but one that promised to be challenging and exciting. Having a dog would change my routine of working with people every day. And besides, a dog couldn't give me orders. I figured that would be an advantage!

A prerequisite for assignment to this company was to have a primary Military Occupational Specialty of 11B, Infantry. I assumed I could qualify for the job and decided to volunteer. The personnel clerk reviewed my record, got the assignment approved, and cut my orders. I was reassigned from the 1st Logistical Command to the 267th Chemical Company, Suikran, Okinawa.

When I reported to the 267th Company orderly room, the first sergeant saw that I wore a Combat Infantry Badge. He smiled and offered me a cup of coffee. Then the company commander shook my hand and told me *Top*, a nickname for all first sergeants, would take care of in-processing.

Top was a WWII infantry veteran who had fought against the Nazis in European campaigns. After trading a few war stories, he told me that I was the only Vietnam infantry veteran in the outfit, which made him proud to have me aboard. He said that we were the only guys with CIBs. With a smile, he looked at me and said, "The Army is either getting younger, or I'm becoming an old-timer."

When Top briefed me on the mission of the 267th, he explained that the unit provided security for and managed the contents of the Army's ammunition supply storage buildings on the island of Okinawa. The job called for a sentry dog handler to guard the buildings. He explained the sensitive nature of the organization's mission, and how important it was not to discuss my work with anyone outside official channels. This restriction included not taking pictures or writing anything about my work in letters home.

Top told me to be careful about strangers who offered free drinks in downtown bars. "There are spies out there," he said. "They want information about what we do. Don't talk or try to figure them out; they're professionals. Report everything immediately to our security officer."

It all sounded mysterious, but I agreed to follow his instructions. I also had to sign an official document, validating that this briefing had taken place. I supposed that if I were suspected of talking with a Communist, the Army would have been able to use that document against me.

I thought, *Hell, the Army doesn't have to worry about me. I'm true, blue American and would never sell my country out to any Communist bastards.*

Top called for his company clerk, "Get this man squared away and in-processed for his new assignment."

Top got up from behind the desk, shook my hand, and told me that the 267th would take good care of me. I sat beside the company clerk's desk and filled out a long personal history form, so I could get a security clearance. This was required for everyone who was assigned to the 267th Chemical Company. My next stop was to meet the men of the sentry dog platoon.

A sentry dog handler named Fred escorted me to my new living quarters on the third floor of the building. Fred was about my size and build with straight black hair, brown eyes, a square jaw, and a neatly trimmed mustache. His uniform was starched stiff and his boots spit-shined. Fred had joined the Army two years before me and held the enlisted rank of SP4 (E-4). I was a PFC (E-3), one rank below Fred.

We entered a huge sleeping bay with neatly made metal bunk beds lined against the walls. A wooden footlocker sat on the floor at the foot of each bed. A green mosquito net, suspended by t-bars, anchored to the head and foot of the bed frame draped over each bed. Gray metal, two-door wall lockers sat between each set of bunk beds. The floors were covered with clean and polished linoleum tiles.

I picked an empty bottom bunk bed and spread out the S-rolled mattress. I opened the empty wall locker next to it and placed my stuff inside. I had to go to the PX to get a combination lock for my wall locker. Later, I was issued a set of white sheets, a blanket, a pillow, and a pillowcase. The latrine was at one end of the sleeping bay. I felt relieved to finally have a new home. I'd slept in ten different places after leaving my tent in An Khe.

Thinking about Vietnam caused me to wonder what had happened to Sergeant Doreman. Was he still alive? Did he finally go home in August? What had happened to Bob Dunn? He was due to leave Vietnam in December. I closed my eyes and could hear Sergeant Doreman yelling, "Saddle Up!" along with the distant noise of Bob's machine gun blasting away.

After Fred showed me my bunk, he said that the entire sentry dog platoon was out either training or on guard duty. I asked Fred about the small, one-inch, square patch he wore above his nametag. It showed the black head of a dog against a yellow background. Fred told me that all the Army sentry dog handlers wore them. I would have to earn my patch through dog training and qualification. Fred asked what I knew about sentry dogs. The only sentry dogs I'd encountered were in Vietnam or behind fences guarding junkyards back home.

His eyebrows raised as he quickly asked, "Dogs in Vietnam?"

I said, "Yes, but I saw them at a distance; I think they were guard dogs."

"Wow!" he replied.

Fred told me that I was the first Vietnam veteran he'd met. With excitement in his eyes, Fred asked me lots of questions about my combat experiences and the war dogs I saw. I only answered him in very general terms. I didn't feel comfortable with Fred yet or with my new surroundings. Everyone I'd met after I'd left the hospital, hadn't served in Vietnam or the infantry. They all had noncombatant, rear-area support experience. Most of them told me that they were glad they'd been assigned to units outside the fighting in Vietnam.

I spent the rest of the day putting my uniforms away and polishing my shoes and boots. Later, several men entered the room. They were all talking and joking with one another. Fred introduced me to the platoon sergeant. We shook hands and spoke about the work everyone did. I learned that there was no platoon leader, only this platoon sergeant.

After checking into the 267th, the first item on my agenda was to visit the kennel and dog training area. Over time, I'd meet the rest of the sentry dog handlers. They all seemed friendly, so I felt welcome.

Fred asked me if I'd ever played a card game called Hearts. I told him that I'd never heard of it. The guys invited me to join them the next time they played a game. It seemed like a good way to get to know them, so I began to play cards and listen to the radio. These pastimes were how dog handlers seemed to prefer relaxing between guard shifts.

Sentry dog handlers worked the night shifts. Days off varied. During mandatory morning formations, everyone had to be present or accounted for in front of the barracks by six-thirty in the morning. The company commander and first sergeant would take a head count, pass out general information, and provide work instructions. The sentry dog platoon had about twenty men who would assemble in four ranks behind the platoon sergeant. The platoon sergeant would march the platoon to a nearby open field. There, they'd perform military exercises such as jumping jacks, squat thrusts, push-ups, and sit-ups. After exercises, the platoon would jog to the cadence calls of the platoon sergeant. Exercise was always followed by breakfast in the mess hall. By eight o'clock, everyone would report to work. That was a typical scenario of life in the 267th and completely different than what I had gotten accustomed to in Vietnam.

The sentry dog platoon was assigned a 2½ ton troop-carrying truck and a jeep equipped with a military radio and antenna unit. The radio was exactly like the ones used in Vietnam, but this one was mounted to a metal carriage and bolted to the jeep. The platoon would load up and off they'd go to the kennel.

I had no idea what to expect the first time I boarded this truck. When it arrived, I heard dogs barking. The dog handlers quickly dismounted the vehicle and entered the kennels. I lagged back a little to observe. Inside the kennels, handlers yelled out the names of their dogs—Wolf, Mike, Rex, Lucky, etc.

After the handlers exited the kennel with their dogs attached to leather leashes, I slowly entered. The smell of dogshit and urine on the concrete floor filled the air. Several dogs stayed behind thick-wired, see-through fencing. Each dog's name was above his kennel door. A metal choke chain hung on a nail outside each kennel door along with a leather leash and muzzle. Silver metal water and food bowls sat inside the dogs' runs.

As I walked by the caged German shepherds, they growled and lunged at their gates. If one of those gates accidentally popped open, I'd have literally been dog meat. It was a horrifying thought. The dogs probably sensed that I was scared shitless. Not one dog allowed me to get close without growling and showing how big and sharp his teeth were. *Maybe I don't want to be a sentry dog handler after all,* I thought.

At both ends of the kennel were walls of wooden bins. They had the names of each dog on them. Each bin neatly stored grooming equipment, long leashes, leather collars, and leather body harnesses. Large boxes of dog food were stacked high against the walls alongside several large metal wall lockers. Water hoses were connected to pipes at each end of the kennel. Two of the dog handlers turned the hoses on and washed down the dog shit and urine through the back of the fenced cages and into a concrete drainage ditch. They laughed as they squirted some of dogs and seemed to enjoy pissing them off.

Outside, the handlers groomed their dogs on small wooden tables. Each dog was tied to a wooden post that was nailed to a table. The dog handlers talked to their dogs while they brushed them, cleaned their teeth, clipped their nails, and checked them for health problems. As I watched, I felt impressed by how fit the animals were, with not a bit of fat on any of them. The platoon sergeant approached and instructed me to observe and help around the kennels for the next few days.

The platoon sergeant was responsible for matching dogs to handlers. Usually a handler was assigned the healthiest dog that had spent the most time being without a handler. Each dog was already trained in basic obedience, but if a dog didn't work, he became lazy. This meant that training the dogs was an extremely important part of the routine. Sentry dogs were trained that their primary functions were to guard and attack on command. Dogs learn through repetition and consistency, and are taught to react to the commands of only one master. I soon learned a basic rule for working with sentry dogs—don't befriend any other animal except for your assigned dog.

Rex held the distinction of being the most vicious sentry dog. His handler, Specialist Aldridge, was a tall husky man. The platoon sergeant assigned me to Hans—the biggest but not the meanest-looking German shepherd in the kennel.

My first task was to spend quality time with Hans—feeding him, cleaning his cage, and talking to him. During that initial getting acquainted period, I didn't touch Hans. Physical distance was okay with me. I had plenty of time and was in no hurry to put my hands on Hans. Every time I visited the dog, he'd growl and try to eat through the wire fence that separated us. The platoon sergeant said Hans growled because it was his way of testing my control and fear. He told me not to show any fear if I was ever going to command a sentry dog.

Over time, Hans stopped growling and became accustomed to seeing me. I was also getting used to him. As each day passed, my fear slowly diminished. The day came when the platoon sergeant told me that it was time for me to take Hans out of his kennel run.

I asked, "Do you think I'm ready?"

The platoon sergeant replied, "It's now or never, soldier!"

I felt as though the dog and the platoon sergeant were testing me. I had to take Hans out of the kennel and deal with him face-to-face.

I thought, *Well, I can't be a chicken shit about it or let the dog control me.*

I took a deep breath, cleared my mind, grabbed the leather leash and connected a choke chain to it. All the while, Hans paced back and forth like a hungry lion in a cage. He knew he was getting out.

The platoon sergeant watched me the whole time. I spread the choke chain as far as possible, so that the dog's head could pass through easily. Then I opened the door to Hans's run and knew that now there was nothing to keep that dog from eating me alive. To my surprise, Hans quickly put his nose and head through the loop and charged past me through the open door, pulling me behind him. Hans headed for the exit and into the open area behind the kennel.

The platoon sergeant ran behind, telling me to yank back on the leash and to command the dog to heel. I pulled as hard as I could and yelled, "Heel! Heel! Heel!"

Hans pulled away even harder. Finally, he got the message and let me catch up, moved to my left side, and paced his walk with mine.

The platoon sergeant instructed me to praise Hans by saying, "Good dog. Good dog." I praised Hans with words, but I wasn't ready to give him a hug yet. While we marched around the training yard, I had a huge smile on my face and felt as if I'd won a blue ribbon in a basic obedience contest. My fear had been replaced with joy.

I obviously had more to learn if I was going to become a sentry dog handler. The platoon sergeant told me I'd have to master the commands for basic obedience and learn to control Hans under all circumstances. Hans already knew what to do but needed a master to make him do it. I had to remain consistent with how I handled him. I learned that discipline was extremely important. It could be achieved only by practicing every day. Through consistent training, Hans would become my companion and maybe we'd make a great team.

Several days passed as Hans and I got better acquainted. It reached the point that, when I dangled the leash in front of his cage, Hans would go crazy with excitement. When Hans stood on his hind legs, he was taller than me. The platoon sergeant said Hans was one of the biggest German shepherds he'd ever been around. All the sentry dogs were healthy, lean, and muscular. They stayed lean because of their diet and rigorous training. There wasn't one fat dog handler either. Each man was in excellent health and physical condition.

I was issued a military dog-training manual and expected to learn and practice what it preached. The manual contained procedures and illustrations of tools for grooming, voice commands, hand and arm signals, and deployment. All the other dog handlers were versed in the commands and advanced dog training techniques. Most had graduated from a formal twelve-week military dog-training school in the States. I enjoyed watching the other soldiers work their animals. Everything they did appeared to be simple and smooth and showed the genuine love between the dogs and their handlers, even though these dogs were trained to be lethal weapons.

The platoon sergeant assigned Fred, who had oriented me on my first day in the platoon, to be my tutor in the finer arts of basic dog training. Fred's happy-go-lucky personality had been quickly rubbing off on me. He always talked about the pretty Okinawa barmaids working at Club Lucky, a downtown bar not far from the base. This was where the dog handlers frequented and considered their own special place to hang out.

Fred taught me that positive reinforcement was critical throughout the training effort. My first lesson included the voice commands: *sit, heel, come, down, stay, no,* and *good dog.* Fred taught me how to use inflection in my voice when calling out commands to Hans. I practiced for hours each day until I could bark out the commands like a drill sergeant.

At first, Hans was slow or lazy and wouldn't commit to each action I commanded. When I told him to sit, he took his time. When I voiced the command, down, Hans would get down only partway and then get up and sit. After several training sessions with me, Hans became more responsive. I finally learned how to make him obey basic voice commands.

Eventually, I was ready to join the rest of the platoon for group training. Uniformity was the key. Each dog handler had to carry the same equipment attached to specific places on his pistol belt. Each pistol belt contained a canteen of water, an eight-foot leather leash, a leather collar, a choke chain, a twenty-five foot nylon leash, a leather muzzle, a first aid bandage, and a .45 caliber pistol in a black leather holster.

Outside the kennel, the platoon sergeant would assemble the twenty dog handlers with their dogs in a formation of four ranks. The platoon sergeant would position himself several feet in front and center. When he'd call the platoon to attention, everyone assumed the standing position of attention—feet together, shoulders back, heads and eyes forward. The position of attention for the dogs was a full and proper sitting position on the left side of the handler.

Dogs weren't allowed to slouch or sit leaning on one hind leg. There was a little more than an arm's length between each handler and his dog. The handler usually gripped near the end of the choke chain with his left hand close to the dog's neck. This way, he could easily control the dog if it decided to attack another dog or handler. After all, the dogs were trained to attack and kill on command. Fellow dogs were no exception. The handler's right hand held the brown leather leash.

The platoon training area was across the road from the kennel. A schoolyard-type fence surrounded it. In the center of the yard, the platoon would assemble in a platoon formation below a platform painted infantry blue and made of wood with handrails on all four sides. The ground in the training area was mostly dirt with large spots of short grass. The sergeant would stand on top of the platform to command his platoon.

When the platoon sergeant commanded, "Sit, dog," the dog handlers would repeat the command, saying in unison, "Sit." When all the dogs sat, the platoon sergeant would command, "Down, dog." Again, everyone followed by giving the voice command, "Down." The platoon sergeant would yell at the dog handlers if they didn't execute the command together. He'd always be looking for rhythm and precision.

The sergeant would call the platoon to the position of attention and command by saying, "Move to the end of the leash." To carry out this command, the handlers would command, "Stay." Then they'd move to the end of the leash and turn to face the dogs. Sometimes the dogs wouldn't stay, but would follow behind the handler. When this happened, the platoon sergeant would get pissed off at the handler and yell at him. I got yelled at many times during the exercises, because Hans would lie down when I turned my back on him. After we'd all be at the end of our leashes and facing our dogs, the platoon sergeant would bark, "Down, dog!"

We practiced many other basic obedience drills: *sit, stay, right face, left face, about face, down,* and *forward march.* We weren't allowed to praise our dogs until the platoon sergeant gave the command, "Okay," which was after we successfully completed a movement. When the dogs were warmed up, he'd give the command, "Okay," after we did three or four successful movements.

I soon mastered the basic voice commands and graduated to voice command with a hand signal. Hand signals were generally taught with the handler facing the dog at the end of the leash. To get Hans to sit, I'd simultaneously signal him with my hand and voice and command, "Sit." We'd practice hand and voice signals for all the movements of advanced basic obedience, including the dead dog, roll over, and crawl commands.

I wore out the command, NO! After many weeks of training, Hans responded repeatedly to silent hand signals. It fascinated me that a dog could learn to do so many tricks on command. I often thought while training Hans, that he'd have made a great patrol dog for Vietnam. He was so big that the Viet Cong would have run when they saw him.

After about a month, I was ready for another phase of my education. I had to learn how to get Hans to attack and stop attacking on command. This was the most frightening part of our training experience.

One day the platoon sergeant marched us into the fenced training yard. He selected two handlers and directed them to put on heavy burlap attack suits. The rest of us removed the choke chains, quickly attached them to our pistol belts, and buckled the leather collars around our dogs' necks. The collars were used only when a dog was on official guard duty.

We formed a single line, facing away from the person in the attack suit. The platoon sergeant instructed us to turn around and face away from the platform. Once the leather collars were on our dogs, they seemed to sense what was coming next. The handlers had a difficult time keeping their dogs in a sitting position, facing away from the action.

One soldier outfitted in a heavy burlap suit, protected his face with a steel mask that looked like a baseball catcher's. The dogs growled but stayed at their masters' sides. Hans sat and stared at the man in the burlap suit. We were instructed to hold the dogs still. Each sentry dog team would be given the opportunity to attack. There were three commands to the attack phase—watch him, get him, and out. The command, get him, meant that the handler wanted his dog to attack the target. The command, out, meant that the handler wanted the dog to stop attacking and release the target.

The platoon sergeant called one of the handlers by name and said, "Attack dog command!" The man in the burlap suit assumed a crouched position about thirty feet in front of the dog. The handler commanded, "Watch him!" His dog watched the target and moved slowly toward the burlap-suited man who raised his arms and growled. The handler commanded, "Get him." In a flash, the handler released his dog, and the sentry dog charged and lunged at the crouched man's throat and then at his groin.

I'd never witnessed a sentry dog move so fast. Each time the dog lunged, the man in the burlap suit moved backwards from the force of the hit. The dog bit down on the arm of the suit, then backed off, and lunged again. At one point, the force of the dog's lunge knocked the man over and onto his back. Relentlessly attacking the man's throat area, the dog bit down and thrashed his head from side-to-side like a shark.

The platoon sergeant gave the command, out dog. The handler responded by saying, "Out!" The dog released his bite and backed off the man on the ground. The handler commanded, "Heel!" and the dog returned to his side. The handler praised his dog by patting him and telling him, "Good boy! Good boy!"

The dog's gums bled, but he was still excited. The man in the burlap suit got up and took a short breather before preparing for another attack. After four attacks, the platoon sergeant ordered a different man into the burlap suit. After each attack, more dogs' bloodstains joined the others on the arms and legs of the burlap suit.

Soon it was my turn. I was nervous and not sure how I'd handle Hans throughout the attack. The platoon sergeant gave me the signal. The man in the burlap suit began to kick up dirt and wave his arms. From about thirty feet away, I commanded, "Get him." When Hans reached the end of the leash, the force of his charge pulled it out of my hands. He was all over the guy in the burlap suit. I ran and grabbed the end of the leash, while Hans had the man on the ground biting and twisting his entire body and trying to rip off the man's leg.

The hair on the back of Hans' neck stood straight up and his teeth buried deep into the burlap. The guy in the suit screamed, "Call him off! Call him off!" I frantically yelled, "Out!" several times and kept pulling back on the leash. Finally, Hans let go. It took every bit of my strength to keep Hans back and away from the man on the ground. I was exhausted, even though the action lasted less than a minute. The platoon sergeant told me, in what was surely an understatement, that I'd have to learn to control my dog better.

After the attack, Hans's gums were bleeding and the muscles in his shoulders and legs were tense and hot to the touch. I praised Hans as he sat with his ears pointed high and forward, and alerted to the man. This had been quite an experience. I realized that my sentry dog would have killed that man if he hadn't been protected. That was a scary thought. Later, the soldier who had worn the suit told me that he could feel the powerful jaw pressure of Hans's teeth clamped on his leg near his groin. He said Hans had the strongest crushing bite of all the animals that had attacked him even though Hans hadn't punctured the man's flesh.

Back in the barracks, several of the dog handlers commented on how well my training was coming along. Fred invited me to go to town for drinks at Club Lucky that day. I didn't have any civilian clothes at the time, so I bought some at the PX. I thought it was great that I didn't have to pay taxes for anything.

Being overseas also made me exempt from paying taxes to the IRS. Anyway, I didn't make very much money as a Private First Class. In Okinawa, we were paid cash with regular American greenbacks on the last day of each month. Some soldiers owned civilian cars, but none of the dog handlers I knew had one. They all lived on base in the barracks and traveled everywhere by foot or cab.

One day after work, I accepted Fred's invitation to go downtown with him to Club Lucky and several sentry dog handlers joined us.

Outside the main gate, skoshi cabs parked alongside the road. In Japanese, *skoshi* meant *small.* Fred instructed the driver to drive to Club Lucky. The car wasn't that comfortable or roomy inside, but I didn't care. Its engine whined loudly as it went at about thirty miles per hour.

Every sign we passed was in Japanese until we drove closer to the heart of the bar district. The streets were crowded with people walking, riding bicycles, and driving funny little cars. The name of one of the main streets was BC Night. The signs above the bars were in English—Club BC Night, Club California, Club Texas, and so on. Japanese men, dressed in black slacks and white shirts, stood outside bars hawking at people to come in. Most of the people on the crowded streets were American servicemen— sailors, marines, soldiers, and airman.

My new friends and I entered Club Lucky as the Japanese hawker bowed and opened the door. I was warned not to mess with the hawkers. Although they were little guys, hawkers were karate experts and club bouncers.

I said to Fred, "You mean these little shits can fight?"

Fred replied, "I've seen the little fellows take down some big boys."

Well, that was enough to convince me. Besides, I'd never been one to pick a fight. I'd been a champion wrestler in high school. I'd liked wrestling because it was a fast one-on-one competition. Wrestling meant I'd fight against another guy of the same weight. We'd often refer to wrestling as the fastest six minutes in sports. Everything relied on *individual* talent, speed, training, and the desire to win.

During my brief tour in Vietnam, I'd learned that winning there, in contrast to wrestling, was a *team* activity with human lives at stake. The prize for winning in this war was to go home in one piece after twelve months. The punishment for losing was to get wounded or sent home in a body bag. The prize for the enemy was to rule the land by whipping the heavily armed Americans and running them out of the country.

War with the enemy was a deadly game of cat and mouse, played inside a giant labyrinth of treacherous terrain and weather conditions. The enemy, unlike a wrestler, wasn't easy to identify, find, or engage in a fight. The rules of fighting in Vietnam weren't as clear as they had been on the wrestling mats. No referee called a foul in the heat of an exchange or awarded the opponent points for a takedown. Body counts seemed to be all that mattered to American commanders.

Back in high school, I'd trained hard several hours every night to be the best 120-pound wrestler. My goal had been to win every match. Each week, I had to defend my first string varsity status against other seniors, juniors, and sophomores who were trying to earn the right to represent our school colors at the Friday night wrestling competition.

I loved winning and had remained undefeated in my weight class for my junior and senior years. I won two conference championship medals and two first place invitational tournament medals. I competed for the Colorado State title, but lost in the third round to a returning state champion.

Since I'd never heard of any wrestlers from Okinawa, I now wondered if I could teach these hawkers a few tricks. I knew nothing about judo or karate, but, I thought, *I'd love to go one-on-one with one of those little hawkers.*

After the hawkers let us into the club, I noticed that it was dark inside with lit candles on each table. Neon Japanese beer signs hung on the bar wall, which had a large colorful display of American military shoulder patches, rank insignia, and assorted badges. The place, set up like an American military bar, was very comfortable, although the air had a peculiar scent of fish mixed with cigarette smoke. It seemed as if everywhere I traveled in the Far East — Vietnam, Japan, and now the island of Okinawa — I encountered a variation of this same smell. The bar could hold about seventy-five people. It wasn't well-ventilated; the ceilings appeared lower than usual; the floor was a concrete slab.

From behind the bar an older Japanese woman greeted our crowd. She gave us a big friendly smile as if we were all old friends. Everyone called her Mama San. There were several other Oriental women dressed in colorful long silk dresses. They sat at the bar and tables talking Japanese to one another. Fred ordered a round of Japanese beer and we moved to an empty table to sit down.

The jukebox filled the air with the sound of American rock and roll tunes. One of the women came over and asked for money to put into the jukebox. Someone gave her change and off she went. Soon, several other young and attractive barmaids came to our table. Everyone except me knew them by name.

When the drinks came, we ordered a round for the girls. I was introduced to each of the barmaids who smiled and talked in broken English. Gradually, I learned that some of the guys considered certain ones their girlfriends, which meant they were off limits to everyone else. Fred pointed out the women who weren't taken and this didn't leave many to pick from. Besides, I didn't want to find a Japanese girlfriend. I was having too much fun watching everyone else.

I quickly learned that if I didn't buy a barmaid a drink, she'd leave and sit with someone who did. It was the barmaids' job to rotate to all the customers. The Ryukuans, local nationals, were poor people and basically survived on the money Americans poured into their economy. By local standards the bars created big business. The only way these women made a living was by working in bars, selling drinks, and becoming prostitutes. Fred told me that none of the women at the Club Lucky were prostitutes, but I found this hard to believe.

Communication with the Japanese girls was so difficult that I soon became frustrated with it. What I wanted was to meet and date a girl who didn't work at a bar, but that seemed impossible. Most of the island girls my age who didn't go to bars also didn't want to date American soldiers. Meeting decent girls in a foreign country wasn't as easy as back home.

Fred said that every barmaid he'd met believed all Americans were rich. By their economic standards, working in a bar was a top-paying job. Rich wasn't a word in my vocabulary. Each month I lived from paycheck to paycheck. Even so, I figured I was economically better off than many of them.

Many of the young women on the island were looking for a way to get to the United States. The best method was to marry an American serviceman. This would ensure them a home on a military base, money, medical benefits, and an easy way into the States. Many of the higher ranking soldiers paid for their girlfriends' apartments in town, so they'd have a place to shack up on weekends. Apparently, this was a common practice. As soon as a soldier got reassigned off the island, another soldier was in line to rent his apartment. Some of the servicemen had even fathered illegitimate children and had abandoned them when they left the island.

The Japanese beer we drank that night was okay, but not great. We had a pretty good buzz by the end of the evening. I believe I only spent a few dollars because beer cost about thirty-five cents a bottle. There was no such thing as draft beer and mixed drinks were served in glasses.

A midnight curfew for all military personnel forced them out of the bars and off the streets. MPs from all the military services roamed the streets and checked the bars for soldiers who caused problems or violated curfew. The local island police force also roamed the streets on foot to enforce local law and order. We left the bar at about eleven-thirty at night, flagged a skoshi cab, and were back on base before midnight. Everyone understood the negative consequences of missing curfew or being picked up by the MPs. I wasn't one to get into trouble with MPs or to become involved in a military court martial.

By January 1967, my Secret clearance was finally approved. I could now patrol the classified military sites with Hans. I looked forward to working the dog in a live situation. My first four-hour guard duty was on the night shift. I was driven by truck to the kennel at around ten o'clock. The dogs barked as if they knew what was going on. I got my gear together and filled two canteens of water for Hans and me. Each canteen had a metal cup, neatly attached to the bottom, and I resolved to remember which cup belonged to the dog.

The dogs had already been fed. They ate a diet of Purina Dog Chow and water, once a day, at a designated time. That was it. They weren't given any treats. I'd learned that pets get treats, not military sentry dogs. Fred said that the only praise I should give a dog is to pat him on the back and tell him that he's a good dog.

I had two seven-round clips of ammunition for my .45 caliber pistol. I wasn't supposed to insert a loaded clip into my pistol until I arrived at the work site. I put on a pistol belt and strapped the leather collar on Hans. I attached my poncho to the pistol belt in case it rained. The gear weighed four pounds, which seemed light, compared to the sixty pounds I used to carry in Vietnam. My right knee felt stronger, and I experienced little pain now when I stood for extended periods of time. Dr. Bogumill had done a terrific job patching me up. Even the hair around my knee had fully grown back, except along the long and wide scar tissue.

There were six dogs on a guard shift that first night I worked with Hans. We boarded the back of the troop truck. It was exactly like the one I'd ridden to Bong Son plains. For protection, we muzzled the dogs when they rode in the back of the truck. The dogs always had to be under control in a sitting position between the handlers' legs. I took up the slack in the leash and held Hans by his collar. The sentry dogs always seemed to want to attack each other or anyone who got close to them. I'd already learned what they could do to a man in an attack suit. I was relieved to see them in muzzles.

The sentry dog teams arrived at the entrance gate of a fully lighted fenced area. The truck stopped in front of an armed guard. He checked us over and opened the gate to let us into the compound. The truck stopped inside the gate. The driver dropped the tailgate and the sentry dog teams exited.

Armed guards in jeeps patrolled between two electric fences that encircled the compound perimeter. Sentry dogs patrolled the inner fenced perimeter. The munitions buildings were located there. The inner perimeter contained about fifty munitions bunkers covered with dirt and grass. Shaped like and called igloos, the munitions bunkers looked exactly alike. They were well-spaced apart and lined up in rows. A paved road and a driveway led to the igloo's only entrance, where a huge steel double door was attached to a thick windowless concrete wall. That was all that was showing, the rest was under dirt and grass. From the sky, the area must have appeared to be a flat grassy field.

My assignment was to guard five igloos. Fred instructed me to check each door to ensure that no one had tampered with the locks. I was to initial the security sheet attached to the door every hour. He told me that I was to patrol the grounds all around the igloos. Fred also said to load my pistol and keep it in the holster. Each sentry dog handler carried a flashlight, which we weren't to use, unless absolutely necessary. We also carried two rubber gas masks—one for the handler and a special one made to fit our dog's head.

I asked Fred what was inside the igloos. He told me that was classified information. I said that I had a Secret clearance and needed to know what the hell I was guarding. Fred gave in and told me that the military kept a stockpile of chemical warfare weapons inside. He said that I now had a classified secret to protect and I was never to discuss the issue with him again. He didn't want to compromise security information.

Fred instructed me to frequently check the cages near the vents of each igloo and to look for unusual behavior by the rabbits housed in them. I was supposed to also check on the goats that roamed around the area. I asked Fred why they kept goats and rabbits inside a high security compound. He explained that if chemicals leaked from an igloo, the rabbits' and goats' behavior would be my first clue that the ground or air had been poisoned. He said that if I felt anything weird, like an upset stomach, eye, or skin irritation, I had only nine seconds to put on my protective mask before I became a casualty. After that, I must put a mask on Hans and immediately sound the silent alarms near the bunkers. Fred told me that if the shit hit the fan and there was a chemical spill, I'd have company within seconds trying to contain the damage. If a perpetrator entered my guard post area I was to command the dog to attack or shoot to kill.

The 267th Chemical company was responsible for the maintenance and security of the entire compound. *No wonder there are electric fences and so many guards around this place*, I thought.

By the time my first shift ended, all the rabbits and goats were fine and I was thankful that nothing had happened. As I sat in the back of the troop truck returning to the kennels, I wondered if I wanted this job. I began to conclude that I'd rather take my chances in Vietnam, fighting the hardcore North Vietnamese army, than guarding a bunch of igloos full of chemical weapons. I didn't like the idea of having to worry constantly about becoming a casualty of a nerve gas leak or some other killer chemical agent.

Hans and I got along fine. I really loved that dog. For many nights we guarded those igloos. I never had to report an unusual incident, but I began to grow bored with the whole routine. On those long nights, I had plenty of time to become homesick. I missed the majestic Rocky Mountains, towering over Denver from the west. I remembered how I'd drive twenty miles to lookout point, high above the city, and felt as if I could see forever from there. I recalled how especially beautiful Denver was all lit up at night, and how brightly the stars shone from a mountain top view.

My house in Denver had been about forty-five minutes away from the tranquillity of mountain wilderness. I longed to again listen to the whispering aspen tree leaves, to watch water rushing over the Rocky Mountain streams, and to breathe fresh, cool air.

While I lived in Vietnam, Japan, and on the island of Okinawa, life was very different from that in the States. The beaches of Okinawa were thousands of miles from the shores of California, and I couldn't easily get away to them by myself. The island was small and heavily populated by every branch of the U.S. military. All my friends wore military uniforms, and I didn't have any civilian buddies. The local people, culture, food, language, and natural surroundings were beautiful, but their appeal was wearing off. Even if I'd been a civilian, I wouldn't have wanted to live in Okinawa for any length of time.

Some nights, while Hans and I stood guard over the igloos, rabbits, and goats, I thought about my friends back home, Joe and his sisters, Tena and Ruth. They were great friends. I really had loved visiting the Poljanec family. His mother and father had always treated me as one of their own children. I also thought about Kenny Mook. He used to tell me how beautiful the Pennsylvania countryside was and how much he missed his family farm.

Kenny would say, "Someday, when we get out of this hell hole, Johnny, you have to come visit me in Pennsylvania,"

I'd answer, "I will, Kenny. And you have to come see me in Colorado."

Kenny would say that he'd visit me as long as I didn't try to take him on a camping trip. We'd both burst into laughter.

When I wasn't on guard duty, I grew tired of hanging around the same old bars and women on BC Night Street. I was fed up with playing Hearts and staying around the barracks when I was broke or didn't feel like going downtown.

By this time, I'd met a local barmaid, Kiko, who worked at Club Texas. She was the most beautiful Japanese girl I'd ever seen. Kiko looked like a model from some magazine. Every time I went into Club Texas, soldiers surrounded Kiko and sat at her table. We all thought she was a knockout.

Many nights I'd go to Club Texas and try to get her attention. I'd sit by myself for hours, patiently waiting until Kiko would sit with me. After many visits, Kiko finally started greeting me as soon as I'd come into the bar. I rarely had to buy her drinks to keep her at my table. It wasn't long before I was taking her to the local Japanese theater and dining with her in Japanese restaurants off the main bar strip. We seemed to enjoy each other's company.

Gradually, I began spending most of my off-duty hours with Kiko. We'd go to the beach together, and that was where we started to fall in love. I enjoyed hearing the way Kiko talked. She spoke excellent English and loved to read. It impressed me that Kiko could even write in English. She'd never been outside the island of Okinawa, but had learned how to speak and write English from Americans. Kiko wanted to have children and make a home with me in the United States. I thought about it many times and even checked into the military administrative procedures.

There was a lot of legal paperwork involved, but deep down I knew I wasn't ready for marriage. The only girl I'd ever loved, so far, was Joe's sister, Tena. Joe and I had been members of the Littleton High School varsity wrestling team. Through my friendship with him, I'd gotten to know Tena. As much as I loved Joe's whole family, I'd do anything to get a chance to visit his house, so I could look at Tena. She'd been so beautiful in high school. By now, she'd be entering her freshman year at the University of Colorado. I wondered if she'd found a steady boyfriend in college.

I'd been only one of the many boys Tena had dated. Although we'd gone out only a few times and had not gone steady, thoughts of her continued to melt my heart. Tena had been the girl of my dreams, but she was only a dream.

The more I thought about marrying a shy, petite Japanese girl, the more

I realized that I didn't want to take home a girl from a different culture and face problems and prejudices. Like most guys my age, I was lonely for female companionship, but I concluded that marriage to Kiko would be too big of a step for me. I had to admit that Kiko wasn't someone with whom I wanted to spend the rest of my life. This relationship had become too much for me to deal with. Breaking it off gave me another reason for trying to leave Okinawa.

I was wound up all the time, thinking about leaving my current assignment. The Army wasn't going to let me off the island for another year. I kept pondering the idea of volunteering to go back to Vietnam to finish my twelve-month tour. After leaving Vietnam, I could return home to Littleton and attend a state college. These constant thoughts made me feel unfulfilled and depressed.

Gradually, I realized that being an infantryman was all I was skilled to do. I convinced myself that fighting in Vietnam wasn't such a bad job. Although I hated the idea of leaving Hans, I felt that requesting reassignment to Vietnam was the best thing for me to do. I figured that if I returned to Vietnam, I could select an assignment to become an elite paratrooper there. With all this in mind, I made an appointment with the personnel office to volunteer for a return trip to Vietnam.

My friends thought that I'd gone out of my mind. Returning to Vietnam as an infantryman was the worst thing anyone could imagine. Countless people told me, "You'll be killed if you go back there."

I tried to justify my reasons but I couldn't convince my friends that I wasn't insane. Their words—dead, killed, blown away, dying, pine box, body bag—weren't affecting me. These terms didn't trigger the belief that anything tragic could happen to me. I had confidence in my decisions and in myself and I didn't fear dying.

I thought about what I needed to buy in Okinawa to help me survive in South Vietnam. Many crazy ideas went through my head. One of the things I'd regretted about my Vietnam experience was that I didn't have any pictures of it. I didn't have a camera to record the people or places. Now I had a chance to go back and record what I'd missed previously.

From the PX, I bought my first camera—a Canon 35mm half-frame model. The camera could produce twice the exposures from a standard roll of film and was small enough for me to carry in a pocket or ammo pouch. The next thing I wanted was a shiny pair of handmade patent leather paratrooper boots. I'd wear them in base camp when I wasn't hiking the jungles. The last item I wanted to buy to carry in my pistol belt was a bone-handled hunting knife with a six-inch, sharp-as-a-razor blade. With these items, I started preparing for my planned return to Vietnam.

When I went to see the personnel clerk, he told me that I had two options. The first was to fill out the paperwork and request transfer and reassignment to Vietnam. That option would get me to Vietnam as a replacement with no guarantee that I'd be able to choose my assignment. The paperwork process for this option could take a few months. That didn't appeal to me in the least. I wanted control over where I was going, if I was volunteering to return.

The second option was to re-enlist in the Army for an additional year and get assigned to the outfit of my choice. The paperwork process would only take a week or so, and I could be on my way quickly. I didn't think twice about giving the Army another year of my life. In reality, I would only be extending my original enlistment of three to four years. The Army called this type of re-enlistment a *short*.

I told the personnel clerk that my decision was to pursue option two. The clerk directed me to the office of the Re-enlistment NCO. In about two hours, I signed up for more service. I re-enlisted for the 173rd Airborne Brigade, an elite paratrooper outfit operating in the southern jungles of South Vietnam. A week later, I received official orders to my unit of choice. It went that quickly, and I was on my way back to the war in Vietnam.

Don Vestal, a good friend of mine at the time and a former infantryman, told me that I had the balls of a real American fighting soldier. He said, "To go back to that hell hole after being wounded is a choice only you can understand. No matter what happens to you in life, John, I will always respect your decision." Don had been wounded in Vietnam and had received the Army Commendation medal for valor in combat. He was counting the days until he went home to Texas. I spent my last days in Okinawa hanging around with Don until I departed for the Republic of Vietnam (RVN).

I had enjoyed my time with Hans and hated to leave him behind. Learning about German shepherds as sentry dogs had been a great experience. The role of sentry dog handler was exciting, but guarding a chemical weapons site was not.

When I made the important decision of re-enlisting for one more year of military service and returning to Vietnam, I was only nineteen, bored, and feeling the need for a change. I was also escaping from my relationship with Kiko because it was becoming more complicated. I viewed Vietnam as an opportunity to get out of Okinawa.

What I couldn't foresee, as I prepared to enter the Vietnam war zone for a second tour of duty, was how the sentry dog training in Okinawa would save my life.

Chapter 8

I Asked for It, I Got It —
My Return to Vietnam

Iarrived in South Vietnam on March 23, 1967, two days after I turned twenty years old. I flew in on a military cargo plane. It was loaded with new recruits who were getting their first glimpse of Saigon and Ton Son Nhut Air Force base. Their innocence and fear of the unknown contrasted with my eagerness to get in-processed and be on my way to the 173rd Airborne Brigade.

The air was hot and humid with the familiar smell of stale fish. The airfield was busy with the sounds of equipment moving about and the deafening roar of fighter jets speeding down runways.

I saw the olive drab buses, the same as I'd ridden on before, with steel mesh covering the windows and crammed to the last seat with soldiers. Military officers still were separated from enlisted troops and boarded separate buses. The buses cruised through the airfield and passed armed guards and manned bunkers.

While I passed through the main gates into the city of Saigon, I noticed that everything looked much as it had one year earlier. Saigon was extremely crowded with people, bicycles, rickshaws, strange-looking foreign buses, and little cars. Again, I saw no signs of war. Outside the city limits and into the jungles, I now knew, was a different story. Soon my bus entered the gates of Camp Alpha. As I stepped off it, I noticed that the camp looked about the same as I remembered it.

In a drill, similar to my first tour of duty, the replacement troops were quickly shuffled into a large reception building. I again heard the person-nel clerks say, "Give me a copy of your orders, soldier. Wait right here and don't move. We'll get you processed as soon as possible." I was accustomed to the hurry-up-and-wait routine. Nothing the personnel folks did was ever fast enough for me. Now I wanted to get to the 173rd Airborne Bri-gade and didn't like the idea of hanging around in the replacement pro-cessing camp for a week.

I heard my name called over a loudspeaker, so I reported to a wooden building, where a sergeant sat behind a gray metal desk. He asked me to sit while he prepared my assignment. When he finished, he told me I was going to be assigned to the 3rd Brigade, 4th Infantry Division in Dau Tieng.

I couldn't believe what I was hearing. "What do you mean?" I asked. "Didn't you read my orders? There has to be some kind of mistake here, Sarge. Are you sure you have the right guy? Look, Sarge, I have orders guaranteeing my assignment to the 173rd Airborne Brigade."

The sergeant looked annoyed when he said, "Look, soldier, I process hundreds of men through here each day. You're not special because you were here before or because you have orders to the 173rd. Uncle Sam re-serves the right to change your orders anytime he desires."

Heatedly, I said, "Well, I'm not going to accept this. I was guaranteed an assignment to the 173rd Airborne Brigade. That's the only reason I came back to Vietnam."

The personnel sergeant didn't respond as he sat with his head down and shuffled the papers on his desk.

I shouted, "Are you listening to me? Look! I want to talk to the officer in charge here!"

The personnel sergeant pointed to an officer sitting behind a desk and reading documents in the corner of the building. I marched over to him. The personnel sergeant was right behind me carrying a brown folder con-taining my military personnel file.

The major looked up from his desk and asked, "Can I help you, sol-dier?"

I blurted out, "Sir, I have a guaranteed assignment to the 173rd Airborne Brigade and this sergeant changed my orders. I want to know why, Sir!"

The sergeant handed the major my file. The major asked me to sit down and dismissed the personnel sergeant. The major opened my file folder and read my orders. Under normal circumstances, he explained, it would be no problem to process me for assignment to the 173rd. However, the camp commander had directed that the 3rd Brigade, 4th Infantry Division be given the highest priority for infantry replacements. The 3rd Brigade had suffered numerous casualties recently and was operating far below combat readiness strength. The major was under direct orders to process all available infantrymen to that unit.

Again, I couldn't believe what I was hearing. I said, "This is my second tour. I should be given priority since I re-enlisted to come back to Vietnam as an infantryman."

The major patiently listened but kept telling me that there was nothing he could do. As I began to comprehend that I was being screwed out of my assignment, I became more pissed-off. I told the personnel officer that if I'd known such a thing could happen I would never have volunteered to come back to Vietnam.

The officer sympathized with me and told me that the timing of my arrival was unfortunate. He told me that I was a brave man for going back into the infantry after having been wounded in action, but there was nothing he could do to change my assignment. He pointed out that he'd processed only a few soldiers who had returned as infantryman.

"Sir, is there anyone else I can talk to?"

"No! And seeking counsel with the base camp commander is also out of the question," he barked.

The personnel officer assured me that he would give my assignment top priority. I picked up my orders from the major's desk and stomped out of the building. There was really nowhere I could go. The Army had me hooked. I felt completely helpless. I paced around the replacement camp growing more infuriated by the minute.

After passing the chapel for a third time, I decided to step inside. It was quiet and dimly lit with candles. I sat at the end of a pew and stared at a wooden cross above the altar. An older soldier sat nearby. He turned and smiled at me. I immediately recognized the railroad tracks, two parallel bars on his shirt collar, the symbol for an Army captain. A white cross, sewn to his collar, signified that he was also a chaplain.

The chaplain came over to me, shook my hand, and welcomed me to the place of the Lord. We talked for a while. I explained my situation and how unfair I thought it was for the Army to treat me in such a way. The chaplain patiently listened. Then he told me that he'd talk to the personnel officer and see what he could do.

I stayed in the chapel and said a few prayers. When the chaplain returned, he told me that he was sorry. There was nothing he could do to help. I was visibly distraught, got up, and walked out of the chapel.

The next morning, I heard my name called over the loudspeaker, so I reported to the personnel office. When I got there, I was told to see the major. He told me that my out-processing was complete and that he had dispatched a jeep to transport me to the airfield. We shook hands, exchanged salutes, and the major wished me luck. I grabbed my gear and climbed into the jeep. It was a short ride to the airfield. I still couldn't quite believe it. I was going to the 3rd Brigade, 4th Infantry Division. My new assignment was located at the U.S. Army base camp of Dau Tieng, seventy miles west of Saigon and not far from the Cambodian border.

When I arrived at the airfield, I didn't have to wait long before boarding a Chinook re-supply helicopter. It felt like old times flying over the rice paddies, villages, and jungle. I didn't know any of the other men who were riding along with me. I sat quietly and thought of Kenny and our first helicopter ride with the 7th Cavalry. My mind drifted back in time. It had been only a year earlier when I'd been a brand spanking new guy. A few months later, I'd been in deep shit in Bong Son. *Now I'm an old guy*, I thought.

I had a lot of questions and concerns: What kind of shit had the brigade run into to that caused it to lose so many infantrymen? What would my fellow veteran infantrymen think of my volunteering to return? What platoon and squad would I end up joining? What was I getting myself into?

In a strange sense of timing, the entire scenario of my plan to return to Vietnam had taken a sharp turn off-target. I was beginning to question my decisions, and this insecurity was having a negative impact on my psyche. I had no idea what was in store for me. I was having too many questions, not many explanations, and too much speculation.

Will my new assignment provide the answers and the challenges I'm so eagerly seeking? I wondered.

There was no way of knowing then, that the strange twist of fate, which had turned me away from my goal of becoming an elite paratrooper, would place me on a lifelong path. Because of this forced reassignment, I'd meet, befriend, and one day, tell the story of my life and death experiences with Vietnam war dogs.

Chapter 9

44th Scout Dog Platoon

T he Chinook helicopter began its decent into a small base camp in the middle of a huge rubber tree plantation. Raised in the inner-city and suburbs of Denver, I hadn't ever seen an orchard of trees that size, so I enjoyed the view. From the air, the base camp appeared small, remote, dusty and temporary. A Vietnamese village lay outside several rings of connecting barbed wire that separated it from both ends of the camp. The village was only a rock's throw from the nearest parked chopper. Close to the airstrip, a low mountain range bordered the north side of the camp.

The two rotary blades of the huge Chinook kicked up dust as it landed on four wheels. The airstrip was covered with interconnected, perforated steel plating (PSP) that overlaid the packed dirt. When the helicopter landed, I grabbed my duffel bag and walked down the ramp.

So, this is Dau Tieng, I thought.

A buck sergeant in dusty jungle fatigues waved the replacements over to him. We handed him copies of our assignment orders. Then we rode in the back of a utility truck to the replacement facility on the camp's main dirt road. It passed slowly by the field hospital with large red crosses painted on the sides of its tents. Further down, on the left side of the road, an encampment of armored tanks and a small motor pool of jeeps and trucks were parked in rows according to vehicle type. The utility truck finally squeaked to a complete stop at the entrance of the replacement center. Barbed wire fence enclosed its perimeter.

I asked, "Are they trying to keep the replacements from running away, or what?"

No one answered me.

After we jumped out of the truck, we moved inside the main wooden building. Sandbags, piled waist high, surrounded them. As we sat in a small classroom, the non-commissioned officer in charge, a Master Sergeant (E8), stood before us. He was a towering figure with the presence of an old drill sergeant.

In a deep penetrating voice, he welcomed us and emphasized the importance of the 3rd Brigade, 4th Infantry Division's mission. He explained that the base camp was strategically located as a buffer between Cambodia and Saigon. The area was called *III Corps* and *War Zone C*—military names that meant nothing to me. High level commanders made a ton of decisions on how Vietnam was strategically divided for military operations. No one at my lowly level of the military machine ever saw or communicated with the top brass.

The Master Sergeant explained that the entire area surrounding Dau Tieng had a high concentration of VC who regularly waged mortar attacks on the airstrip. He said that if the VC overran this camp we'd be issued weapons and ammunition stored in bunkers inside the replacement compound.

I quickly learned the answer to one of my questions: Why did this division need replacements so badly?

The master sergeant explained that on March 21st, the 3rd Brigade's 2nd Battalion, 12th Infantry had fought a victorious battle with the NVA at LZ Gold not far from Dau Tieng. The battle had started as a result of a *mad-minute*.

I flashed back to my experience with the 7th Cavalry. I remembered that the *mad-minute* is when old ammunition is shot up at a scheduled time. It is both an impressive display of firepower and very noisy, because an entire company opens fire all at once. Unknown to the Americans, Charlie had several regiments operating in the immediate area. The enemy had been preparing to attack our unsuspecting infantry battalion. When the mad-minute commenced at LZ Gold, all hell broke loose around the entire perimeter. In the end, the enemy had lost the battle. There were so many dead enemy bodies that the Americans used bulldozers to dig mass graves. The enemy bodies were gathered and piled into the mass graves

Members of the original 44th Scout Dog Platoon in the back of a 2½-ton truck shortly after arriving in Dau Tieng in January of 1967. Wearing glasses is Mike "Mac" McClellan.

and covered with dirt. Although the number of American casualties was low, compared to the large number of enemy who had been killed, the Master Sergeant told us that we were desperately needed to fill vacancies in the ranks of the 2/12 and 2/22 infantry battalions.

The Vietnamese town of Dau Tieng, we were told, was hostile and off-limits at all times. At night, the military police patrolled the village. The Army Republic of Vietnam (ARVN), the *Vietnamese good guys* on our side, ran a command post in the center of the village.

Oh wonderful, I thought. *How many of those little Gook bastards are using that village to spy on us?* I felt that the Americans were doing most of the fighting, and I had little respect for the South Vietnamese Army.

Before release from the replacement center or reporting to any unit, we had to have some initial training. This consisted of going through orientations, learning how to use an M16, hearing the history of the 3rd Brigade, memorizing the different enemy names and their uniforms, and being shown what the VC were using to kill Americans. It all sounded too familiar. I'd had the same indoctrination with the 1st Cavalry Division. A year later, nothing had changed. For the new recruits, though, it was their first time hearing such information.

The Master Sergeant used a pointer and a large military map, thumbtacked to the wall, to provide a geographical overview. He pointed out the base camp location in relation to other military camps scattered throughout Vietnam. The 3rd Brigade's camp split the district town of Dau Tieng into two parts. The Dau Tieng business district was outside the west end of the base camp. A dirt road ran east and west, straight through the camp, connecting both ends of Dau Tieng. A military airstrip was north of the replacement center.

Dau Tieng was large enough to contain a brigade-size unit of three battalions of infantry and an assortment of small unit attachments. Each battalion of infantry was strategically placed around the perimeter. The Saigon River snaked its way north and south, less than a mile west of the perimeter. The Ben Cui rubber tree plantation was situated west and south of the Saigon River.

Tay Ninh, the next largest populated province, was several miles northwest of Dau Tieng. Southwest lay Cu Chi, the home of the US Army 25th Infantry Division, nicknamed the Tropical Lighting. Cu Chi was big enough to fit five Dau Tiengs inside its perimeter. The three base camps formed a large triangle on the map.

After the briefing, I walked up to the master sergeant and boldly stated, "I've been through all this shit before. Can I skip the training and join a unit right away."

The master sergeant replied, "No! You will be treated like everyone else with no exceptions for past experience. Besides, you can be of value to me by helping the others learn from your combat experience."

I impatiently replied, "I didn't come back to train fucking replacements."

The master sergeant got pissed and said, "You, soldier, have a bad attitude. If you don't back the fuck off, I'll put your ass in a sling!"

I quickly backed off. My only ambition was to get to a unit. Besides, I didn't want any trouble or to get my name on his shit list and be labeled as a troublemaker. The Master Sergeant looked as if he could kick my ass into next week. In those days, it wasn't uncommon for a person like him to take a young trooper to the wood shed and beat the crap out of him. He was too damn big for me to piss off, anyway. I had no choice but to go along with all this in-processing bullshit.

The next day, everyone formed up for training outside the wooden hooch. The training area had mock booby traps, mines, bamboo punji pits, and a huge ball of dried mud with bamboo spikes sticking out all over it. A vine attached to a large branch of a tree suspended it. In reality, the trap would work like this: The spiked ball, which was rigged by a trip wire or vine, suspended above a trail in the jungle. When tripped, usually by some poor soldier's foot, it would swing down with all its weight, gathering momentum, until it hit the soldier about chest high. The victim would probably have no chance of surviving the hit.

The Gooks were very clever at creating all kinds of nasty booby traps for their round-eyed American foes. I already knew what it felt like to be penetrated by a bamboo punji stake. I wasn't afraid that I'd be wounded a second time or killed. This wasn't something a soldier thought about when he was at the beginning of his twelve month tour in Vietnam.

One day two scout dog handlers, who had dogs on leashes, came from the 44th Infantry Platoon Scout Dogs (IPSD) to the replacement center. They were trying to recruit dog handlers. The news perked me up. I thought, *Scout dogs. Cool!*

I was excited to see the scout dog teams make their casual introductions and presentation. One of the team, Oliver Whetstone, whom everyone called Ollie, hailed from Kenosha, Wisconsin. Ollie was a tall, skinny, blond hair, blue-eyed, friendly guy with a Midwestern accent that sounded odd to me. Ollie told us about the scout dogs, trained at Fort Benning, Georgia, and their mission in Vietnam. He and the other dog handler ex-

K-9 handler sleeping quarters in the rubber trees of Dau Tieng base camp (1967).

plained that scout dogs provide early silent warning for the 3rd Brigade infantry units.

Scout dogs used their natural instincts and training to alert specially trained handlers, who determined what the dog smelled, saw, or heard. It was up to the handler to signal an alert to the patrol and provide an explanation of the dog's signal. Ollie explained that their dogs alerted on things like booby traps, VCs in foxholes, and even other animals. I was completely fascinated by what scout dog teams could potentially achieve in a combat zone. I immediately started mentally comparing the scout dogs' duties with the experiences I had with my sentry dog, Hans.

The handlers provided a short demonstration of basic obedience. When they gave their dogs the command sit, the dogs sat and stayed. When the handlers commanded the dogs to lie down, the dogs obeyed. Each time they gave the dogs a command, the dogs obeyed immediately. The discipline between the handlers and their dogs thoroughly impressed me. The handlers demonstrated the dogs' ability to attack on command. This reminded me again of Hans.

At the end of their presentation, the scout dog handlers asked, "Is anyone interested in joining the 44th Infantry Platoon Scout Dogs?" They assured us that we'd be trained before we went out on a mission. All we had to do was sign up. They said that being a scout dog handler meant loving and caring for animals. Ollie told us that if we didn't love animals not to consider handling a military war dog.

As I listened to the scout dog handlers describe their job, I knew I'd be good at this assignment because I love animals of all kinds. Hans was my first dog and I'd enjoyed my experiences with him. By working with him, I'd learned how to care for dogs. Hans had been a special partner many ways. Even his name, *Hans,* translated into English, was my name, *John.* I missed Hans and wanted the chance to be with another German shepherd.

I thought, *I'm not going to let this window of opportunity pass by. Could it be my destiny to be with a dog?* I didn't know. As the handlers talked, I was getting more inclined to volunteer to work with them.

Then one fellow popped a question that was probably on all of our minds. He asked, "Where is the scout dog team positioned in a tactical formation?"

The handlers looked at one another as if to say, "We were hoping no one would ask that question."

After a short pause, Ollie answered it. He told the soldier that the scout dog and handler always walked point. In other words, they led the way. Handlers and scout dogs were first in a combat formation, first in the jungle, first across clearings, first down roads and trails, and, it was hoped, first to find the enemy before being fired upon. He went on to explain that, after the dog alerted and enemy contact had been made, the dog and handler pulled back inside the perimeter.

"Our job is done after we make contact with the enemy. Remember, we're only the warning system, but we fight the enemy when we have to, because we're infantryman first."

Ollie explained that dogs must have the best possible chance to use their natural senses and instincts. That meant working them up-front and on-point, where the air is fresh and the scent is unobstructed. I concluded that walking point was apparently the most effective way to deploy a scout dog team.

Another fellow asked, "How many dogs and handlers have you guys lost?"

Ollie replied, "A few have been wounded, but no one has been killed."

Everyone in the small training area was quiet. Ollie broke the silence by asking if any of us had experience working with dogs. I stood up and stated that I'd had some sentry dog training in Okinawa. Each dog handler asked me several questions. Apparently, I answered to their satisfaction.

They finally asked me if I wanted to join the 44th IPSD. Without hesitation, I said, "Yes!"

Out of the entire group of replacements, I was the only one to volunteer to join the K-9 platoon. I was also the only one in the group with any experience handling a military war dog. Not one other replacement wanted the job of being a pointman in Vietnam. The other replacements thought I was crazy for coming back to Vietnam and now they thought I was doubly crazy for wanting to be a pointman. Maybe I was a little different, but I wasn't crazy. I figured that I'd rather take my chances, having a well-trained dog lead the way, than trying to survive with my own experience and instincts.

The Master Sergeant said, "If you really want to go to the dog unit, I'll let you leave earlier than the others."

I replied, "Let's do it now. In fact, I want to go today."

My answer made it a done deal and the Master Sergeant called the 44th on the landline to confirm my assignment. I felt relieved to be on my way to doing something that I believed I could do successfully. My assignment orders were soon typed up.

My parting words to the Master Sergeant were, "This isn't the 173rd Airborne Brigade, but it's the next best thing for me."

The Master Sergeant wished me luck. I was so glad to get the hell out of that replacement center. I considered these places to be troop traps that could easily be attacked by the enemy.

The 44th IPSD was right off the main road, leading out of the base camp. I walked to the K-9 compound in the company of war dog handler, Ollie Whetstone. As we neared the entrance, I could hear the dogs barking in the kennel. That familiar smell of dogs filled the air and it reminded me of the sentry dog kennel in Okinawa.

After finding my quarters, I was introduced to the platoon leader Lt. Fenner, a thin man, about five-feet-seven inches tall, with short blond hair. He told me that his platoon had graduated together from a twelve-week scout dog training course in Fort Benning, Georgia, and had arrived in Vietnam three months earlier in January 1967. The platoon consisted of about fifteen scout dog handlers and twice as many dogs. Lt. Fenner said that his platoon was definitely undermanned for the number of available dogs they had.

I learned that most scout dog handlers were Officer Candidate School (OCS) dropouts from Fort Benning—home of the Army's OCS program. The candidates who hadn't made the grade, were reassigned to whatever was available. Most of the platoon members of the 44th had college backgrounds and some were college graduates. I wondered how I'd get along with these guys since I'd barely made it out of high school.

Lt. Fenner briefed me on the dog platoon's tactical mission and deployment. The scout dog teams were assigned to support the scouting needs of the 3rd Brigade, 25th Infantry Division, and used extensively. The 3rd Brigade consisted of infantry foot soldier units, mechanized armored units, and the local MP detachment.

Lt. Fenner coordinated the dog platoons' scheduling and assignments when the brigade needed support. His policy was simple — one scout dog team per tactical mission. Lt. Fenner spoke about the need for being fair and ensuring that no one man was doing more than his share of missions. He said that he created his schedules and made all the decisions on assignments to ensure central control and an equitable rotation program. I learned that several of Lt. Fenner's scout dog teams had participated with bravery in the battle for LZ Gold.

Lt. Fenner told me that each scout dog had a unique personality and behavioral pattern. A dog's breed, strengths, weaknesses, and other characteristics determined the role he was trained for in Vietnam. Although the 44th had only scout dog teams, the military deployed Labrador retriever tracker dogs, sentry dogs, mine and booby trap dogs, and even water dogs throughout South Vietnam's war zones.

I knew that my familiarity with German shepherds had taught me a lot about their characteristics and abilities. As I listened to Lt. Fenner describe the work I'd be doing, I realized the importance of the sentry dog training I'd received in Okinawa. This assignment went far beyond anything I'd ever imagined!

Lt. Fenner explained that, over time, an infantryman could acclimate to his surroundings and develop animal-like instincts, but he could never reach the natural skill level of a dog. When a scout dog acclimates to working in the jungle, open terrain, woods, and dry and wet weather, his natural senses and instincts become unbelievably keen. The scout dog's eyes can detect movement at greater distances than any foot solder. A scout dog is capable of hearing sounds a soldier can't. A scout dog's sense of smell is far greater then a man's. When all this is coupled with the dog's unbelievable loyalty and desire to serve his master, it makes the scout dog team an extremely valuable asset to the infantry. The relationship between scout dog and handler is so remarkable that only a scout dog handler can fully understand it. The more frequent the handler and dog train, the more experienced they become as a combat scouting team. They live, bleed, and sometimes die together.

The platoon had its own veterinarian technician specialist, Robert Glydon. He lived by himself in a one-man hooch, fully equipped with medical supplies, across from the row of dog handler quarters. Glydon was qualified to perform surgery on the animals.

A mission for a scout dog team lasted anywhere from three to seven days. The K-9 platoon had compiled a record of many highly successful combat missions, where no one had been killed in action. They'd gained the respect of the patrols they had led. When I arrived at camp, several dog handlers were out on combat missions.

At my orientation, Lt. Fenner had noticed my Combat Infantry Badge. He'd tried to talk with me about my prior Vietnam experiences, but I was reluctant to provide specific details about what it was like to face the enemy. Lt. Fenner didn't ask me why I'd returned to Vietnam. I quickly discovered that my new platoon leader was a soft spoken and easygoing type of guy. He never pushed his rank around like some of the officers I'd met in the past. He was a little hard to understand at first, and I wasn't sure if I liked him, but he was my new boss, and I had no problem following his orders. I knew that I'd need to stay alert, avoid mistakes, and see how things went as I settled into my new job.

The Army corps of engineers had built the dog kennels between rows of rubber trees with floors that were long slabs of concrete. Wood and metal fence sidings and a tin roof formed the rest of the structure. The kennel had a capacity of forty dog runs — twenty on each side. A metal chain link fence separated each dog's run. For privacy, each dog run had waist-high, non-see-through, tin partitions installed. The engineers had wired the kennel for electricity and installed overhead lights. Several empty runs were used for food, supplies, dog crates, and other equipment.. Sandbags were filled and stacked waist-high, around one side of the kennel to provide the dogs with protection from mortar attacks and small arms fire.

The platoon used to employ local Vietnamese laborers to help fill sandbags. Early one evening, several hours after the Vietnamese went home, one of the sandbags exploded. It had a small time bomb inside. After that incident, even though no one was hurt, Lt. Fenner made it a policy not to allow Vietnamese laborers inside the K-9 compound. The dog handlers now had the job of completing the rest of the sandbagged walls when they weren't in the field on missions.

The dogs were kept inside the kennel after dark. During the day, they were tied to the rubber trees outside. Each dog had his own water bucket under his tree. The dogs were fed once in the morning and once in the afternoon.

I soon learned that if a dog handler wanted any comfort in his life, he had to trade something for it. I enjoyed hearing stories the handlers liked to tell about how they'd improved on the original design of our K-9 compound.

One day, a few dog handlers had seen the supply sergeant preparing equipment for transport near the Chinooks and C-130s at the Dau Tieng airstrip. Around him, prefab hooch kits and a collection of corrugated tin sheets for making roofs had been lying in a pile on the ground. The dog handlers had decided to offer the sergeant a fifty-kilowatt generator as a trade for the kits and roofing materials. After making sure that the generator worked, the supply sergeant smiled, indicating that the dog handlers were in position to negotiate a deal. When they'd finished their trade, the dog handlers walked away with four prefab hooch kits, nails, and tin to make roofs. They loaded everything into their 2 ½ ton truck and drove back to the K-9 compound.

The funny part about this creative trade was that the generator had originally belonged to the Air Force. It was even painted Air Force-blue with yellow markings all over. It stuck out like a sore thumb among the Army equipment painted olive drab, or OD. This is an age-old flat green color that the Army uses to paint all its equipment and dye its uniforms. The 44th IPSD had confiscated this generator from the Air Force when it had arrived in Vietnam from Fort Benning.

The generator's history went something like this:

One day the handlers, dogs, and equipment of the 44th IPSD were loaded into trucks and a jeep as part of a convoy headed to Dau Tieng.

While the handlers waited for the convoy to move, someone spotted a huge blue generator sitting on the side of the road unattended. Not knowing what to expect at their new camp, they thought they might need it. A dog handler backed up a truck to the generator and hooked it to the truck's tow hitch. To avoid detection, the dog handlers covered the Air Force-blue generator with an OD canvas tarp and tied it down. Such action was known as an *emergency requisition*. In Vietnam most of us learned never to leave equipment and supplies unattended. Besides, what was the Army going to do if they caught these new guys stealing? Send them to Vietnam?

A short time later, the convoy rolled out with the emergency requisitioned generator in tow for the sixty-mile trip northwest of Saigon to the Dau Tieng base camp. As it turned out, the generator worked fine, but the 44th IPSD never put it into service. It remained hidden behind the kennel until the opportunity came for trading it to the supply sergeant.

At Dau Tieng, with only a few simple hand tools, everyone participated in cutting the timber and hammering nails to assemble the hooch. The K-9 club was the final construction and it turned out to be the most popular building on the grounds. Some of the guys set up a volleyball net between two rubber trees inside the platoon area. They nailed an iron basketball hoop to the side of a tree. Who knows where they got the volleyball or basketball equipment? Building all those things, including the playground, helped morale and killed time when handlers weren't in the field walking point.

And that's how an Air Force generator turned the 44th IPSD's dream of having better living conditions into reality.

Dau Tieng dog handlers found other ways of making life more bearable for themselves. For showering, they suspended two huge metal water barrels on a rack above a wood pallet. A water truck filled the water containers every few days.

I often wondered how a soldier would like to have that job as his tour-of-duty in Vietnam? When he'd go home to the States, people would ask, "Billy, what did you do for your country in Vietnam?"

"Well, Dad," Billy would answer, "I drove a truck in a base camp and filled water containers all day for the troops." Not too exciting, but certainly one of the safest jobs in camp.

The 44th Scout Dog Platoon was assigned to scout for the troops of the 3rd Brigade, 25th Infantry Division, headquartered in Dau Tieng, South Vietnam (1967).

Of course, when Billy came to tell his girlfriend what he did in Vietnam, it would have been a different story altogether. "Well, sweetheart," he'd say, "I spent most of my time in enemy territory, securing the drinking water supply lines, constantly fighting off ferocious North Vietnamese Army saboteurs deep in the jungle. It was a dangerous assignment that was given to only the best trained fighters the Army had, but I really don't want to talk about it anymore."

Actually, jobs such as water-delivery services were given to short-timers — the lucky infantryman with thirty days or less before they'd be going back to the States. Having a job that didn't involve enemy contact was one of those unwritten short-timer benefits commonly practiced throughout the infantry. Another infantry benefit was that if a soldier was wounded in action five times, he never had to serve in the infantry again. I didn't know of one man who had set that as his goal for getting out of the infantry. During wartime, I guess the Army made up these benefits as they went along.

Entrance into the 44th Scout Dog Platoon compound. Kennel is visible, bottom right. The sign depicts the Combat Infantry Badge (CIB) on the left and the shoulder patch (tropical lightning) of the 25th Infantry Division on the right (1967).

A typical day as a dog handler in base camp was different from a typical day in the jungle. In base camp, we got up at six or seven in the morning. We shaved, put on jungle fatigues, and ate some chow. After breakfast, we went to the kennel to feed the dogs, refresh their water, and clean the runs. A few handlers were assigned other cleanup chores, such as burning the shit in the outhouse. Speaking of the shit house, the 44th IPSD painted theirs red, white, and blue. Lt. Fenner was ordered by higher headquarters to have us repaint it, so we painted it infantry blue with a white playboy bunny head on the door.

Other chores included cleaning the K-9 club, driving supplies, filling sandbags, and repairing hooches. The dog handlers worked at a leisurely pace. No one busted ass to get a chore done. Some guys had their noses in books. Dan Scott, for example, could be found most of the time sitting under a tree reading to his scout dog, Shadow.

After the dogs had been put into the kennel for the night, many of the handlers gathered at the K-9 club where they'd get to know one another a little better. Most of the men were in their early twenties. They played poker, read books, drank beer, soda pop, Kool-Aid, and talked about girls and family back home.

To add to the relaxation factor between missions, the 44th IPSD had brought a tiny dog from the States to serve as their pet and mascot. Her name was 44. She had a shiny black, short hair coat, a long snout, floppy ears, and a skinny, long black tail. 44 ran all over the compound and hung around like one of the guys. She was killed by a vehicle when she ran across the dirt road in front of the compound. We gave 44 a proper burial in a secluded place under a rubber tree.

Not long after 44 died, a dog handler brought back to camp a tiny Vietnamese puppy he'd found on a mission. The puppy was about the size of an adult squirrel with white short hair and a few black spots and floppy ears. We named him Hardcore because he was high-spirited and chewed on everything. A handler stored his possessions around or under his cot. If we found tiny teeth marks on our boots, we knew that Hardcore had been there. Hardcore spent a considerable amount of time roaming in and out of our hooches and chewing on whatever he found there. We all loved Hardcore, but after a few months, he was killed when he played too close to one of the more aggressive German shepherds.

Even though Hardcore had an early demise, he fared better with us than he would have in a Vietnamese village. They raised dogs for food like we raised cattle. There were no large Vietnamese dogs, only skinny, small ones. I enjoyed seeing the looks on the faces of Vietnamese villagers when they saw a full grown, muscular German shepherd that would have fed a Vietnamese family for a month. For the entire time I served in Vietnam, I never saw a scout dog be friendly to a Vietnamese. Scout dogs wanted nothing better than to sink their teeth into the Vietnamese, and it was hard keeping the dogs from attacking them. Maybe scout dogs sensed that the Vietnamese had eaten fresh barbecued dog over rice for Sunday's dinner.

Chapter 10

Timber, the Scout Dog

My first assignment was to be a handler for a scout dog named Timber. He had a beautiful mane and perfectly shaped ears that stood at attention all the time. Although Timber was smaller than some of the other dogs, he was high-strung, had a mean streak, and didn't like to be disciplined. Ollie told me that Timber would settle down after he got used to my handling. This comment made me wonder if Timber was like my previous dog, Hans. I thought, *Why do I always get the mean fuckers?*

Training was an extremely important part of preparing to work in real-life combat with a dog. The handlers of the 44th IPSD had built an obstacle course to train the dogs and painted it infantry-blue. The course had a five-foot wall with a window opening big enough for a dog to jump on or through. Another obstacle was a seesaw like the kind you might see in a playground. The dogs learned to walk up one side, balance the board in the center, and then walk down the other side as the board hit the ground. We used hurdles to teach the dogs to jump on command. We connected several fifty-gallon drums together to teach the dogs to crawl through them. We stretched out a twelve-foot section of wire mesh fence, staked it about two feet above the ground, and taught the dogs to crawl under it.

To train the dogs in balance, we used a long log with no branches and made a catwalk with a narrow wooden ramp for the dogs to walk up. Across the top of the catwalk were about twenty small wood slats spaced six inches apart from each other. Since dogs aren't as sure-footed as cats, it was fascinating to watch them try to negotiate the wood slats with their four paws while crossing this horizontal ladder about five feet above the ground.

I had fun working Timber through the obstacle course. This helped to build his confidence, balance, strength and muscle tone, and to reinforce obedience. The scout dogs had to learn to maneuver on command; to go over, around, under, and through whatever they might encounter on a combat mission in the jungle.

Basic obedience was the root of our training. If the dog listened to and obeyed the handler's commands, then the handler could command the dog to negotiate each obstacle on the course effectively. Initially, it was slow for Timber to learn one obstacle at a time. The more I practiced, the better and faster we learned together. I soon discovered that successful scout dog training was all about repetition and consistency. I hadn't attended the formal, twelve-week scout dog training course, so training in camp was all I had. I worked hard to make the best of it.

When a dog performed well, his only reward was love and a big hug and praise like, "Atta boy! Good dog!" One reason dog handlers didn't give treats to dogs was that they had none. The dogs were on a basic diet of water and canned and packaged food issued by the military and monitored by Doc Glydon. More importantly, handlers didn't give treats due to wartime situations. The question became, "What if a handler runs out of treats and he's in deep shit with Charlie out in the middle of the jungle?"

I didn't believe that I needed treats to control my dog in a life-threatening situation, or that my biggest concern would be running out of treats when I needed the dog to do something special, such as locating a booby trap. I already knew things happened fast in combat. A lot was going to depend on how Timber and I trained as a team. Being a German shepherd, Timber was naturally an extremely smart animal and he loved human companionship. The breed is known for its adaptability to almost any climate and environmental condition. That must have been why the Army had decided that German shepherds were the best dogs for scouting in Vietnam.

I learned that you get out of a dog what you put into him. Dogs adapt to the personality of their handler. If the handler is lazy, more than likely, his dog is going to be the same way. If a handler is a go-getter, his dog will probably be energetic. I learned that you have to teach the dog what he needs to know about working with you.

A scout dog has to learn the scent of his master, the pitch of his voice, what type of physical gestures he uses, the pace the handler walks, his general moods and disposition, his touch, and which commands he gives that are more important than others. The more time the handler and his dog work together, the more responsive they'll be to one another. Consistent training creates understanding and teamwork. This strengthens the bond and devotion between them.

The hard part for the handler was interpreting what a dog already knew. I learned more about scouting from my fellow handlers, Ollie and Mike (Mac) McClellan, than I did from anyone else. The key, they told me, was to keep your eyes on the dog at all times. A dog's natural instincts will tell you what he smells, sees, and hears, and when danger is near.

I learned that my scout dog is the real pointman, not me. It would be my job to translate his dog language into English, so I could convey to everyone else what the dog sensed. When Timber and I worked together, he was the one in charge. I had to be his interpreter. This was an ironic revelation, since one of the reasons I'd decided to become a dog handler with my first dog, Hans, was because I'd liked the idea that a dog wouldn't be giving me orders!

Ollie and his dog, Erik, worked with precision as a team. They were something special to watch. In addition to leather eight-foot leashes, we had twenty-five foot leashes. We used the longer leash for training or tying the dogs to their trees when they weren't housed in the kennel. Ollie used silent arm and hand signals to instruct Erik at distances well beyond the length of the standard issue leash. Ollie also worked Erik off leash while in base camp and on missions. Erik responded quickly to each of his commands. Their movements were an art form in motion. I was amazed and hoped I could teach Timber to be as well trained as Erik. Mac McClellan was considered to be another excellent off-leash handler, along with his dog, Archates. They were also a treat to watch.

The other dog handlers were equally well-trained in scouting techniques. We didn't train as a group at base camp. Training was usually at the individual handler's discretion. There was never any pressure for us to train in base camp between missions. The only hard and fast rule was that a handler better be ready to go on a mission when scheduled.

I felt less prepared than my fellow scout dog handlers. Sentry dog training had helped, but it hadn't prepared me for anything like what I was about to face as a scout dog handler in Vietnam. The functional use of sentry dogs was vastly different from that of scout dogs. I preferred the concept of deploying scout dogs over that of sentry dogs. A sentry dog was trained primarily to guard and attack. The scout dog was used in more complex and diversified maneuvers. This made my scout dog assignment much more interesting and challenging. Even though the danger was greater, I wasn't apprehensive about learning and performing my new job.

Now I looked forward to my first real scouting mission with Timber.

After Timber and I had completed several uneventful combat missions, we spent a few days in base camp before going out again. On May 17, 1967 I reported to the Commanding Officer of Company B, 2nd Battalion, 22nd Mechanized Infantry, an encampment which was within walking distance of the K-9 platoon. Part of my job was to brief the CO on where the scout dog team could be best used. The CO introduced me to the platoon leader and platoon sergeant. We'd supported them with scout dog teams in the past.

The platoon leader briefed me on the mission by using a map and grid to point out the objective. The brigade's Long Range Reconnaissance Patrol had recently located a large concentration of VC, operating several miles west of Dau Tieng. A long column of Armored Personnel Carriers (APC) had assembled on the main road leading out of base camp. The first leg of the mission was to travel on several dirt roads, until we reached a point near the target area. Although I knew that riding inside or sitting on top of an APC would neutralize Timber's effectiveness, during the second leg of the mission, when we'd be looking for the VCs bases of operation in the jungle, a scout dog would be invaluable.

After we reached the target area, we were to get off the road and break trail through the jungle for about half a mile, until we reached a large clearing where the APCs would form a defensive perimeter. When the pe-

A column of Infantry Armored Personnel Carriers (APC), 3rd Brigade, 25th Infantry Division, heading across a clearing (1967).

rimeter was set up, Timber and I would join foot patrols to search for VC. The area on the map was considered uninhabited yet hostile. I advised the platoon leader and platoon sergeant that being deployed on foot was the best use of a scout dog team.

I explained that negotiating our way through dense jungle terrain would be difficult. It shortened the distance of a dog's alert to a target and allowed for little reaction time. One of the objectives of the scout dog team would be to locate and check out the narrow paths that zigzagged through the terrain. Trails were dangerous. I believed that with a dog, we had a better chance of getting an alert, than by sending a soldier to check out this treacherous area.

Timber was frisky and eager to go on this mission. The APCs lined up, one behind the other, on the road. With their engines running and ramps up, most of the APCs were ready to move out through the main gate. On top of the APCs, several armed grunts wore helmets and flack vests that uncomfortably increased body temperature in the hot sun. Fifty caliber machine guns were manned in their turrets and radios squawked as we prepared to move out. Timber and I followed at a quick step behind the platoon leader until he stopped close to the front of the column. He turned, looked at me, and pointed to an APC. The smell of diesel fuel filled the air. The APC's ramp was already down, so Timber and I climbed aboard. The driver yanked a hand-lever. A greasy cable slowly pulled the heavy metal ramp door up, until it locked in a closed position, eliminating the light from outside. I thought that watching the ramp close was like seeing a very squeaky and noisy drawbridge go up. Inside the APC, people had to shout to be heard.

I wasn't fond of APCs. Scout dog teams were useless riding inside any type of vehicle. Mostly, I didn't like the way APCs presented big and easy targets for the VC Rocket Propelled Grenade (RPG). The RPG was designed to destroy helicopters and other vehicles. It damaged bunkers and buildings, blew up ammunition dumps, and killed people. Nonetheless, I had no choice about my assignment. This was to be my first scouting mission with a mechanized infantry unit, so I decided that I should make the best of it.

The Russian-made RPGs, which the VC carried, were lightweight, fired very quickly, and reloaded easily. Like their American counterparts, the Lightweight Antitank Weapon (LAW), the RPGs were deployed by resting them on top of a man's shoulder. The RPG and LAW were capable of destroying or damaging similar targets. A drawback was that one LAW fired one shot. That was it. The VC didn't make as easy targets as Americans did. They didn't ride around in jeeps, trucks, tanks, or helicopters. Their strengths lay in their knowledge of the terrain, their ability to strike without warning, and the quickness with which they could escape and evade contact.

Inside the APC troop compartment, two other infantrymen accompanied Timber and me. The manually operated hatch over their heads was open. If a person didn't mind standing, he could look out over the top of the APC, as it motored down the road. Sometimes the rifleman would sit on top of the APC to enjoy cooler air and view the countryside. If the shit hit the fan, and the enemy attacked, the men on top could pile inside through the top hatch and return fire from a standing position. For this ride, I sat quietly with the leash on Timber lying down on the cool metal floor.

I thought about many things during that trip. I didn't know one person on the crew. I had no idea how Timber and I would work out in a mechanized infantry unit. I didn't feel part of the camaraderie that the others displayed. It was still a question whether I'd be accepted by the crew, but I knew that I'd come to do a job, not to make a bunch of new friends.

Each time one of the crew tried to touch Timber, he growled and showed his teeth. They quickly backed off, and I commanded, "No, Timber! No!" Timber stopped showing his teeth as long as the soldiers kept their distance. Since my mission equipment didn't include a muzzle, I held Timber close on a short leash and explained that he was a little aggressive around new people. I told the crew members that Timber would get used to them over time. I was telling a white lie though. Timber was an aggressive dog. Period. He even wanted to bite me many times. I don't think Timber liked his job or Vietnam. He was like a grumpy draftee with a let's-get-this-over-with attitude.

One of the grunts commented, "I have a dog at home. He's a Lab. No way would I send his ass over here to fight this fucking war."

Another grunt said, "Fuck that! I don't know shit about what you and your dog are supposed to do for me. All I know is that he wants to bite my ass."

That crew had never worked with a scout dog team. I did my best to explain how a scout dog team worked in the field. Although the men appeared interested, I didn't think I had gained their confidence. They seemed to take a wait-and-see attitude. Nevertheless, I was at least getting to know them a little better.

I thought, *I hope that they aren't like this for the whole mission. If they are, working with this crew is going to be a real bummer.*

While we rode along, we couldn't hear any war activity. The only noises were sounds of the APC. We rode for several hours before we came to a long stop. The radio started to squawk with chatter. From what I could

Two unknown infantrymen posing with Ollie's scout dog Erik in fromt of their Armored Personnel Carrier (1967).

hear, we were to break up the convoy, get off the road, and head into the thicket. I stood up through the open hatch to take a look around. The dust was heavy and irritated my eyes, so I sat back down.

The APCs moved off the road into the jungle and headed for the clearing that I'd seen on the map. There was no way of knowing where or how far we'd traveled to get to it. The tracks under the APC slowly crawled and ground their way through thick brush. Leaves and small branches, along with bugs and fire ants, began to fall through the open hatch and land on us, so we buttoned it down. Now, we had to quickly kill the fire ants that had fallen inside, because those little predators hurt like hell when they bit.

The APC moved forward, bulldozing everything in its way. It left a wide path of mashed brush in its wake and created a new trail behind it. The engine roared. The brush crackled underneath the APCs' heavy metal plates. It was slow and bumpy. The tracks struggled to get over rocks, stumps, stubborn trees, and bushes.

There was no doubt in my mind that if Charlie was in the area he already knew our location, how many we were, and where we were heading. The lead track was responsible for setting our direction and it forged the trail for the others to follow. Inside my APC, our ride was a little smoother on the path that the leader had created. After about a half-hour of blazing a trail through the bush, the APCs entered a huge clearing. I looked out at the surrounding area and saw that the APCs were assembling into a giant defensive perimeter.

The command APC was easy to spot with all its antennas sticking out. I watched it set up by a clump of trees, near the center of the perimeter. The APCs were forming into a large defensive perimeter. I figured that we must have reached our first objective. We'd position ourselves defensively and organize into foot patrols. That's when Timber and I would get our chance to show what we could do.

When my APC finally stopped, the driver lowered the ramp. I got up and Timber followed me outside. I saw APCs strategically spaced on each side of ours. The gunners on top of the APCs manned their guns to the front. I introduced myself to the track commander, a sergeant, and asked him about the next phase. He said that we'd set up camp for the night, send out some ambushes, and deploy foot patrols in the morning. I told the sergeant that I was ready to take the lead, when the patrol assembled. The sergeant nodded and told me that I'd get my chance the next morning.

It was late afternoon and hot as hell. The ramps were down on the APCs. Crews milled around talking, assembling their gear, checking their weapons and ammunition, and setting up defensive positions. I tied Timber to the track and poured water into my steel pot for him to drink. I'd brought four canteens of water—three for Timber and one for me.

My weapon, the latest model of the M16—a CAR15, had a metal, retractable stock. When extended, it served as a rifle, yet fired the same 5.56 caliber steel-jacket bullets as the M16. Internally, it had the same functional parts as the M16. However, the CAR15 was much shorter, lighter, and easier to carry. I could hang it from my shoulder by a sling and fire it from my hip with one hand. The rifle had little or no kickback, when I fired it that way. This feature allowed me to simultaneously manage Timber on the leash and shoot.

Most of the grunts carried the standard M16 rifle. Some carried the M79 grenade launcher, M60 machine gun, or 22-gauge shotguns. I was the only one sporting the new CAR15. I felt special, because my weapon got second looks from the grunts who hung around the track. I had back-packed twenty clips of ammunition — 200 rounds, two grenades, a hunting knife, food, water, an OD poncho, and a poncho liner for wrapping up in at night.

My backpack held enough food for three days. If I had thought ahead, I could have only carried dog food and two canteens of water, because I was working with a mechanized infantry unit. Inside the APCs, those guys stored all the food and water they needed, making these vehicles their pack mules. I learned that the men who rode in APCs only carry one canteen of water and a few meals of C-rations when they went on patrols because they never ventured far from their supply on the track. Most of the time, they slept inside and under cover of the APC. I was learning new things all the time on this trip. *Leave it to grunts, if there was a way not to have to carry their shit, they would capitalize on it,* I thought. I could understand why they were so proud of the luxuries I didn't have.

I was getting hungry, but I fed Timber first. I checked his food package for bugs before I gave it to him. Bugs were everywhere in Vietnam, and they'd get into anything except a metal can of C-rations. There were probably even some that could eat through cans. Timber ate the semi-moist packaged food as fast as I put it down and slurped up the water I poured for him.

I took a can of beefsteak and potatoes from my stash and soon realized that I hadn't packed a can opener. The Army labeled everything they issued. An infantryman's basic load included a can opener (P38). Most of the time, I had a P38 attached to the dog tags chained around my neck. This time my can opener was missing. I felt embarrassed to ask for one from grunts I didn't know very well. I was a new face to those guys and to have forgotten to pack my P38 might make them think of me as a greenhorn. I was a veteran, but they didn't know that.

I thought, *Ah, what the hell, I gotta eat, don't I?* So I asked a guy from New York to borrow his P38. He was about five-feet-seven, weighed a husky 175 lbs. and had jet-black hair and a black mustache. He spoke with a heavy New York accent and was quite friendly, but had an inner-city tough-guy attitude.

The soldier from New York said loudly, "My P38? Sure, you can borrow it, but I'll have to kill you if you don't give it back." He burst into laughter and told me to keep it as a souvenir of the 2nd squad. I was relieved when he asked me to join him for chow. As we ate our C-rations, we talked about where we were from. Timber lay quietly sheltered from the hot, late-afternoon sun on the ground beside the APC.

Suddenly, radio activity picked up. Troops quickly moved around the two tracks on each side of me. My track commander yelled, "Saddle up! Hurry! Let's go! Come on! Let's Go! Go! Go!"

I hustled to gather Timber and my gear. I clutched my backpack in one hand and Timber's leash in the other. I scrambled up the ramp into the track and sat with Timber between my legs on the bench seat close to the hinged ramp. I'd left my half-eaten can of C-rations on the ground. The other guys quickly loaded their gear and sat facing Timber and me.

Within seconds the driver had the engine going, raised the ramp, and moved forward. The sergeant was on the radio. I leaned over to ask him what was going on. He told me that a bunch of armed NVA troops had been spotted from the air, heading away from the perimeter. His squad was the closest to them, so he'd been ordered to close in and engage the enemy. The sergeant laid his compass on the map and pointed to an area that wasn't too far from where should be heading.

During the pursuit, Timber and I were in the lead APC. It was moving as fast as it could go. We bounced around and hung on. The APC crashed into the brush. Small trees and bushes splintered, as we rode over them. When the terrain became rougher, the APC slowed down and mashed whatever was in its way. The APC dipped down with a jolt, when the tracks hit something solid. It felt as if we were stuck in a ditch. The tracks kept grinding. The APC tried to climb up and over the sides of the depression. With a thick smell of diesel fuel smoke filling the air, the engine revved, and its tracks spun. Our driver backed up and then slammed forward, repeatedly trying to break free. We rocked back and forth inside. Finally, the APC climbed up over the bank and onto more jungle growth.

The machine gunner on top ducked under tree limbs. Looking up, I couldn't see the sky. Green vegetation was falling in on top of us. It felt as if we were inside a blender. Then a deafening BANG! rang out. The APC stopped in its tracks. This felt like being inside a metal drum, and that someone had hit it with a sledgehammer. The explosion's force ripped through the maintenance panel that covered the engine in the drivers compartment. Black smoke streamed from the driver's compartment and filled the inside of the cabin. I noticed that the driver was wounded in the right leg. He scrambled up through his hatch and out of the APC. Simultaneously, the .50 caliber machine gun on top began firing. I looked at the other two soldiers across from me. They looked startled and said nothing. All of this had happened in only a few seconds.

There was no time to reach the handle to lower the ramp, because it was in the driver's compartment. Instinctively, I grabbed the small emergency door handle and yanked it open. With my boot, I pushed the heavy metal door as hard as I could. It swung out on its hinges and latched itself open.

With Timber's leash in one hand, I grabbed my CAR15 and a bandoleer of magazines. I dove through the open door and lay flat on my belly in the dirt just behind the smoking track. Timber was going crazy trying to get away. The loose end of his leash was pinched under the closed ramp, and I couldn't yank it free. This must have happened when the ramp door closed behind me as I rushed to get inside with Timber.

The other two men had already jumped out of the APC and were crawling away. I frantically pulled and yanked to free the leash. It wouldn't budge, so I cut it with the hunting knife that I'd bought in Okinawa. Only about ten inches of leash remained to connect me with Timber. The dog panicked and jumped up and down, trying to get away from me. The shooting and explosions increased to my front and on the left.

I crouched on my knees, leaned against the back of the APC, and tried hard to control Timber. I quickly looked around and realized that the APC was sitting perpendicular on a narrow dirt road. Its back provided some protection from the bullets. I looked to the front of the APC and saw that it was on fire. No shots were coming from the right side of the APC, but the left side was catching hell. Another stationary APC stood directly behind me in the jungle. The rest of the column was somewhere behind it.

The shooting increased. The VC fired on the APC column from its front and left sides. I saw my track commander lying on top of the burning APC and firing directly to his front with the .50 caliber machine gun. The vegetation on both sides of the dirt road was thick and dark. I couldn't see the enemy, but could feel his bullets hammering the APC close to my position.

I aimed to the front of the APC and fired several rounds. Charlie returned fire immediately. I realized that I'd become a sitting duck behind the track in the middle of the road. I decided to seek better cover. I got on my stomach and crawled away, dragging Timber from the inflamed track. We made it into the jungle about fifty feet behind the APC. Timber continued to growl and jerk away from my grasp. I was determined not to let him run. If Timber ran away, I'd never have forgiven myself. He'd surely be killed. We were in this together and it was my job to keep us together.

I scanned the jungle for signs of the enemy. Charlie was still invisible. The column of APCs were stationary on my left. I could hear American weapons firing and the turret-mounted, heavy machine guns blasting away. Small arms fire from the Americans and VC filled the air with constant cracking noises. Another loud explosion erupted nearby causing my ears to ring. I couldn't imagine the pain Timber's ears were feeling. Through the thick vegetation, I saw black smoke and red flames coming from a second APC. I hung on to Timber and hugged the jungle floor.

We were pinned down by enemy fire from the left and front of the column, and two APCs had definitely been knocked out of action during the first few minutes of this fight. Charlie hit my APC first. This probably meant that the ambush had sprung along the left side of our column.

Bullets zinged through the air around my position chopping up jungle foliage everywhere. Nothing was coming in from my right side. This led me to believe that we were in an L-shaped ambush. The small part of the L was the direction the APCs had been heading. The large part of the L was the left side of the column of our four APCs. The VC we chased after had intentionally maneuvered us into their trap.

Timber was going crazy. I crawled around looking for a better fighting position. I met a wounded American soldier and Timber growled at him, but I kept the dog at bay. Timber was scared and didn't want to be in this situation any more than I did. The soldier sat on his knees and stared blindly into nothingness. He didn't carry a weapon or have his helmet on. I recognized him as one of the crew who had been in my APC. A chunk of shrapnel stuck out from his forehead and his eyes glazed over. I pulled the wounded soldier to the ground and tried to comfort him. I had no first aid bandages, only my CAR15, Timber, and a bandoleer of ammunition. With my free hand, I ripped a strip of cloth from my fatigue jacket and used it to soak up the blood dripping down the soldier's face. I located a nearby tree and helped the man crawl over to it.

Timber still struggled desperately to get away. He tried to bite me several times. I was getting pissed off so I slapped the dog hard across the mouth with my free hand. This only upset Timber more. I quickly realized that I'd lost my composure. I shouldn't have struck my dog. There was too much confusion. I had too many things to concentrate on at once. The whole situation was out of control. For the first time, I began to wonder if I'd survive.

The constant rifle fire, exploding grenades, and chatter of machine guns were deafening. I fired into the jungle in front of the track that still burned in the road. Although we received fire from the left, I didn't want to shoot in that direction. I wanted to avoid hitting Americans positioned around the APCs. The shooting and explosions didn't stop. I was fortunate to have a good firing position from behind the thick base of a tropical tree. It had large roots, growing a few feet above of the ground, and connecting to its base. For protection, I wedged between the tree's roots with Timber and the wounded soldier. Even if the wounded soldier had had his weapon, he was in too much shock to defend himself.

There was another APC on fire to my left behind the one on the road. I kept returning fire into the thick jungle. I thought, *I have to conserve my ammunition. I don't want to run out.*

It bothered me not to have both hands free. I figured Charlie would eventually surround and trap us like he did in Bong Son. The difference was the we had clear lanes of fire and could see the enemy in Bong Son. Here it was thick jungle all around and difficult to find a target. I had no idea how large a force we were up against. The non-stop firing was brutal. I thought that there must be more than a platoon of VC for them to be putting out so much firepower. Maybe there were fifty Gooks attacking us. I couldn't be certain.

We had started out with four APCs. Now I could only hear two of them firing their .50 caliber machine guns. Although I couldn't see it, the noise of a .50 caliber machine gun was distinctly American, because Charlie didn't have .50s.

I felt certain that we were trapped in an L-shaped ambush. This allowed for interlocking fire and maximized the killing zone without causing casualties on the side executing the ambush. Charlie had pulled off this attack very well.

I thought, *Charlie is going to be coming around on my side. I'm not prepared to hold off an all-out assault. He's going to overrun me.*

I was on the right side of the burning APC and receiving intense fire from across the road in front it. I could see from where the bullets were landing that Charlie knew my exact location. I couldn't see the VC through the jungle, but I knew they were close. I had no idea if I was hitting any of them when I returned their fire. Charlie must have been dug in and he seemed to know where all the Americans were positioned.

I kept reloading and fired on semi-automatic. Trying to maintain my confidence, I thought that Charlie probably realized American reinforcements would be here soon. On the downside, I also knew that the enemy's bullets and rocket-propelled grenades would take less than a second to kill us. My confidence was weakening as I thought that reinforcements wouldn't reach us in time and we were all going to die.

This attack wasn't typical of how Charlie operated. Usually, he'd hit the Americans fast and run like a rabbit before we could regroup and reinforce. This time, Charlie wasn't running. This led me to believe that he was preparing to move in for the kill.

Timber kept on fighting to get free. I refused to let him go and tried talking softly, hoping to calm him down. The wounded soldier was still alive and lying quietly on the ground between the roots of a tree. If Charlie charged across the road, I decided that I'd switch to full automatic and take out as many of them as I could.

I didn't see any other Americans near me, so I assumed that I was the only one who could defend the APC's right side. My mind raced with frantic thoughts: *If Charlie realizes I'm the only man defending this side, he'll overrun my position. Why hasn't he attacked already? Maybe he's getting ready to. Maybe he knows I'm low on ammunition. I must make every shot count.*

Reinforcements have to get to us soon. I can't hold out much longer. My grenades are in the burning APC. Going back there to get them would be suicide. Timber has gone mad.

All these crazy thoughts were driving me out of my mind. For the first time, while serving in Vietnam, I felt completely isolated.

BOOM! The noise of a tremendous explosion filled the air. The ground shook, and so did I. The APC I'd escaped from had blown sky high. Timber let out a painful cry and went down on his side. At the same instant, I felt the heat of sharp stings burning into my face, body, and left hand. Blood trickled down my cheeks from small cuts in my face. My hands and arms had small cuts, too. My muscles were tense. Timber was bleeding badly from his right rear flank. I had no bandages, so there wasn't much I could do to cover my dog's wound. Timber lay on his side in pain and panted quietly. I'd been lucky once more. The tree had taken the brunt of the shrapnel. Afterwards, I looked to my left front where the explosion had occurred. The APC had been reduced to a smoking slab of metal resting on it tracks in the middle of the dirt road.

The soldier lying on top of the burning APC firing his .50 caliber machine gun had disappeared with the explosion. I knew that there was no way that brave American could have survived. Several brass casings of .50 caliber machine gun bullets, hot to the touch and split wide open from the exploding powder, were scattered near my feet. Their black metal links were still connected the bullets.

It became strangely quiet for a few moments and I anxiously scanned the area looking for any kind of movement. I saw nothing, but heard groans nearby. The shooting started again on the left side of the column of APCs.

The other APCs on my left were close. One of them was still smoking, and I figured that it was only a matter of time before it blew up, too. Soldiers moved around on the ground, using the protection of the APCs to defend themselves. I decided to help another wounded man nearby, so I left Timber and crawled over to him. Timber didn't follow me. He was too hurt to move. I recognized the soldier as the fellow from New York who earlier in the day had given me a P38 to open my C-rations. Then I saw the most penetrating, mind-boggling sight I'd ever witnessed in combat.

This poor soldier, suffering from severe wounds, was crawling on his hands and knees aimlessly. The sleeves of his shirt were torn away, exposing nothing but the remains of his arms—white bones and joints. Most of the flesh was gone. Chunks of flesh had ripped away from his thighs and back. I couldn't understand how this man could still be alive and crawl around in such a condition. It was shocking to watch.

The wounded soldier grabbed me by the shoulder and stopped crawling. He looked as if he recognized me. Then slowly, he rolled over on his back. His eyes stared up at me. He moved his mouth and tried to talk, but I couldn't understand a word he said. I couldn't stop staring at him, either.

Then something happened that I knew I'd never forget for as long as I lived. The wounded soldier stared at me and muttered sounds I couldn't understand. Then his body began to glow a soft white, as if a light fog was slowly covering him. This only lasted a few seconds. When it disappeared, the soldier stopped breathing. I knew that he was dead. I closed his eyes and slowly moved away. I'd seen my share of men die in Vietnam, but I'd never witnessed anything like this. Had I watched this man's spirit leave his body? I didn't really know, but his face would be forever burned into my memory.

I felt helpless and hopeless. The shooting didn't stop. I returned to the tree to check on Timber and the other wounded man. Their conditions hadn't changed. Timber wasn't moving anymore, but he was breathing. I told Timber that he was going to be okay. I assured him that I'd get him out of there. I don't know if Timber understood a word I said, but his eyes were wide open and he didn't move.

The other wounded soldier was alive but still in shock. Small arms fire poured in on us. I spotted movement in the jungle across the road. I fired on semi-automatic. The movement stopped. I believe that I silenced one VC.

I could hear the enemy but couldn't see where they hid. I kept firing single shots wherever I heard something. I looked around and spotted more wounded Americans, huddled in the vegetation behind nearby trees. Some were lying curled up on the ground crying in pain and unable to continue the fight. I left my position again to try to help. I found the platoon leader I'd met at the start of this mission. Badly burned, he sat with his back propped up against a tree. His smoking fatigue jacket had welded to his flesh. His right arm was mangled.

With the numbness of a man in shock, the lieutenant asked, "Do I look okay?"

"You look fine, sir. Everything's going to be all right," I said, trying to give him some shred of hope to hang on to.

The lieutenant said, "Before we abandoned the burning APC, I radioed for air strikes on our position."

There was nothing I could do for the lieutenant, so I returned to the tree to check on my scout dog and the other wounded man.

American artillery and air strikes zeroed in on our positions and dropped their loads. Nothing is more frightening than the incredible cracking sounds of exploding artillery shells and bombs falling within a stone's throw of a soldier's position. Those jets couldn't possibly see us within the jungle's canopy. I hugged the jungle floor near a tree, kept my head down, and held Timber to the ground. Even though Timber had lost some blood, he came to life when the artillery shells and bombs exploded. He wore himself out, struggling to get away from me, and finally gave up and lay still. I felt so sorry for him.

The fighting seemed to last forever, and too much was happening around me. It was hard to believe anyone was going to make it out of this trap alive. I knew it was only a matter of time before I'd be hit. I tried to keep my wits about me and to stay focused on the VC who were still out there.

I began to feel a strange numbness coming over me. I had never experienced such a feeling before. I've seen plenty of combat before, but for some reason I now felt mentally and physically strange. Numbness spread quickly throughout my entire body. Something weird was happening. I couldn't shake it off.

Suddenly, I heard commotion in the brush to my right. It was the first time there had been noise on that side of the jungle.

My numbness intensified. I thought, *This is it! The Gooks are coming for me now. It's all over! Charlie is at my doorstep. Charlie won't be taking prisoners. I will fucking kill myself before I let those fuckers get to me.*

The noise grew closer. My adrenaline flowed. Nervously, I aimed my CAR15. I shook like a cold chill had come over me as I listened and waited for something to happen.

Then I heard English-speaking voices calling out from the brush. They yelled, "Don't shoot! We're Americans!"

I dropped my weapon in my lap and sat there, staring. American soldiers poured into the surroundings.

Timber and I had been saved.

The Americans were going to prevent all of us from being completely wiped out.

I was still in a daze when one of the soldiers came over. He stooped and brushed the ants and dirt from my naked arms and offered me water from his canteen. I couldn't speak or stand up, and I couldn't shake that strange numb feeling. The soldier told me to stay where I was and that he'd be back. Another soldier tended to the wounded man lying next to me. Several fresh troops moved all around the area.

Leaders commanded, "Let's get these wounded men some help over here! Check out those APCs for survivors! Help that man over there! Set up a firing position! Oh, my God, we have a lot of dead Americans over here, sir!"

The shooting and explosions had stopped. The only noise was the sound of American voices. I sat, silently clutching the short leash still attached to Timber. I watched as American troops helped the wounded and covered our dead. It was a complete mess. I couldn't budge to help.

Why is this happening to me? Why can't I get up?

A huge armored wrecker drove past the tree where I sat. Right in front of me, it ran over a land mine that exploded violently, rocking the armored wrecker. Everyone nearby instantly hit the ground. I didn't even flinch. Dirt and debris flew everywhere. I only sat there and watched without responding or talking. It was as if I was deep inside myself, looking out.

Our rescuers loaded the dead and wounded into an APC that idled on the road. Two soldiers came over to me. I recognized Mac McClellan, my fellow scout dog handler from the 44th Scout Dog Platoon.

Mac said, "John, I'm going to take care of Timber. You need to release the leash and let these guys get you into the APC and to a hospital."

I shook my head and yelled, "No! No! No!"

Mac pried my hand open to take Timber's leash. He picked up my wounded dog and carried him away. Two soldiers helped me to my feet and into an APC. As we rode away, I sat, not saying a word, not moving. I felt completely useless. When the APC stopped, the soldiers helped me get up and out. They put me on a stretcher. I lay very still, staring up at the darkening sky. I heard and saw choppers everywhere.

A face appeared and looked down at me. His eyes were fixed on mine. I glanced at his collar and noticed a white cross. He was a chaplain. My eyes welled up with tears and blurred my vision. The chaplain hugged and blessed me. He told me that the Lord was with me now and not to worry. He said that I was safe. The chaplain walked beside the stretcher. Two soldiers carried me to the awaiting medical evacuation chopper. The chopper lifted off and I was on my way to a field hospital. I still felt paralyzed. By now, my mind was clear and active.

When the chopper landed, I was carried into a tent that smelled like medicine. I realized was in inside a field hospital with its bright lights overhead. Wounded men on stretchers and tables were all over the place. A nurse with a mask over her mouth asked me where I hurt. I couldn't speak. I lay there on my back and stared aimlessly, unable to respond. The nurse pointed a bright light into my eyes. I didn't even blink. She cut away my fatigue jacket and trousers and checked over my entire body. The nurse cleaned the cuts on my face and arms and then stuck me with a needle. I soon passed out.

I awoke the next morning in a recovery tent. I sat up on my cot and looked around the room. I felt a little sore but, otherwise, perfectly fine. I no longer felt the strange feeling and numbness in my face. *What happened to me out there?*

The tent was filled with soldiers all bandaged up and lying on cots. A doctor came over and told me to lie back down. I tried to explain that I felt fine and wanted to check on Timber. The doctor said they didn't have a patient by that name. He said that I had no serious wounds. He'd soon release me. I'd suffered a bout of traumatic combat shock and battle fatigue. I told him that nothing like this had ever happened to me before. I'd been on many missions and seen plenty of combat prior to that incident. Why, this time?

The doctor believed that this type of medical condition occurred when a soldier's resilience to violent combat wears down and his system decides it has had enough. He explained that the consequences of combat could linger for a while, but that I should recover soon. He told me to take it easy for a few weeks before heading out on another mission. The doctor said that he'd release me from medical care the next day.

When I arrived back at the 44th scout dog compound, Mac welcomed me and said that Doc Glydon had patched up Timber. Most of my gear had burned up in the APC, but Mac had put my weapon on my cot. I went to my hooch to rest. It was hard to believe, but I'd only been gone for a few days.

I pondered over the events that had led to the ambush and all those casualties. I thought about Timber jumping all around and how difficult he'd been to control. I was still pissed off that he'd tried to run away. I felt even more upset that I'd struck him. I most certainly didn't want to ride in another APC for as long as I lived.

I looked at the P38 attached to my dog tags, and instantly flashed back to that poor soul from New York who had given it to me as a souvenir. That young man had died in the middle of nowhere and there had been nothing I could do but watch it happen. I played the battle over and over in my thoughts. All the faces of the nameless men I'd fought beside flashed through my mind. *God rest their souls,* I prayed.

I briefed Lt. Fenner on the mission. He listened intently and was happy to see that I was okay. That was about it. Lt. Fenner wasn't one to dwell on the details of what had happened. I guess that as a leader he wanted me to recover and try to forget.

Doc Glydon told me that Timber had been a frightened animal when he'd arrived back at base camp. Timber's right rear flank had been badly chewed up by shrapnel, and he'd lost a lot of blood, but would recover over time.

I went to the kennel and found Timber lying on his concrete run, his upper leg and back wrapped in bandages. He didn't respond when I called his name. I went inside Timber's run and sat beside him. I talked to him as I gently petted his head and back. I apologized for striking him and asked for his forgiveness.

Timber didn't show any excitement or spunk. It was too early to expect much healing from him. Timber was obviously having a hard time dealing with all that had happened to him. I could certainly understand. I knew how he felt. I wondered if Timber and I would ever get over what we'd gone through in that jungle. Would he ever be the same dog as before? I knew I'd go on other missions, but would I be okay? Time would tell.

I continued feeding and caring for Timber, and his wounds started to heal. I took him out of his run several times to exercise his leg. He limped but steadily improved. Over time, I slowly worked in some basic obedience exercises. Timber didn't respond to commands as he had before. He had no snap and lacked his usual aggressiveness. My instincts told me that Timber wasn't going to be ready for any missions in the near future. I wasn't sure what I wanted to do. I felt sorry for my dog.

As much as I loved Timber, I decided that the best thing for both of us was to ask Lt. Fenner for a different scout dog. The lieutenant authorized me to replace Timber with any other available dog. It was not our policy to put a dog to sleep just because he couldn't perform. In fact, Timber never went out on another mission. Although he recovered physically, he never fully recovered mentally from that mission.

Many times I thought about that mission. I hadn't had the chance to work Timber the way we'd trained together. Regardless of the job description for a scout dog handler, in reality I was an infantryman. We'd entered the ambush with four APCs. Each had at least four to six men. Charlie's L-shaped ambush had surprised, trapped, and picked us off one by one. Enemy RPGs, grenades, rifle and machine gun fire had kicked our Americans butts that day, but the final VC deathblow which I had been so sure would come, never did.

I didn't know how many of the enemy troops had paid with their lives.

I thought I'd killed a few of them, but I never saw their bodies. No doubt Charlie had drawn us into that spot on the map to kick our asses, and we fell right into his trap. Only a handful of us survived that ambush. Without timely rescue, Timber would have been killed and I would have gone home in a pine box.

Later, I read a poem Mac wrote. It expressed so well what it had been like to ride in an APC and become a vulnerable target for the enemy.

Kaiser Coffin
Aluminum-hulled hearse, carrier of cattle.
Made by Detroit to take men to battle.
Gas tank high on the left hand side.
Charlie found out, and a lot of men died.
Gasoline tanks in the floor and wall,
One rocket hit, and you're in a fiery ball.
Beer can aluminum, two inches thick,
A browning fifty will go through slick.
Can it stop anything except a trifle?
You're safe as can be from a Daisy air rifle.
— Michael (Mac) McClellan, 44th Scout Dogs, 1967

Now, with all my strength, I had to put this traumatic experience behind me and heal. My task would be to prepare for my next mission. I'd have to go on it with all the uncertainties of learning how to handle a new scout dog. My life and the lives of others would depend on my succeeding.

Chapter 11

Clipper, My Second Scout Dog

It took several days for me to decide which of the available dogs I wanted before I selected Clipper. I felt excited the first time I saw this dog, and he took to me as if we'd worked together before. Words can't express how much I wanted him, and Clipper responded to me as no other dog had.

The military permanently identified Clipper by tattooing serial number 12X3 in his left ear. It was ironic that Clipper and I both wore dog tags.

Each scout dog in the 44th Scout Dog Platoon had an official military medical record. It contained his age, weight, height, date, the place where he began military service, his training record, and a picture of his profile. Doc Glydon maintained the file and a veterinarian record of all the medical treatment he provided to the scout dogs.

Clipper was docile but very smart. He had a beautiful black and brown coat, big brown eyes, and great-looking tall, pointed ears. He weighed eighty muscular pounds and walked with a sense of pride, confidence, and control. In my opinion, Clipper was a perfect specimen of a German shepherd. He'd let any American soldier pet him, no matter where we were.

Whenever Clipper was around a Vietnamese though, he became aggressive. One reason was that the Vietnamese looked, talked, smelled, and ate differently from Americans. Secondly, a Vietnamese worker had planted a time-bomb in a sandbag inside the K-9 compound. Ever since then, Vietnamese weren't allowed in the compound or near the dog kennel. The dogs knew that the Vietnamese weren't supposed to be around, and they treated them as trespassers.

In scout dog training, command and control are the most important issues. A scout dog, trained in the basics, learns to walk in pace with his handler. He also must master a technique that takes much practice—not to pull the leash tightly or to drag the handler. When the dog and handler move as a team, there should always be a little slack in the leash between them. After a while, it should seem as if the leash has become invisible. However, if a dog gets startled the handler still has control when the leash is fastened. Military policy required that dogs be leashed at all times when not in the kennel. Several dog handlers, like Ollie and Mac, trained to patrol with their scout dogs off-leash.

Ollie and Mac were great scout dog handers. They were in tune with their dogs and could work them off-leash with complete confidence and control even under the duress of a combat situation. Working a dog off-leash was really a matter of training, confidence, and choice. I wasn't confident enough to try off-leash scouting. My combat experience with Timber had left me in doubt about working a dog off-leash. I wanted complete control of my animal under all conditions and combat situations.

If Clipper and I were on a live mission, I'd brief the two men behind me and they would act as my bodyguards and security. My job was to concentrate on the dog. This left me somewhat blind and vulnerable. The soldiers behind me had to be my eyes, ears, and security net. If the enemy got the edge, the grunts would be right there to give me fire support and security.

The K-9 compound provided plenty of room for training. In between missions, Ollie and I decided to do some dog training together. We found a perfect place within the base camp's outer defensive perimeter in the rows and rows of tall rubber trees behind the kennel. The trees offered the added advantage of providing shade from the hot Vietnam sun.

One of the things I wanted to teach Clipper was how to recognize and alert me to the presence of trip wires. I needed to learn how to identify clearly when and how Clipper alerted, so I knew what his signals meant when on a mission. For instance, I had to know what Clipper would do when he sensed danger, when he suspected VC were hiding in foxholes, behind or up in trees, moving at a distance, or standing in full view. How far out could Clipper alert when he detected movement or noise? Did he alert the same way when he found a man as he alerted for an animal or a booby trap? To learn the answers, I had to work with Clipper in mock situations.

In one mock situation training scenario, I'd send a fellow dog handler out into the woods far enough so that I wouldn't know exactly where the decoy was hiding. While the decoy hid, I'd keep Clipper distracted from what was going on by walking and playing with him in another area. I'd allow several minutes to pass before we'd begin the hunt. When enough time had passed, I'd command Clipper by slapping my hand against the side of my left leg. This would be Clipper's sign to automatically heel and sit.

When it was time to go, I'd work Clipper on an eight-foot leather leash. I'd tug the leash to signal Clipper to move to the end of it. I'd keep the pace of this training slow, as if we were walking point on a live patrol. I walked behind Clipper, keeping my eyes on his head and ears at all times.

As we headed toward the hidden target, I observed Clipper's neck and head rising sharply and his ears popping straight up and forward. Clipper stopped, stood erect, and stared straight ahead. He turned and gave me a quick glance. I interpreted his reactions to be a strong alert. I looked in the direction Clipper's head was pointing and knelt on one knee. Clipper sat. I put my weapon on ready and scanned the area to our front but I saw and heard nothing. We moved only twenty or thirty yards toward where I assumed the target decoy must be hiding.

Since this was a training session, I got up and tugged Clipper to move out again. Clipper obeyed, moved a few more feet, and again gave the same strong alert. I knew that he'd spotted something to the front, but I couldn't tell how far away the target was.

There were hundreds of trees in every direction. The question was, which one hid the decoy? I decided to continue to move forward. Clipper headed in a certain direction and when we were within thirty yards of one particular tree, he alerted again, then he stopped and stared at that tree. Clipper stood erect and refused to go any farther. The decoy came out from behind the tree and I grabbed Clipper around the neck and hugged and praised him for doing a great job at finding the target.

The author with Clipper in the Dau Tieng K-9 compound (1967).

As it turned out, Clipper's first alert took place about one hundred yards from the decoy. We also used captured equipment and clothes from the VC to teach dogs the scent, by hiding them in the woods. Using these training techniques, I learned how Clipper would alert me to the enemy.

I began to repeat the training exercise over and over, even in the rain. I learned that weather conditions such as wind, heat, humidity, density of vegetation and terrain, surrounding noises, and the movement of others, all played an important role in how far and strong a scout dog could alert.

139

During our sessions, Ollie was a terrific tutor, always patient and understanding, as he thoroughly explained and demonstrated the training techniques.

Sometimes we dug foxholes for men to hide in. A soldier hiding in a foxhole would lightly tap a stick against a tree or quietly carry on a conversation. In this way we were able to determine the distance at which the dog picked up sound. Over time, I learned to read Clipper's reactions by concentrating on his head and ear movements and I gained confidence in what Clipper could do.

The question remained: How would he work in the rubber tree plantation outside base camp? We couldn't conduct training missions outside the Dau Tieng base camp. Everything beyond the barbed wire fences was considered hostile. We had to be on an actual mission for me to learn if Clipper's alerts, during our training sessions, would be the same in the dense jungle, open terrain, or in tall elephant grass.

Everyone was expected to go on missions. It was normal for a scout dog handler to be a little nervous or apprehensive about leading the way on a patrol. If the handler felt he wasn't ready, even though he'd trained for it, he had to overcome his fears and do the job. A dog handler's natural instincts also played an important role in surviving the bush. He had to do his best in combat situations to provide early silent warnings of danger and return home, alive.

Walking point was one of the most dangerous jobs in South Vietnam. Since this is what a dog handler did, he had to constantly stay focused. The enemy usually had the advantage of spotting the American point men first. With a scout dog team though, the tables were turned. The Americans gained the advantage, because a dog's sense of smell, hearing, sight, and instinct was hundreds of times greater than a human's. Clipper was like a walking radar beam. I learned to trust him more than my rifle — he was that good.

I carried my own ammunition and equipment, and Clipper's water and food supply. Clipper relied on me to recognize when he was thirsty, hungry, tired, hurt, or sick. We bonded as a team because we took care of each another.

The expectation of becoming a casualty in Vietnam was extremely high. With a scout dog, a handler had a better chance of spotting the enemy first. This advantage could make the difference between his living or dying.

When a scout dog alerted, the handler's job was to drop down on one knee immediately, determine what the alert meant, and as quickly and quietly as possible, relay the information to the men behind him. The platoon leader would then assess the situation and determine if the patrol should act on the alert, check it out, ignore it, or proceed with caution. Even though a handler would have briefed the platoon leader ahead of time, if the leader had never worked with a scout dog team, it was difficult to figure out how he'd react when a dog alerted.

Most of the patrol leaders, I worked with, trusted the dogs' natural instincts and my assessment of the situation. However, some leaders didn't like the idea of a scout dog team making decisions. Often they'd ignore the scout dog team's warning. Sometimes they'd get away with it, but other times they paid a price. When I worked as pointman on a scout team, I insisted that every strong alert my dog gave should be checked out. I didn't like the crapshoot of ignoring the dog's signals.

If soldiers checking out a scout dog's alert didn't make enemy contact, the dog team resumed the lead and continued pushing in the mission's direction. If a dog's alert resulted in enemy contact, the scout dog team quickly moved back inside the patrol's main body.

The scout dog team's job was considered complete after the enemy was engaged. Standard operating procedure for every mission was that when the fighting was over, and if casualties were light, the scout dog team resumed the point position and continued the mission. If casualties were heavy, the entire platoon was usually relieved from its mission and replaced by a fresh unit. I'd been trained as an infantryman and scout handler to follow this process, but it didn't always work as planned. Sometimes, the scout dog handler and his dog were so far out in front that they got caught during a fight between the Americans and Viet Cong.

Since I'd been in combat Vietnam before I took my base camp training with Clipper seriously. I knew that I'd have to rely on him. I'd experienced dealing with jungle conditions, open terrain, rivers, creeks, villages, hills,

141

valleys, rice paddies, night-time operations, and various weather conditions. Now I had to adjust to working with a dog under those same conditions.

This time, my dog was a highly trained and lovable dog. My job was completely different from anything that I'd done in the past. I knew I had to make us work as a team by taking the lead and pointing out danger. The patrol behind my scout dog team would watch out for me. They depended on Clipper for an early, silent danger warning. I wanted to earn the men's respect and confidence. I needed Clipper to be successful.

I soon discovered that the enemy also knew that when we pitted scout dog teams against them we gained the advantage and were able to beat them at their own tactics.

Chapter 12

Death in the Kennel

ission after mission, scout dogs alerted American patrols of snipers, ambushes, and booby traps. Their bravery saved many American lives. The enemy counteracted the success of the scout dog teams by rewarding their soldiers who killed the dogs.

On November 9, 1967, several scout dog teams from the 44th scout dog platoon in Dau Tieng were out on combat missions supporting local infantry units. That evening, I walked to the kennel to say good-night to Clipper. It was a quiet evening in base camp; all of the dogs were sheltered in the kennel for the night. Most of the other dog handlers had already turned in for the night, and I did, too.

After midnight, I awoke to the deafening sound of a nearby explosion. I could hear and feel the shrapnel splintering the outside walls of my hooch. I jumped up, grabbed my CAR15, slipped my bare feet into jungle boots, and ran out, only to go flying into the screen door. I tripped and fell to the ground outside, then clad only in my underwear and unlaced boots, I darted to the nearby bunker. It was pitch black except for the blinding flashes of light from exploding missiles.

Everyone was hurrying to the two bunkers outside our sleeping quarters. After I entered the bunker, I couldn't stop shivering. My hands and body were shaking uncontrollably. It was a terrifying experience to wake up at night in so much danger.

While everyone ran for their lives to the safety of the bunkers, I heard at least ten explosions. Dog handlers crammed inside the bunkers and huddled tightly in the small floor space. When I looked around, I realized that I wasn't the only one in underwear and unlaced boots. Hell, some guys were barefoot. We all looked shocked and we were definitely wide awake by now. It was the first time the K-9 compound had taken direct hits from enemy mortars. It was definitely a VC surprise attack. After we were safely inside the bunkers, another volley of shells whistled down and exploded in the trees and on the ground. I shuddered with fear at each metallic sound of shrapnel striking and piercing stationary objects all over the compound.

The bunkers provided us with the only safe area on the K-9 compound from which to fight. Enemy troops had set up mortar tubes in the nearby rubber trees, not far from the base camp perimeter. From the sounds of the explosions, Mac McClellan suspected that the VCs were launching 82mm mortars, which were more deadly than the American infantry platoon's portable 61mm mortar tubes.

The two bunkers where we hid were huge steel containers, once used as shipping crates, buried in the ground under dirt and sandbags. Portholes, cut through the steel on all four sides, made ventilation possible and provided the ability to create a 360-degree field of fire. We had no radio communication between bunkers on the K-9 compound. Although there was no way to account for men, it looked as if, by some miracle, no one had been wounded while running to the bunkers.

The K-9 compound was several hundred yards inside the primary defensive perimeter of Dau Tieng. The bunkers, where we had taken refuge, were fully stocked with weapons, grenades, and plenty of ammunition. Between barrages of mortar fire, the dog handlers nervously waited to see Charlie assault the compound. If we spotted the VC, this would mean that they had breached the base camp's primary perimeter of defense.

We loaded weapons, pointed them out of the portholes, and anxiously waited for a target to appear. During the relentless VC barrage, one round exploded on top of my bunker, and everyone inside ducked simultaneously. The bunkers had never been tested like this. We didn't know how safe they would be. Fortunately, the bunker held up and made us feel more secure.

The kennel was in an open area two hundred feet away from the bunkers. We could see the kennel and hear the dogs among the dark shadows

44th Scout Dog Platoon kennel with repaired roof (1967).

of the rubber trees. There were no sand bags on the backside of the kennel to protect the dogs from shrapnel or the bullets that flew around just above ground level.

During the attack, the war dogs barked in panic. They were accustomed to their handlers' being with them during dangerous situations like this. I knew Clipper felt confused, wondering where I was or when I'd be coming to move him out of harm's way. Because of the frequent volley of explosions inside the compound, it was too dangerous for us to leave the bunkers. As long as the dogs kept barking, the dog handlers assumed they were okay. However, several of the men wanted to get their dogs and bring them inside the bunkers. Lt. Fenner directed us to quiet down and stay where we were.

We could hear small arms and machine gun fire in the near distance. We assumed that Charlie had decided to assault the main perimeter of defense, which was well-fortified and manned twenty-four hours a day, seven days a week, 365 days a year. If Charlie somehow got through the perimeter, the K-9 compound was the second line of defense. I wondered how long the dog handlers would be able to hold off an all-out enemy assault.

The scout dogs were the only ones unprotected from an enemy ground attack. Caged inside their runs, they couldn't get out. If Charlie and his sappers got to them, the defenseless dogs would probably all be killed.

Every dog handler's worst fear became a reality when several 82mm mortar rounds hit the tin roof over the kennel and exploded, sending a shower of lethal shrapnel in every direction.

"Oh, my God!" one handler screamed.

Another handler yelled, "They hit the kennel! They hit the kennel!"

The scene inside the bunkers was chaotic. We strained to see through the portholes. The tin roof of the kennel had been visibly damaged. We knew that some dogs had been hit or killed. The question was, which dogs? Several of us started to leave the bunkers. Lt. Fenner screamed, "Everyone stay in the bunkers! That's an order!"

Indescribable dismay filled the eyes of the dog handlers. We couldn't do anything but wait as more rounds exploded outside. I worried that Clipper had been hit. *Maybe Clipper is okay and lying low,* I thought, hopefully.

Several more explosions damaged trees near the entrance of the compound. I figured that the VC were directing fire with a nearby spotter. To our surprise, a jeep with its lights on and no doors or canvas top, suddenly roared through the compound's entrance. Someone screamed, "That's our jeep! Who is it?"

A man jumped out of the jeep and ran toward the bunkers. Sergeant Barnett was halfway out of the bunker motioning the man to hurry when a mortar exploded. We watched in horror. The impact of the explosion blew the driver to the ground face first. The jeep lurched forward. Its engine died when it was a few yards from the bunkers. A large piece of flying shrapnel shattered Sergeant Barnett's elbow.

Sergeant Barnett and another man dragged the jeep's driver inside the bunker. Someone turned on a flashlight to identify him. It was Kentucky, one of the new men in the platoon. His backside was bleeding from head to buttocks, and peppered with gray and silver slivers of shrapnel. He looked more frightened than filled with pain. A quick look at his wounds indi-

Wade Evans and Robert Glydon, Veterinarian Technician, giving scout dog Buckshot a shot. Picture taken after Doc Glydon returned from trip (1967).

cated that he wasn't in a life-threatening situation but definitely needed medical attention. A dog handler got some field dressings from the first-aid kit and wrapped up Kentucky's larger shrapnel wounds. He also patched up Sergeant Barnett's elbow.

Kentucky's pain would have been unbearable if he sat down or rested on his back. Two dog handlers helped him to stand, which was less painful. The front of his body and hands were unscathed. He didn't complain; he tried to tough it out. Most of the dog handlers had experienced the brutality of combat. It was easy for us to imagine how bad Kentucky felt. We knew that when the blood dried from his splinter wounds Kentucky would experience pure agony if he tried to move.

Lt. Fenner asked Kentucky why he'd driven a jeep into the middle of a mortar attack. Kentucky explained that he'd been visiting a friend across the compound when he saw the flashes of light and heard explosions. The area he'd been in wasn't under attack and Kentucky wanted to help us and the dogs, so he drove the jeep as fast as he could. Kentucky forced a smile and said, "Hey, I almost made it through, when that mortar hit me from behind."

An angry voice in the bunker blurted, "Kentucky, you're fucking nuts! You should have stayed put!"

Shortly after we brought Kentucky into the bunker, the mortar shells stopped dropping. The only noises we could still hear were the pitiful sounds of our scout dogs in the kennel. Lt. Fenner finally let us check on the dogs. In underwear and boots and carrying our weapons, one-by-one, we darted from the bunkers. We moved quickly over shards of glass from the jeep's blown-out windshield and debris from the trees and kennel.

There was danger that one of us might step on an unexploded mortar round lying armed on the ground. We knew that the VC might have breached the perimeter. They could be waiting behind rubber trees. Even so,

Sergeant Dan Barnett having his morning coffee in the bush. Sarge, his scout dog, is nearby (1967).

148

Death in the Kennel

Ollie and Erik out in the field (1967).

we braved the dark unknown to reach our dogs. The closer we came to the kennels, the louder the dogs howled. They knew we were coming. The dogs couldn't wait to get out of the runs where they'd been trapped and helpless.

A few of us stepped inside the open entrances at both ends of the kennel. Others checked the surrounding area for signs of the enemy. In the darkness, we could hear the dogs groaning in pain.

Someone suddenly screamed, "My dog's hit!"

I was only a few feet inside the kennel. I stopped in my tracks, apprehensive about what I might see. Clipper's run was close to the middle. I took a deep breath. I hoped I'd find my dog alive and unhurt. I moved closer to his run. Unexpectedly, someone flipped on the overhead inside lights to reveal a sickening sight. Large pools of blood in the aisle marked the entrances of several dog runs. Splinters of wood and structural debris littered the concrete floor. Gaping holes filled the tin roof.

By now, most of the dog handlers had made it inside the kennel. Several handlers sobbed as they held their wounded and bleeding companions. Some of the dogs lay still in pools of blood inside their runs. Others limped from their wounds.

I hurried to Clipper's run. He was pawing at the door and trying to get out. I opened the door and went inside. Clipper jumped all over me with

(Left to right: Sergeant Shelton, "Mac" McClellen, "Doc" Glydon, and Dan Scott (1967).

his bloody paws. I touched and examined every inch of his body. Although Clipper's paws were bloody from clawing at the door, he didn't have any wounds or life-threatening injuries. Clipper was so excited to see me. I sat on the floor, hugged him tightly, and cried like a little kid. I told Clipper how sorry I was that I hadn't been able to protect him. I felt terrible that my dog had been helplessly caged during the attack.

The sight of the other suffering dogs completely devastated me. The smell of blood saturated the air. Doc Glydon, the K-9 veterinarian, was away on R & R (Rest and Recuperation) so, he wasn't there to medicate the wounded and dying animals.

On that awful night Ollie, who was scheduled to rotate back to the States in only a few months, found his scout dog, Erik, serial number 36X3, in his kennel run bleeding to death. The dog's body had taken many shrapnel wounds. Both of Erik's lungs were punctured. Ollie held his limp friend in his arms and cried. He was crushed to know that his best friend suffered painfully and was dying slowly.

No one could save Erik's life.

Mac, sadly, came over to Ollie and offered him his weapon. Ollie told Mac that he couldn't bring himself to use it even to relieve Erik's pain and suffering. He asked Mac if he'd take care of this terrible task. Visibly shaking, with tears streaming down his face, Ollie stood on unsteady legs. Without looking back, he walked away from Erik and Mac. After Ollie left, a single shot rang out. I knew that Erik was dead.

Ollie had made the hardest decision of his life by releasing Erik. The thought of losing his best friend must have been devastating to him. Ollie had trained with Erik back in the States and worked with him on countless missions in Vietnam. Many people considered Ollie and Erik to be one of the best-trained scout dog teams in the platoon.

I'd learned a great deal about scout dogs from Ollie and held him and Erik in the highest regard as soldiers and friends. Ollie and Erik had been through countless scrapes with the enemy over the past ten months. No telling how many lives had been saved as a result of Erik's alerts and courage under fire. One thing was for certain, in ten months Ollie was never wounded when Erik was in the lead. Now, on this tragic night, Ollie had to watch helplessly from a distance as the kennel was attacked, only to find his dog dying of multiple wounds. The experience was unbelievably painful for Ollie and for the rest of us.

Dan Scott's dog, Shadow, serial number 9X00, was next to Clipper's run. Shadow, barely breathing, lay in a large pool of blood. Dan hadn't been in the K-9 compound during the mortar attack and couldn't to get back in time from the other side of base camp.

After Sergeant Dan Barnett knew that his own dog, Sarge, was okay, he tended to Shadow. Sergeant Barnett had arrived in Vietnam with the original platoon in January 1967. He was mature beyond his age and pulled his share of scout dog missions. Many of the other dog handlers in the platoon respected him as a leader. Barnett and I had something unique in common. We both wore the 1st Cavalry Division patch on the right shoulder sleeve of our uniforms, meaning that we'd served in a different combat unit before. We'd gotten along well from the day we met. Sergeant Barnett loved Sarge, as the rest of us loved our dogs.

On this tragic night, It was Sergeant Barnett's sad duty to make the tough decision about whether to put Shadow out of his misery or allow the dog to continue suffering in hopes that he'd somehow recover. He assessed Shadow's wounds and decided that the dog was too badly hurt to be saved. Shadow was slowly dying from a massive loss of blood. In the absence of Shadow's handler, Dan Scott, and the veterinarian, Barnett had to decide Shadow's final fate. He fired a single bullet into the dog's head. It's one of the hardest calls a dog handler ever has to make. Barnett was very sad about it.

When Scott returned later that night to find Shadow dead from a gunshot wound and covered with a poncho, he went berserk. Several dog handlers had to restrain Scott from attacking Sergeant Barnett. Scott believed that Shadow hadn't been so badly wounded and didn't need to be killed. Scott felt that if Shadow had received proper medical attention and a blood transfusion, he'd still be alive. He pointed out that another handler's dog had been saved, even though he'd suffered severe face and jaw wounds. Scott thought that Shadow could have recovered, too. Sergeant Barnett had done what he thought was best for the dog. He stood his ground and defended his decision, but Scott called Barnett, "The Dog Killer." Scott and Shadow had worked together for eight months and become inseparable. I wondered if Dan Scott would ever recover from Shadow's death.

A medical vehicle took Kentucky and Sergeant Barnett to the Dau Tieng field hospital. We all pitched in to help clean wounds and patch up the dogs that had survived. I washed the bloodstained concrete floor of the kennel. Other dog handlers picked up debris and hunted for unexploded 82mm mortar rounds.

Before long, it was daybreak and the sun was shining. Even with all we'd gone through, none of us looked tired, probably because we were so keyed up. That morning, we paid our respects by giving Erik and Shadow a proper burial. While someone led us in prayer, Dan and Ollie buried their part-

Michael "Mac" McClellen and Achates (1967).

ners. We marked the dogs' graves in the scout dog cemetery, which was in a quiet spot away from the kennel and sleeping quarters, under the shade of rubber trees.

Later that morning, someone yelled, "Formation!" We assembled in front of the orderly room next to the K-9 club. Lt. Fenner made an announcement that Major General Mearns, commanding officer of the 25th Infantry Division, was flying in from his headquarters in Cu Chi. The Commanding General (CG) planned to visit the 44th and evaluate the damage to our K-9 compound. Lt. Fenner ordered us to clean up, shave, and get into proper uniform. Most of the time we ran around the base without hats and shirts.

Someone spotted a clean jeep heading our way. We gathered in the parking area in front of the K-9 club, having moved the jeep with the shrapnel damage and shattered windshield next to our truck. Several jeeps drove under the 44th IPSD sign and into the compound. When the vehicles stopped, Lt. Fenner walked to the lead jeep with two white stars on its red flags and saluted. Major General Mearns returned his salute, stepped out of the vehicle, and shook the lieutenant's hand. This was the first time that a distinguished military officer had visited the K-9 compound.

Fifteen dog handlers gathered to greet him. We hung out in a very loose group; I hesitate to call it a military formation. The dog handlers weren't showing disrespect, but we weren't known for our snappy protocol. However, we were properly dressed and had baseball caps on our heads.

Major General Mearns addressed us, expressing his sorrow over the scout dogs we'd lost, and the handlers and dogs who had been wounded. He explained how important scout dogs were to the Army in Vietnam. He also described how the 44th IPSD had successfully contributed to the mission of the 3rd Brigade, 25th Infantry Division. He cited two specific instances where our dogs had saved patrols from walking into ambushes. It was obvious that the CG was well-informed of several recent K-9 missions that had saved American lives. The look in his eyes was sincere as he shook each dog handler's hand.

The CG took Ollie Whetstone and Dan Scott aside. He asked Ollie how long he had before rotating back to the States. Ollie told him that his rotation date would be in January, only two months away. Major General Mearns promised Ollie that he'd be home for Christmas. Dan said that he wasn't scheduled to rotate for four months. The general told Dan that, regrettably, he had too much time left to justify having an earlier rotation date. After talking to Ollie and Dan, Major General Mearns toured the damaged area and walked into the kennel. None of the dog handlers accompanied him, just our lieutenant. When they returned, the general ordered one of his staff officers to make sure that repairing the kennel got top priority.

With great sorrow, I prepared for my next mission. I felt grateful that Clipper had lived to help me and others make it through the battles yet to come.

Chapter 13

Trapped with No Way to Escape

A few weeks after the demoralizing attack on our K-9 compound, the kennel was repaired and we were going about our business as usual. Along with our dogs, those of us who were healthy continued to support the infantry units of Dau Tieng.

On November 25th, Dan Scott, Mike Eply, Ed Hughes, Ollie Whetstone, Mac McClellan, Dan Barnett, and a few others were playing cards and hanging out in the K-9 club. A fight broke out between Eply and Hughes. During the scuffle, Eply went flying through the screen door and hit the hard ground. Hughes ran after him to punch Eply again. Lt. Fenner seemed to come out of nowhere and stepped between them.

Mike had hurt his ankle when Ed knocked him to the ground. Mike complained to Lt. Fenner that his ankle hurt so badly, he couldn't go on his assigned mission in the morning. Lt. Fenner, clearly angry, told Ed that he had to take Mike's place.

Ed turned to Mike. With hostility in his voice, he said, "Eply, if I get killed out there tomorrow, I'm gonna come back here and kick your fucking ass."

Mike said nothing as he limped away.

In spite of the brawl between Ed and Mike, we all liked Ed and nicknamed him *The California Boy*. He and I were good friends. He liked to tell about how, before joining the canines, he was assigned to the Old Guard to guard the Tomb of the Unknown Soldier at Arlington National Cemetery in Virginia. Ed explained that, for a soldier to be an honor guard, he had to project the right image and look like a Hollywood model with a certain height and weight, and the right physique. Short and stumpy guys were rejected. Ed explained that the public visited the tomb every day. The guards had to stand tall and always look great. There were no excuses for failure.

Ed was tall and had a perfect soldier's physique. He said he had to wear a perfectly tailored Army dress blue uniform. His shoes and boots had to be spit-shined every day. Most of the dog handlers had never seen dress blues, and hadn't spit-shined a pair of shoes since basic training.

Ed demonstrated how to march properly with stiff, sharp, and snappy movements as he paraded around like a toy soldier. Ed had learned a marching rhythm that we had never seen before. We got a kick out of watching Ed demonstrate Old Guard rifle drills with his M16.

Thanksgiving morning, since I was also assigned to the mission, I got up early and greeted Ed in the kennel, while he was with his dog Sergeant. I let Clipper out of his run. As usual, Clipper raced to his tree and waited there until I hooked him to his twenty-foot leash. I changed the water in Clipper's bucket and set it by his tree.

Each dog had a tree with his name on it. I had nailed a small piece of wood from an ammunition box to Clipper's tree and painted CLIPPER on it in large black letters. Below his name, in smaller letters, I wrote, "War is Good Business. Invest Your Dog." At the time, I thought this was a pretty cool slogan.

While I cleaned Clipper's run, I couldn't help noticing the faded stains of blood in Shadow's and Erik's empty runs—a constant reminder of what had happened to them. I wondered if these dogs would be replaced. We'd had no new dogs since the canine platoon had arrived almost a year earlier.

It always amazed me how a dog knew when it was time for a mission. When I returned to Clipper's tree with my field gear, he became excited, wagged his tail, and paced back and forth. He knew he was going somewhere and would soon have freedom from the kennel area.

I met Ed near the entrance to the compound. He and Sergeant were ready to leave. As the sun peeked over the trees, we walked onto the main dirt road leading to our respective units of assignment. Along the way, we talked and agreed to get together to exchange stories after the mission. I didn't ask Ed about the incident with Mike the night before, because it didn't seem like an appropriate thing to talk about then.

Ed and I split up when we reached the infantry battalion area, so I could search for the "Company A" sign while Ed looked for his outfit. Military units weren't usually difficult to find, because pride and esprit de corps is an important part of Army life, so they identify everything with signs and company logos. We knew we'd found our mission assignments when we saw men milling around and preparing their gear.

When I arrived at Headquarters, Company A, I recognized the company commander by the two black bars attached to his helmet. He stood outside talking to several lieutenants. He acknowledged my presence and introduced me to the platoon leader Clipper and I were assigned to support. We shook hands, and the lieutenant knelt to pet Clipper. "Shake, Clipper," I commanded. Clipper put his paw out and the platoon leader shook it and grinned. He seemed happy to have a scout dog team with his unit.

The platoon leader briefed me on the mission. My platoon was assigned to be the company's point platoon. The scout dog team would lead the first platoon when we hit the ground. This would be a battalion-size operation. Choppers would fly the platoon into a landing zone close to the Cambodian border and west of Dau Tieng.

Other platoons were to follow when the first platoon landed. Then each platoon would split up and maneuver into tactical sweeping formations. The orders were for us to sweep the South Vietnam side of the Cambodian border for several miles. Battalion reconnaissance teams had reported large numbers of North Vietnam Regulars and Viet Cong throughout the area. The location was remote, and a primary NVA infiltration route from the Ho Chi Minh supply trail, which lay just inside Cambodia and stretched all the way into North Vietnam. No other American units were operating in this area.

The field map showed terrain that appeared to be fairly flat with thick vegetation and jungle. There were also a few large natural clearings run-

The author and Clipper wait for a patrol to assemble.

ning alongside the border. American troops were not allowed to cross into Cambodia in search or pursuit of the enemy. I told the lieutenant that while I was on point, someone needed to direct my forward movement to ensure that I didn't venture into Cambodia. The lieutenant smiled and assured me that I'd stay advised. He instructed me not to get too far ahead of the platoon.

Even though the border between South Vietnam and Cambodia was clear on the map, it wasn't marked on the ground. Where we were going, there would be no villages, signs, fences, walls, outposts, roads, or other significant ground markers to show the border separating the two countries. On the ground, Vietnam and Cambodia looked the same. It would be easy to accidentally cross the border. Besides, who would've reported us?

The area of operation was designated as a hostile, free-fire-zone. This meant that I could lock and load, fire first, and ask questions later. I liked that scenario best. I didn't like the limited fire zones where I could only lock and load when the enemy fired at me first. No-fire-zone rules sucked because they placed us in densely populated areas that were always dangerous. Firing back when Charlie fired on us could result in civilian casualties. Evidently, it was okay for us to have casualties, but we couldn't inflict them. I didn't think that the people who made these rules had ever served as infantrymen.

American and Vietnamese government and political leaders were making and controlling the ground rules of war, and I didn't like it. Even though this wasn't a declared war, soldiers were killing each other. Setting ground rules for fighting this *conflict* should be left up to the men who were fighting it. Besides, Charlie didn't abide by rules of war, but Americans did. This was no gentleman's war. Soldiers on both sides were serious and used every trick possible to hunt and kill the enemy. American soldiers were handicapped by fighting within the guidelines of those ridiculous rules.

I told the lieutenant, "Get real! It's a bunch of bullshit that we shouldn't pursue Charlie into Cambodia. The multiple restriction fire zones are a crazy idea!"

The lieutenant replied, "Just do your job."

I learned that the company's strength was 150 fighters—about the same as four platoons. My platoon would be breaking trail, when we reached the landing objective. The other platoons would follow not far behind.

Ed and I had both been assigned to this mission, but I didn't know anyone in the platoon where I'd be working for the next several days. I wondered where Ed and his dog, Sergeant, were positioned in relation to us.

The platoon split up for transport into small chopper-size groups. The morning was heating up and it felt like it might eclipse one hundred degrees before the day was over. My backpack was jammed full with stuff for three days. I expected to be re-supplied in the field. I listened to some grunts complaining that they were carrying more than seventy pounds of gear on their backs. No one felt sorry or offered to carry another man's load. I had at least three hundred rounds of ammunition for my CAR15, but I forgot to pack a few grenades.

I moved out to the Dau Tieng airstrip with my chopper group and the rest of the platoon. The choppers warmed up and prepared to go. I climbed aboard with several infantrymen I didn't know.

When we were airborne, Clipper stood up, leaned forward, and stuck his head out the open door. He seemed to enjoy the cool air blowing hard in his face. Clipper blinked his eyes with his mouth wide open and his tongue hanging out to one side, flapping in the wind. He must have figured I had a solid grip on his leash and wouldn't let him go of him. This was Clipper's typical tactic when he rode in a chopper.

The weight of Clipper leaning forward out the open door quickly tired my arm. After a while, I'd yank him back inside. Clipper lay down beside me for about a minute. Because the view and cool air must have felt so good, Clipper got back up and assumed the leaning-out-the-door-position. Again, I yanked him inside.

What was a dog handler to do? I took up a little slack in Clipper's leash and clutched it tightly in my fist. When Clipper got up and assumed the leaning-out-the-door-position, I let the slack go. Clipper freaked out. He fell forward enough to think that he might be falling out of the chopper. His ears and the hair on the back of his neck stood straight up. His eyes got as big as baseballs. He dropped to all fours so fast that he scared him-

160

Checking out a path near the Cambodian border after Clipper alerted.

self. Clipper hugged the metal floor of the chopper and scooted backwards to get next to me. He gave me a look, which probably meant, *Fuck you, John,* but he didn't stand up again. Dog training sometimes happens right on the spot.

The chopper formation in the air was quite a sight. Gunship escorts followed low in the formation. Twenty or thirty ships flew in small groups of the large spread-out formation. Through the open doors, I saw well-armed soldiers sitting inside the other ships that flew alongside us. The door gunners' M60 machine guns were loaded and pointed downward. Flying into our target area with such a formidable display spiked my adrenaline and gave me a huge feeling of confidence and a complete sense of power. *With a force like that, how could the lesser-armed NVA and VC possibly whip the Americans?* I wondered.

Below, the enemy probably wondered where in hell we were going to land. We were flying too high to be in any danger from ground fire. I was delighted that the VC didn't have surface-to-air-missiles. The ships began their descent into a large LZ onto flat ground with short grass. When we landed, I immediately ran in a crouched position with Clipper following me. I headed to the tree line away from the landing area. With the choppers blowing the scent away, the noise and movement of troops all around, made it impossible for Clipper to alert us to danger. This was the type of situation when the capability of a scout dog team is neutralized and vulnerable.

We didn't draw enemy fire when we moved into the trees. The soldiers spread out quickly and crept into the woods. We made no contact with Charlie. The squad leaders directed their men to stay spread apart, keep their eyes open, and have weapons on the ready. We moved into a swift, defensive position almost immediately after the entire platoon was on the ground and in the woods.

The platoon leader quickly took control. He assembled the lead squad, including Clipper and me. Ships, landing and dropping off troops in the clearing, were creating a lot of noise. The platoon leader gave me a hand signal, pointing out where he wanted me to go. He assigned two men as my immediate security. I told them to stay far enough behind us for Clipper to have full scent capability in the direction of travel. I instructed my security not to get in front of the dog or me until I signaled them. I told them that I'd turn periodically to check for signals to direct my progress forward. I didn't want to get too far ahead or off track.

Clipper and I moved out through the lightly wooded terrain. The rest of the platoon followed and eventually stretched out behind us. I stepped forward slowly and watched Clipper's head and ears. Occasionally, I glanced to the rear to check my security net and get directions. Using hand signals, the troops behind me made sure I stayed on the compass azimuth, which kept us heading in the direction we wanted to go. The further we moved away from the landing zone, the quieter the woods became, and the more effective Clipper could be.

Clipper didn't alert at all. I wondered if his ears were still ringing from all the noise we'd left behind. Since he kept moving forward, I had to assume that Clipper wasn't sensing danger at his end of the leash.

162

It wasn't too long before Clipper gave a slight alert by flicking his ears and canting his head ever so slightly. I stopped and knelt on one knee and Clipper sat. Everyone behind us stopped too. I listened closely and heard nothing. I looked at the area where Clipper had alerted, but I saw nothing. I wasn't sure if Clipper had given a strong enough alert to signal for help, so I got up and tugged his leash.

Clipper moved forward again. He continued to walk without alerting for another one hundred yards and then he alerted with his ears straight up and forward. I stopped and signaled for one of the security guards behind me to come up. I told the soldier that Clipper had alerted the same way twice and I thought this warning was worth checking out. I couldn't tell him what Clipper had sensed or how far away it might be. The soldier quietly moved back to deliberate with the platoon leader who then came forward. He signaled the two men to cautiously sweep the front about fifty yards out and report back.

When they returned, the men reported seeing fresh footprints, that didn't resemble a GI's jungle boot, about forty yards directly ahead. I couldn't believe it. I wondered if these footprints were what Clipper had alerted on earlier. A dog's sense of smell could pick up the scent left behind by the enemy long after he was gone. It was good to see that Clipper was no exception. I immediately praised Clipper and hugged him for alerting so well.

The platoon leader signaled for me to keep moving forward. As Clipper approached the footprints, he sniffed the ground and moved in the direction of a scent. I followed for several yards and then stopped. The path of the prints headed away from our direction of travel.

I was standing in tall grass about fifty yards ahead of the rest of the platoon. I signaled the man behind me to come forward. While we knelt down and talked about our situation, the platoon leader arrived. I whispered to him that Clipper was getting a fairly good scent and seemed to want to track the trail of footprints. The platoon leader directed a squad of men to follow the fresh tracks for a short distance and report back. When the squad leader returned, he reported that there were fresh footprints all over the place but nothing else. We stayed attentive for a few minutes while the platoon leader got on the radio and made his report. Shortly after-

wards, we were ordered not to follow the suspected trail of enemy footprints, but to continue in the direction planned for this mission.

We moved out of the grassy area and into the woods. Several hours into
our mission, it was fairly quiet except for the commonplace sounds of birds
and insects. Clipper, with his head rising above the vegetation, moved forward without a problem. He headed into woods with low vegetation and
vines climbing up the trees. I had clear visibility. Navigating through these
woods wasn't too difficult. Clipper paused and lifted his head high as if he
sensed something directly in front of us. I stopped and dropped to one
knee. I scanned and listened for anything unusual. Again, I saw and heard
nothing out of the ordinary. I motioned the closest man behind me to come
up. I told him that Clipper's alert was fairly strong and straight ahead.

The platoon leader assembled a rifle team to search the forward area.
They reported a huge clearing about seventy-five yards immediately ahead,
but said that there were no signs of the enemy. The platoon leader looked
at his map, nodded his head, and signaled for me to push on. I
complimented Clipper for the alert, "Good boy! Good boy!" I gave him a
big hug and pat on the back. My dog was doing a great job.

Clipper and I went ahead, but in accordance with standard operating
procedure (SOP), we stopped before entering the clearing. No one was
supposed to enter a clearing when coming out of the woods, unless directed by the platoon leader. The platoon leader always had to assess the
situation and decide how he wanted the platoon to maneuver across a
clearing.

We stayed at the edge of the clearing inside the woods, waiting for orders to cross. I noticed that Clipper began sniffing a small pile of bamboo
shavings a few feet away. I figured that this was probably where the enemy
had made a bunch of punji stakes. As I pondered over the pile, Clipper
alerted to the rear. I quickly spun around only to find Clipper standing
erect and staring at a man who stood in front of us. He was tall and had on
clean jungle fatigues with only a pistol belt and a holstered .45 caliber pistol side arm. I recognized the two black stars sewn into his camouflage-
covered helmet. He carried a field map inside a plastic sleeve. I couldn't
believe my eyes. It was Major General Mearns, the commander of the 25th
Infantry Division, who had visited our base camp after the VC attack.

I wondered, *What the hell is he doing out here? Is he trying to earn his combat pay, or what? And how the hell did he get here in the first place?*

I quickly rose to a standing position and nervously greeted him without saluting. "Good Morning, Sir," I said quietly. It wasn't customary to stand at attention and render a snappy salute in a combat zone. If Charlie was watching and saw me salute, the Commander General (CG) could get a bullet between the eyes.

The CG smiled and asked, "What's the name of your dog, soldier?"

"Clipper, Sir!"

The general knelt and said, "He sure is frisky."

"Shake the generals hand Clipper, Shake!" Clipper put his paw out and the general smiled and shook it.

The general asked me several questions about how scouting worked while he examined his map and gazed across the clearing ahead. *Is he looking to see how far we are from the Cambodian border?* I wondered, but didn't ask.

The general's radio operator and several of his staff officers, all wearing clean jungle fatigues, were close behind him. The CG's staff didn't say a word to me but kept looking and smiling at Clipper. I chatted with MG Mearns for a few minutes before he turned and headed back into the main element of the platoon.

I looked down at Clipper and said, "Clipper, you met the CG of the 25th Infantry Division!"

Clipper didn't seem excited.

Ed Hughes and his scout dog, Sergeant, were working somewhere nearby. During the mission briefing, we were told that there would be an entire battalion in the area. I figured the general had landed with us on the choppers and beat the bush all morning. It was quite rare for a general officer to show up in the jungle and hump with his troops. Unlike during World War II, Vietnam had no front lines. Everything outside a base camp had to be considered hostile and dangerous. For a general officer to walk with the soldiers, who were putting their lives on the line, really impressed me.

After the CG departed, the platoon took a break. I gave Clipper some water and hugged him for doing such a terrific job. I was extremely happy with how Clipper and I were working together as a team. In these very hostile places, Clipper was a source of loyalty, comfort, and satisfaction.

Even though I'd worked with Clipper many times up to that point, each mission was different, and we learned new things every time we went out together.

After about fifteen minutes, I heard some choppers flying low overhead through the treetops. They landed in the clearing, picked up some passengers, and took off. I figured Major General Mearns, the *two-star,* was on his way out of there. Clipper sat, facing the clearing and remaining on guard duty. He moved his head back and forth as if he was searching the clearing, sensing clues about what might be out there.

Ed and Sergeant were out in this same area somewhere. I recalled telling Ed that we'd trade stories when we got back. *Oh boy,* I thought, *would I have a tale to tell about Major General Mearns coming up to me and shaking Clipper's paw. It was Clipper's way of saluting!*

The platoon leader finally gave me the command to move out across the clearing. Clipper and I slowly entered it. I could see the other side several hundred yards away. Left and right, visibility was clear. If a jackrabbit jumped and ran through the knee-high grass, Clipper could spot it on the ground. As I walked farther ahead, I glanced to my rear. The two bodyguards spread out ten yards behind me and didn't intrude. The rest of the platoon spaced themselves apart and cautiously walked behind them. With only a light wind, I had confidence that Clipper wouldn't miss a scent of danger.

As we moved deeper into the open clearing, my eyes stayed glued to Clipper's head and ears. Then Clipper's ears stood way up. He cocked his head slightly to one side and gave his strongest alert of the day. I immediately knelt down low on one knee. I looked and listened, but could hear nothing unusual. I turned around and saw that everyone behind me had also stopped and gone down on one knee.

My right knee was beginning to hurt a little from kneeling on the hard ground. A long time had passed since I'd jumped from that chopper and had a punji stake rammed into it. That was a hell of a memory. Now I had to keep moving and deal with the lingering, annoying pain from that old injury.

166

I felt uncomfortable being in the open with vegetation no higher than the top of my boots. Clipper's ears and head remained erect, so I decided not to push our luck by proceeding. I turned and motioned to the man behind him. The platoon leader, in a crouching posture, jogged to my position. He asked for my thoughts. I told him that I had a bad feeling about going any farther.

The platoon leader didn't waste any time. He motioned for the nearest squad leader, who directed two fire teams of three men each, to move forward and sweep the area. After reconnoitering, the two fire teams returned and reported that they saw a long, wide, and recently used trail about fifty yards away. They'd made no contact with the enemy. The platoon leader hand-signaled for me to lead them to the trail.

When Clipper and I reached the trail, which ran perpendicular to the mission's direction of travel, we saw many fresh tracks from footprints, wheeled carts, and oxen. Several columns of deep footprints appeared to be moving into South Vietnam from Cambodian.

We knew that when peasant farmers moved their equipment, they didn't travel in this manner. Besides, there were no farms or any signs of villages nearby. The platoon leader figured the Cambodian border must be less than a half mile away. This had to be a branch trail leading off the main Ho Chi Minh trail. Since the tracks were so fresh, the platoon leader thought that a heavily armed battalion-size NVA or VC force must have moved into South Vietnam from Cambodia within the past day or so. He used a grease pencil to mark enemy movement on his map.

I took the lead and crossed the trail, heading toward the facing wood line, that was less than seventy-five yards out. Now the platoon's direction of travel was parallel to the Cambodian border. Before long, Clipper stopped and stood erect with his ears pointed high and forward. Twitching muscles in his shoulders grew tense.

I got down and looked back, but my security guards motioned for me to keep going. The platoon leader must have decided to ignore Clipper's alert. I was a little puzzled, but got up and tugged on Clipper's leash. Clipper started stepping side-to-side as if he didn't want to go forward. Several shots rang out over our heads. In an instant, we dropped flat on the ground. Clipper's was on all fours with his head up and pointed in the direction of the tree line ahead. I hugged Clipper close and told him what a good dog he was. In response, he licked my face.

There was a brief moment of silence as I strained to spot the shooter. I couldn't see anything but a wall of green ahead. Behind me, everyone was lying in a prone position in the short grass, trying to figure out where the shots had come from. Someone decided to fire an M16 over my head into the trees. Almost instantly, everyone else started shooting.

I knew that if the sniper were hiding in a tree, the entire platoon was visible to him. From the direction of the shots, I thought that Clipper may have been Charlie's first target. We were definitely not out of the sniper's range of fire, because the rounds had gone over our heads. Charlie was either a bad shooter, or Clipper and I had been mighty lucky.

The firing stopped, after it became apparent that the Americans were doing all the shooting. Then there was another long moment of silence. The platoon leader ordered two squads to fire and maneuver until they reached and secured a position in the tree line ahead. As they tried to fire and maneuver, several more shots rang out from the woods. Voices behind Clipper and me were giving orders to get up and move out on-line. I got to my feet and tugged Clipper to move forward along with everyone else.

Several more shots rang out from the woods ahead. The entire platoon again dropped to the ground on their bellies and poured bullets into the trees. I placed several rounds where I thought the shooter was positioned. Clipper didn't move, while I fired. I patted him on the back and told him that he was a good boy. Several men behind us moved ahead to our left and right on-line.

A voice cried out, "Get up and move out on-line, soldier."

I ignored the voice and remained on the ground. When I looked up, I saw a tall man standing over me with two black bars on his helmet. It was the captain, the company commander I'd met that morning. I was startled to see him glaring down at me with a disgusted look on his face.

The captain shouted, "Get up and assault the tree line!"

I looked at him as if he was crazy and replied, "Sir, why don't you call for artillery or air strikes before we go into those trees?"

"Soldier, I said get up and assault."

I obeyed and I got up from the ground to move forward with everyone else. Charlie didn't fire a single round while the platoon closed in on the tree line.

By the time Clipper and I reached the edge of the trees, there was a lot of fussing and shouting going on. The rest of the platoon was in a state of commotion and confusion. Clipper and I stopped among a bunch of troops, who were standing around, waiting for the next command. There was too much activity and noise for Clipper to be effective. At this point we were useless as scouts.

The platoon leader approached me. He told me that one of his men spotted a bunker not far from us. He asked me if I'd use my dog to check it out.

I told the lieutenant, "Clipper doesn't like going into holes in the ground, but I'll go with you to see if he gets an alert."

On other missions, Clipper would always avoid going into bunkers, foxholes, or tunnels. I never forced Clipper in that type of situation.

The lieutenant told me that he'd lead the way to the bunker. He moved out at a quick pace. Clipper and I followed him closely. A few yards after I passed the last man in our platoon, Clipper raised his head and alerted up into the trees. I didn't give it a second thought, because there was too much activity all around us.

It wasn't long before the three of us were by ourselves. The lieutenant snaked a path through the dark jungle that was thick with tall vegetation. The closest American was at least twenty yards behind us. Almost at point blank range, muzzle flashes lit up in my face. The lieutenant's body slammed into my chest like a sack of rocks, knocked me backward onto my back, Clipper rolled over on top of me, my helmet fell off my head and rolled away. All hell broke loose as I hung on to Clipper's leash.

Directly in front of us, Charlie opened up with automatic rifle and machine gun fire. Fortunately, I'd fallen near a small tree. I rolled behind it with Clipper by my side. Rifle and machine gun fire opened up from behind. Clipper and I were caught in the crossfire between the enemy and Americans. With my arm around Clipper, I hugged the ground. Firing became intense from both sides and chopped vegetation like the blades of a lawnmower. Charlie was dug in and firing from camouflaged positions.

I was trapped and unable to move. I knew the lieutenant had absorbed the initial burst of bullets. He had to be close by, but I couldn't see him through the thick vegetation. The lieutenant wasn't crying for help or calling for a medic. After a few minutes passed, I assumed he must be dead.

Charlie and the Americans fired furiously, back and forth, over our heads. *Charlie must not have seen Clipper and me,* I thought, *or maybe he thinks he's already killed us.* I decided not to make any sudden moves to give Charlie a second chance. I slowly moved my rifle to a firing position. As I got the barrel up by my face, I noticed that the muzzle had a plug of mud jammed inside. It must have happened when I'd fallen backwards hard onto the ground. Trying to clear it with my finger, only forced the mud plug deeper into the muzzle. I thought of using grenades, but then remembered that I hadn't packed any.

It would have been suicidal, under those circumstances, to break down my weapon and run a cleaning rod through the bore and chamber to clear the plug. Right then, it was more important for me to stay alive than to figure out a way to shoot. If I had to, I could fire my weapon, but the round in the chamber would explode in my face. The only weapon I had was my knife and dog, and I was too damned scared to try anything heroic.

Clipper and I lay fifteen feet from Charlie's entrenched positions. Between the exchange of small arms fire, I could hear Charlie whispering in Vietnamese from his foxholes. I knew Clipper heard them too, but he didn't make a sound. I believe he realized we were in deep shit with no easy way out. My heart pounded and my adrenaline spiked.

This situation was much different from when I'd been ambushed with Timber in the armored personnel carrier. This time, I was closer to the enemy, had no helmet, no functional weapon, no grenades, and could be killed by either side. I didn't dare make the slightest movement or noise to draw attention to us. Unlike the frightened and skittish Timber, I was grateful that Clipper wasn't jumping around or trying to get away. "God, please get us out of this death trap," I prayed.

Minutes seemed like hours. Thinking that my time on earth was running out, I wanted to melt into the dirt to get away from it all. I was scared, and Clipper shivered underneath my arm. I wasn't feeling as numb as I'd been during the APC ambush. This time, I was fully alert and in control of my senses.

I found it peculiar that I could simultaneously hear Charlie whispering in Vietnamese and the Americans shouting in English. Not long into the firefight, I heard the deafening sound of a volley of artillery rounds exploding behind Charlie's positions. The shrapnel splintered the trees and shredded vegetation all around us. The Americans were walking the artillery in closer and closer. In between volleys, Charlie and the Americans exchanged small arms and machine gun fire.

I lay silently, holding Clipper and trying not to move a muscle. To my surprise, I felt something touch my foot. I spun my head around in fear and saw the black American soldier who was one of my designated security guards. We exchanged no words as we made eye contact. He gave me a thumbs-up and motioned me to move back to the rear.

During the next volley of artillery rounds, I slowly turned around on my belly with Clipper at my side. When I tried to crawl away from the tree, my backpack got caught in some vines and moved the vegetation. I broke free and crawled away on my stomach with Clipper at my side as the firing picked up again. I anticipated feeling the pain of a bullet entering my body or hearing Clipper groan from being shot. Charlie was either shooting too high, or we were as flat as leaves on the jungle floor.

The distinct sound of an M16 echoed through the jungle behind me. The soldier who relieved me was providing cover for our escape to friendly lines. I flinched at the sound of a grenade exploding behind me. I briefly hesitated but didn't turn to look.

An American soldier appeared and motioned me to stay down. He fired over our heads. As Clipper and I passed, I saw a dead Vietnamese in khaki clothes dangling from a tree by his bare foot. His arms hung down over his head and almost touched the pool of blood dripping from his body and soaking into the jungle floor. I quickly moved Clipper around the hanging body to take cover behind a tree.

A short while later, when I was safely behind American lines, I looked around to see dead and wounded Americans on the ground everywhere. I broke down my CAR15 and ran a cleaning rod through it while the fighting continued. After the clump of mud fell out, I took up a defensive firing position. I quickly checked over Clipper's entire body, looking for blood, but Clipper didn't wince in pain anywhere I touched him. I had to assume that he hadn't been wounded. Artillery pounded the jungle around us. A few minutes later, the artillery halted and the shooting drizzled to a stop.

In the usual way that these firefights started and stopped, Charlie had either been eradicated or decided to break contact. It was hard to tell. Reinforcements from another platoon reached the perimeter and took up firing positions. A medic frantically worked on a wounded soldier who screamed that he was going to die. The medic tried to stop the bleeding, patch him up, and calm the wounded man. When the soldier died, the medic quickly moved on to assist another wounded man.

I saw the lieutenant's limp, dead body being carried in a poncho. Now the platoon sergeant was in charge. He told me that the company commander had killed the VC, hanging from the tree, after this VC had shot the captain in the foot. Then I remembered that, before the firing had started, this was the tree that Clipper had alerted on. At the time, I'd disregarded the dog's alert. Now I realized that Clipper had sensed danger in that tree and he'd been right. By getting wounded, the captain, who had ordered us into this trap, had paid a price for both our mistakes.

The platoon sergeant told me that the soldier who had come to save us when we were trapped in the crossfire had also been killed. After he'd killed several NVA, hiding inside a bunker near the dead sniper's tree, the soldier was gunned down.

Most of the casualties had happened during the first few seconds of fighting, because everyone was standing around waiting for the lieutenant to check out the bunker. The platoon sergeant said that there had been a lot of commotion and chaos, while everyone was getting out of the open clearing and under the jungle cover. He argued that his men should have automatically formed a defensive perimeter and assumed firing positions on the ground. Small patrols should have been sent out to probe for the sniper in the jungle. Instead, they had all moved in at once, and many of them were standing or milling around waiting for something to happen. Charlie had sucked the main element into his trap by baiting it with the sniper.

I told the platoon sergeant that Clipper did his best under the circumstances. The platoon sergeant didn't blame me. He argued that Clipper had alerted them to danger before the sniper opened up in the clearing. The platoon sergeant assured me that we had done our duty and were lucky to be alive. When the shooting started, he thought we were killed instantly, along with the lieutenant.

I mentioned to the platoon sergeant that I had asked the CO to shell the tree line before sending in troops. I told him that the CO had ignored me and ordered me to get up on-line and assault. The platoon sergeant didn't appear too surprised. With a hardened look on his face, he said, "We needlessly lost a lot of good men today."

The platoon sergeant knelt on one knee, patted Clipper on his head, and told him that he was a good dog. Then he shook his head and walked away.

Helicopters, small arms, and machine gun fire echoed in the distance, signaling that someone else was getting into the shit. The entire area must have been loaded with pockets of hard-core NVA troops. The reconnaissance team that scouted that area had done a good intelligence job. Now it was up to the infantry to fight smarter and defeat the bastards. Even though there was another fight going on nearby, my platoon wasn't alerted to assist, so I rested under a tree with Clipper. I listened to the distant noise of that firefight and watched my fellow soldiers receive medical attention.

One soldier came up to me and asked, "Is your name Burnam?"

"Yes!" I answered.

"I thought so; you are the only one without a helmet on."

The soldier handed me my helmet; my name was written on the headband of the liner, as was common practice. I thanked him and asked where he'd found it. He said it was found near a bunker next to the bodies of the lieutenant and another soldier. He couldn't understand how the dog and I had survived without a scratch.

I got cold chills thinking about it. My mind raced for answers to the unspoken question: Why was I spared? I could only come up with one answer — it hadn't been time for me to meet my Maker. Maybe there was a higher purpose for my life, something I was supposed to do with it, but I wasn't comfortable thinking about that at the time. I silently thanked God for not taking Clipper or me that day. The look in Clipper's eyes told me that he was also happy to be alive.

Before I put on my helmet, I checked it over. There wasn't a mark on it. Clipper didn't have a scratch either, and he also appeared to be dealing with the whole situation better than I was.

Clipper had been a brave soldier that day. Many troops came by to touch Clipper for good luck and to shake his big paw. One person called Clipper "the invincible scout dog." I chuckled at that. Clipper had survived by being silent and brave in the face of danger. I was so proud of him.

I looked at Clipper and said, "Clipper, in my book, with all the hell you've been through, you just earned yourself a Bronze Star and a Combat Infantry Badge for all those great alerts."

I knew the Army didn't award medals or badges to war dogs for exceptional performance of duty or for their bravery and heroism. The Army officially recognized scout dogs only as military combat equipment. In four months, I'd be rotating back to the States. Clipper, on the other hand, didn't have a rotation date. His orders were to serve his country in Vietnam for the rest of his natural life or until he died. I didn't want to believe the naked truth about Clipper's likely fate.

What the hell do the Army brass and the politicians know about Clipper and what he's done to save so many lives? I thought. I viewed Clipper as a soldier, not as equipment. He displayed uncompromising loyalty and obedience. His memory was magnificent. He knew what he'd been trained for, and in carrying out his duties he was a hell of a lot more responsive than some humans I'd met during this war.

How did the Army know what my dog could take mentally and physically? How many lives did Clipper have to save to be recognized as something more than equipment? I thought it was cruel and unjust to punish a dog by making him walk point for the entire war. The Army had trained Clipper to save lives. Shouldn't they treat him with respect and give him a rotation date, too? War dog handlers all asked these questions, but they never reached the ears of anyone who could make a difference. As a lowly grunt, I had to follow orders and never openly question or disregard the decisions made by higher levels of authority.

I sat under the tree, pondering the mystery that Clipper and I were still alive, and thinking about my dog's upcoming fate. When the platoon's casualties during this skirmish were summed up and considered light, with six men killed and eleven wounded, it was decided that we hadn't suffered enough losses to be relieved of our mission. The platoon sergeant briefed me on our new orders. I was to join the rest of the company to set up a defensive perimeter for the evening in the very field we'd crossed. The next day, the company would continue its mission of hunting NVA along the Cambodian border.

After the short mission briefing by the platoon sergeant, it was time to move out. Clipper and I assumed our usual position in front of the platoon formation. We headed into the clearing to join the rest of the company. Clipper alerted like crazy. We didn't have to check out his alerts, because American soldiers were in the area all around us.

A sister company had reconnoitered the battlefield to clean up any remaining pockets of enemy troops. They'd discovered a small but empty enemy base camp. It looked as if Charlie had ambushed us in his back yard. Now, except for leaving a few dead bodies near our positions, the enemy had disappeared.

Charlie probably ran for the Cambodian border, knowing that we couldn't pursue him there. In my mind, I kept reviewing the events of this battle. If this had been my old unit, the 1st Battalion, 7th Cavalry, the CO would have dropped artillery and napalm before sending even one soldier after a sniper, especially after Clipper had alerted on all those signs of danger leading up to the sniper's first shot. The 1/7 Cavalry learned early that using a sniper to lure Americans into a trap was a typical Charlie-baiting-the-Americans tactic. Charlie was good at this maneuver, as long as we fell for it. Even when the platoon reached the tree line, Clipper and I had been useless during the commotion. When Clipper alerted toward the tree where the sniper hid, I now believed that Charlie intentionally let us go by, probably figuring that Clipper and I were going to be dead meat, anyway. I'd missed that alert in the tree and felt responsible for the CO getting shot in the foot.

There was no way Clipper could have alerted on that bunker, because the lieutenant was walking directly in front of us. If Clipper and I had taken the lead, it would have been *lights out* for both of us. We had a

175

Clipper taking a well-earned nap after the ambush.

guardian angel watching over us that day. I just hoped that angel would stick around.

Clipper and I entered a company-size perimeter deep inside the clearing. Soldiers everywhere were digging chest-deep foxholes, clearing firing lanes, planting claymore mines, and setting up trip-flares. The company prepared for a counterattack. Every man was on full alert. There would be little or no sleeping on the perimeter that night. None of us wanted to get caught by surprise.

Clipper and I took up a position where I felt a little more secure—behind a bush well inside the perimeter. We got lucky and didn't have to pull perimeter guard duty that night. In the past, when I had guard duty, Clipper was so naturally good at it that I could sleep all night, if I wanted. I wasn't a heavy sleeper, while in the field or base camp and tended to wake up at the slightest unusual noise. This night I was sure that, with all we'd been through, I'd awaken easily.

176

Darkness settled in as a helicopter appeared overhead and landed under the green smoke signal inside the large perimeter. I figured it was a re-supply ship and paid little attention to it. Besides, I didn't need any supplies. A few minutes after the chopper took off, I recognized fellow dog handler Sergeant Durbach from the 44th IPSD. He slowly walked over to me. I wondered what Durbach was doing out here without his scout dog. As Durbach approached, I noticed that he looked fresh and clean-shaven with jungle fatigues that weren't dirty. I, on the other hand, was filthy from a long day of humping and crawling along the damp jungle floor.

Sergeant Durbach carried a CAR15 and a light pack strapped to his back. We greeted one another with a smile and shook hands. As we sat on the ground, Durbach stroked Clipper's head and back. Sergeant Durbach appeared nervous. His facial expressions conveyed that something was bothering him. He forced a smile and asked me how I was doing. "What's up?" I asked.

"John," he said, "Ed Hughes and Sergeant were killed not far from here today."

"What!?"

Durbach filled me in on what had happened. After Ed's chopper had landed, he and Sergeant ran for cover along with the rest of the troops. When Ed reached the jungle, he had moved inside to seek cover and was shot down at pointblank range and killed instantly. The enemy had hacked Ed's dog to death with a knife or machete. Sergeant Durbach speculated that the dog had died fighting, but Ed was caught by surprise. I couldn't believe what I was hearing. My eyes welled up with tears.

Durbach said that the NVA had overwhelmed Ed's platoon and forced them into a hasty retreat across the landing zone. The platoon had set up a defensive position and held off an enemy assault. The NVA then retreated into the jungle where Ed and his dog lay dead.

I asked Sergeant Durbach how he knew so much if he hadn't been there. He said that Lt. Fenner had received a call from 3rd Brigade headquarters in Dau Tieng. They reported that a dog handler and his dog were killed in action while on patrol near the Cambodian border. They told Lt. Fenner that all the casualties, except for the dog handler and his dog, had been recovered. It was apparently too risky to try to recover Ed and his dog at that time, so they'd left them behind.

I interrupted by saying, "This is a bunch of bullshit! Those fuckers can't leave Ed and Sergeant out there alone all night. So they must have sent you to get me to help recover Ed and Sergeant? Well, I'm ready. Let's go get some more men and fucking do it!"

Sergeant Durbach put his hand on my shoulder and said, "John, sit down and let me finish."

Then he told me that Lt. Fenner had sent him out about three hours earlier to size up the situation and report back. There was no fighting going on when he had arrived by chopper. Since the attack, Ed's platoon had been reinforced by two more platoons that were set up in a defensive position, not far from Ed and Sergeant.

Durbach had received a status report from the company commander of Ed's unit. The CO had already decided to assemble two squads and send them across the clearing to locate and recover the bodies. Durbach arrived in time to accompany the patrol. When they'd found Ed and his dog, the NVA were long gone. Ed's body had been stripped of his weapon and gear, including his boots. Sergeant's body was lying near him. The Gooks had even taken Sergeant's leash and harness. Both bodies were recovered without incident and sent home to Dau Tieng. Durbach's next task had been to locate me.

By using a field radio, Durbach had been able to find my exact position within minutes. I was less than a mile from where Ed and Sergeant died. Durbach caught a ride on a re-supply chopper operating in the area. I told Durbach that I'd heard a nearby firefight going on after our battle. I hadn't realized it was Ed's unit under attack.

Sergeant Durbach asked me for details about our fight. I gave him a blow-by-blow account of our near-fatal encounter with Charlie.

On this Thanksgiving Day of 1967, I was thinking, *What the hell do we have to celebrate or be thankful for?* Even after I listened to every detail about Ed's death, I still couldn't believe he was gone. Ed had been killed before he'd even had a chance to fight back.

Durbach and I sat silently for several minutes. I reflected on how much I'd enjoyed Ed's friendship and humor. Even though I'd only known him for six months, I thought Ed was a wonderful person. Now he was dead, and I'd never see him again. The incident between Ed and Mike Eply, which led to the two of them switching places, so that Ed went on this mission instead of Mike, now played over and over in my head.

"Eply, if I get killed out there tomorrow, I'm gonna come back here and kick your fucking ass."

Sergeant Durbach coordinated my return to Dau Tieng, so I could provide a field-report to my unit. We left in the morning on the first available chopper. Shortly after arriving at the 44th IPSD compound, we saw Lt. Fenner. Sergeant Durbach briefed Lt. Fenner on Ed Hughes. I provided the details about what had happened during my mission. After the briefing, all I wanted was to take a shower and put on clean clothes.

No one in the platoon could believe Ed and Sergeant were dead. Of course, every dog handler wanted to hear about it. I must have repeated their story twenty times. I didn't talk to Mike Eply about his fight with Ed at the K-9 club. I could only imagine how he must have felt about having switched places with Ed for this fatal mission.

The day after the debriefing, the entire 44th IPSD assembled at a chapel to pay their last respects to Ed and Sergeant. At the chapel, which was a large green tent with several rows of folding chairs and a makeshift altar, we held a funeral without bodies. By now, Ed was in a morgue somewhere in Saigon.

To my distaste, the chaplain gave a sermon filled with military jargon. He said, "Ed hasn't left us. He's gone on to serve a higher commander, the celestial six."

This term *six* was used in common military radio jargon as part of a commanding officer's call sign. I wasn't the only one to interpret the chaplain's comments to mean that Ed was serving under a higher military leader. Dan Scott and many of the other handlers were livid about the chaplain's choice of military words for this service. Instead, we wanted to hear something beautiful and poetic from the Bible, not language that sounded like a military mission. I vowed that this would be the last time I'd ever attend a formal religious military ceremony for a fallen comrade in Vietnam.

Edward Hughes, killed in action with his scout dog
Sergeant, November 26, 1967, two weeks after the
mortar attack on the kennel.

A few days after Ed's death, Lt. Fenner asked me to join Sergeant
Durbach to escort Ed's dog, Sergeant, to a military morgue in Saigon.
Apparently, they wanted to complete an autopsy on the dog, and Saigon
had better medical facilities. The second part of my mission would be to
identify Ed's body in a military morgue. The Army wanted to make sure
that they were shipping the right man to Ed's home in Garden Grove,
California.

Sergeant Durbach and I flew by chopper from the Dau Tieng airstrip.
Ed's dog, Sergeant, was already zipped up inside a black plastic body bag
and lying on the ship's floor. After the chopper landed on a helicopter pad
inside the military complex in Saigon, two medical technicians waited beside the helicopter pad for us. After identifying themselves, they carried
Sergeant's body into a building. When we went inside the building that

housed the morgue, Sergeant Durbach was asked to fill out and sign some paperwork.

Then we were escorted to the morgue and entered a room full of metal wall lockers. Every so often, the medical attendant would stop, read a nametag, and move on. Finally, he grabbed a handle and pulled open a large metal drawer. A black body bag slid out of it. The attendant unzipped the bag enough to expose the head of the soldier inside. We looked down and recognized Ed. I quickly turned away. I felt sad to see my friend for the last time this way.

Edward Cowart Hughes III, nineteen years old, now rested in peace. He'd be going home to his grieving family in Garden Grove, California. I'd be returning to Dau Tieng to go on more missions with my scout dog Clipper at the risk of our lives.

Chapter 14

Booby Traps

Dense forests and jungles surrounded the Ben Cui and Michelin rubber tree plantations that stretched about ten square miles east and north of Dau Tieng. Fifteen hundred yards north of the airstrip stood a small range of steep foothills covered by a thick jungle canopy.

On a military grid map, the rubber tree plantations were identified by thousands of tiny green circles divided into grids. Access to harvest the rubber tree was by dirt roads. Resident Vietnamese, who lived in small hamlets scattered throughout the rubber plantation, maintained the trees. Since Vietnamese names were hard to pronounce, numerals and letters identified the location of each hamlet on the military grid maps. Letters represented hamlets; for example, AP 2, AP 12, and AP 13.

Every so often, a blue and white civilian helicopter flew into base camp. It would stick out like a sore thumb, since all the military aircraft and equipment were painted olive drab. Civilian choppers belonged to business partners of the Michelin and Ben Cui rubber tree plantations. Scuttlebutt had it that these companies were concerned that the Army was destroying their rubber trees, and they wanted payment for each damaged or destroyed tree. They were also unhappy that we were tying our scout dogs to their rubber trees, because the leashes rubbed the bark raw, and the scout dogs dug too many holes. They complained about the wooden hooches that the dog handlers had built between rows of their rubber trees.

None of us knew if the Army paid for damaged and destroyed rubber trees. In the K-9 platoon, "Fuck 'em all," was a general response to the businessmen's complaints. We had no idea what kind of diplomatic relations the Army had or the deals they'd made with the rubber trees' owners. All we knew was that we certainly didn't want civilian businessmen snooping around our K-9 area.

We figured that we owned the rubber trees while we occupied them and fought the war for the South Vietnamese. Yet the rubber trees offered no safe haven for us. The VC and NVA mined the trees and dirt roads between them. American infantrymen knew that Viet Cong sympathizers lived outside our barbed wire perimeter in the rubber tree plantations' hamlets. Most of these villages were hostile to us.

I found the scout dog business to be a never-ending learning experience. Since booby traps surrounded us, I needed to know if Clipper could detect their tripwires. When conditions were favorable, Clipper was better than I was at seeing, hearing, smelling, and sensing things from great distances. Like most of his breed, Clipper was bright and already had the natural instincts to be a good scout dog. I didn't think that Clipper would ever intentionally walk through a tripwire, stretched between two trees. I assumed he'd avoid that type of danger, but I had to learn what alert Clipper would give when he came close to one.

One morning, before I cleaned Clipper's run, I walked to the rubber trees behind the hooches. I had a roll of regular olive drab (OD), thin, fairly strong, and easily pliable tripwire from a trip-flair. I tied it knee-high between two trees and twanged the wire with my finger to assure that it was tight as a guitar string.

After I cleaned the kennel and played with Clipper, I put him on-leash and we headed in the direction of the tripwire. Clipper walked ahead, and I followed him, as we did when we worked on a mission. We went to an area with short grass that was clear of obstacles. I'd set up the tripwire about seventy-five yards away from us. Occasionally, I tugged Clipper's leash left or right to direct him through the rubber trees. I didn't want to walk a straight line to the target. As we moved farther into the rubber trees, Clipper didn't alert. We approached the tripwire I'd planted, but I still didn't see any signs of an alert from Clipper. When he was about fifty yards away from the target, Clipper gave a weak alert with a slight movement of his ears, but he didn't stop walking.

When the wire touched his head, he ducked under it, so I jerked the leash and said, "No, Clipper, no!"

Clipper turned and looked at me as if to ask, "What did I do wrong?"

I took Clipper back to the wire and clutched it in my hand. I got down on one knee, looked Clipper in the eye, and showed him the thin green wire. Then several times I gently tapped the wire on the black tip of Clipper's nose. Each time I tapped Clipper's nose, I raised the inflection in my voice and said, "No, Clipper, no!"

I talked to him as if he were a trainee. I said, "Clipper, this is a fucking tripwire. Do not cross it. Do you understand? Do you have any idea what might happen to us if you crossed it? BOOM! That's right, BOOM!"

Clipper responded to the word *no,* but I doubt that he understood anything else I said.

I walked Clipper around a bit to calm him then let him approach the wire again. This time, Clipper gave a weak alert and walked under the wire. We continued to practice with the wire, but Clipper did the same thing each time.

I wanted Clipper to try again, even though he surely must have been tired of hearing me say, "No, Clipper! No, Clipper!" Finally, Clipper stopped and sat a few feet in front of the tripwire. I felt so excited and proud of him. We actually accomplished a new trick. I hugged and praised him, "You're the greatest fucking dog in the world! The best scout dog in the platoon! Good boy! Good boy!"

Then I made Clipper repeat the exercise. I wanted to be sure his behavior hadn't been a fluke, and that we were on the same brain wave. Sure enough, Clipper had really learned not to go through the tripwire. He completely avoided it by going around the wire. We continued to practice the tripwire exercise for several hours that day, and Clipper routinely went around it. After a while, I decided to stop, because we'd had enough training for one session.

Over the next several days, we practiced the tripwire routine for a few hours each day. To make the training tougher, I put several wires in different locations. I wanted to examine how Clipper would negotiate more than one tripwire. From our work together, I learned that if Clipper came directly upon a tripwire, he'd sit in front of it more often than go around it. I also learned that if Clipper sensed the wire from a distance, he'd go around it. I was quite pleased that I'd made so much progress with Clipper in only one week of training. This dog had smarts that continued to impress me.

I still had no idea how Clipper would work in thick brush, open terrain, or moving down trails. I always dreaded going down trails and tried to avoid them, especially the deep jungle paths. Pathways around populated areas weren't as hard to negotiate. It was only common sense that staying inside the bush was safer than walking on smooth dirt. Jungle trails were perfect for the enemy to place ambushes and booby traps.

Americans set up ambushes beside jungle trails in hopes of surprising the enemy. The Viet Cong were smarter than Americans at fighting this type of jungle warfare, because the bush was their natural turf. Most of us young teenage grunts had never traveled outside the United States, let alone seen a jungle. The closest I'd ever come to a jungle was thumbing through a *National Geographic* magazine. I knew that the NVA were masters of jungle warfare hit-and-run tactics long before I was born. We Americans were infants, still learning how to walk and talk our way through the jungle.

By conducting these training sessions, I'd learned one more way to keep my dog and me alive, while we walked point. Still, I didn't intend to volunteer our services as an expert booby trap-detection team.

Soon enough it was my turn to go on another mission. This time I'd be working with the 2nd Battalion, 12th Infantry, which consisted primarily of foot soldiers who walked, except when they rode in trucks or choppers to drop-off points. I preferred working with foot soldiers. After the experience of being ambushed, working with the mechanized infantry had become one of my greatest fears. I'd asked Lt. Fenner not to assign me to any more of those units.

I reported to the 2/12 down the road from the K-9 compound. One good thing about living in a small base camp, is that everything is within walking distance. Brigade G2, military intelligence, had information concerning a VC buildup around our base camp. The enemy was reported to be operating out of hidden base camps in the nearby jungles that surrounded the rubber tree plantations. At night, the VC were infiltrating the hamlets and reconnoitering our base camp's perimeter. They knew all about our capabilities, how many helicopters we had, and how many troops were inside.

At least twice a week, they attacked our airstrip with mortars, creating too much havoc for the aircraft. The mortars arrived from jungle foothills northeast of base camp. Retaliatory artillery, helicopter reconnaissance, and gunships pounding away at the suspected locations hadn't silenced the problem.

It was up to the infantry foot soldiers and scout dog teams to find the VC's hidden base camps. Someone once told me that the infantry was called the *Queen of Battle.* When no one else could get the desired results, the Queen of Battle was called in to finish the job.

I learned that we'd be going on a two-day mission. My platoon was to helicopter several miles east of the base camp to a clearing where we were then to search the surrounding jungle. First, we were to patrol the jungles east of the Michelin rubber tree plantation; then we were to sweep west through the rubber tree plantation and back to our base camp.

Another company of the 2/12 had the job of conducting search-and-destroy operations in the northern mountain sector of the rugged foothills. Most of the VC mortar attacks had been coming from that area.

The mobile VC's mortar teams were deployed for close-in support of the fighting. Their small mortars consisted of an 81mm mortar tube, a base plate, and a sighting mechanism. Charlie easily and quickly assembled, disassembled, and backpacked mortar components along with their ammunition. These highly mobile mortar units were deadly anti-personnel weapons. It was difficult to detect them fast enough to make accurate retaliatory strikes.

The Americans had similar capability within their infantry units' arsenal of weapons, but American artillery required vehicular or aircraft transportation. The smallest artillery pieces, the 105mm Howitzers, had artillery rounds that were bigger and increasingly more deadly than a mortar round. Inside South Vietnam, Charlie wasn't equipped with artillery pieces. Since their mortars could reach targets only at close range, it was easy to

186

conclude that the mortar positions Charlie was using weren't far from our base camp.

We had to find Charlie's base camps or run into him and fight it out. The battalion of 2/12 infantry was given the order to hunt down and eliminate Charlie's mortar teams. This would be a two-day operation, unless headquarters decided that we needed more time to complete the mission.

To get to the mission site, we flew east in helicopters, accompanied by gunship escorts. Clipper and I were in the lead formation's second ship. The door gunners had post-mounted their M60 machine guns, loaded and ready for firing. It was a short ride over the rubber trees to the nearby jungle. The choppers descended into a small clearing and landed under the all-clear green smoke signal.

After the chopper landed, Clipper and I jumped out and darted to the jungle wall. Its outer skirt was too thick to get through without a machete. The platoon leader ordered one of his men to take point and cut a path for the rest of us. Clipper and I followed the man with the machete, as he hacked his way forward. We were useless at this point in the mission. The machete's loud hacking noise distracted Clipper's capability to sense if there was danger ahead.

With such thick vegetation, the platoon leader had to pull in the flank guards. He tightened up the column so he could maintain visual control of the platoon. The pointman continued to slowly cut his way through the vegetation. This was the thickest jungle that Clipper and I had been through. It reminded me of the central highlands which I'd seen a year earlier with the 7th Cavalry.

My knee had been bothering me a little bit more with each mission. I was hoping it would hold for several more months until I left Vietnam. The platoon continued to slowly make its way deeper and deeper into the dark, green jungle. When I looked up, I couldn't see the sky or sun through the jungle's canopy.

If we were going to get hit by Charlie, this ground situation would pose a major problem, because gunships couldn't see us to offer clear and accurate air cover. It would be nearly impossible to pinpoint our exact location on a map. This area of Mother Earth was colored dark green for thousands of yards around us. If we needed artillery support, it would have to be walked in from a map's point of reference. If we relayed the wrong map coordinates, we risked having artillery dropped on our heads. Regardless of the what-if factors, we had no choice but to keep moving under this thick canopy of vegetation. Since another entire company of infantrymen was operating in our same area, we had the assurance of safety in numbers, if we could only get to one another in time.

Not long into the journey, thunder roared overhead, and it soon began to rain. Drops of water made their way through the thick canopy and down on top of the platoon. Millions of raindrops, splashing on the leaves and branches, helped to muffle the sounds of our movement. Switching his machete from hand to hand, the pointman helped us maintain a steady pace through the rain-soaked jungle. The pace man walked behind Clipper and me. His job was to count the number of steps we'd traveled. Periodically, the lieutenant halted to use his map and compass and get the pace-man's count so he could check our distance and direction of travel.

Our jungle fatigues and boots were soaked from the constant rain and tracking through the jungle floor's wet and rotting debris. The trail which we forged would disappear in a few days. The jungle grew back amazingly fast after vegetation was cut or mashed into the soil. As we moved more deeply into VC-occupied territory, the unavoidable, thorn-sticker bushes, which we called *wait-a-minute* vines, scratched deep into our exposed wet arms and hands. Rain and sweat washed away trickles of blood from the fresh scratches and cuts. When we rolled up our sleeves, these cuts, scratches, and healing scars on our arms made it easy to identify an infantryman in a crowd of soldiers. Infantrymen, who were fairly new to the bush, could be easily identified by the amount and age of their scars. They were usually the ones that complained the most. A veteran took his licks from Mother Nature without crying about it.

As we moved forward, Clipper startled me by jumping up and down as if he was stepping on hot coals. I looked down to see what was wrong, because Clipper was groaning and furiously biting at his paws. That's when I realized that the pointman must have stepped on a decaying log and crushed it open. Hundreds of large wingless insects had swarmed out. Clipper had stepped right on top of them, and they attacked his bare paws. I leaped over the decaying log and tried my best to slap and brush off as

188

Clipper gets ready for a ride on a helicopter in Dau Tieng (1967).

many bugs as I could. I stomped on the ground to keep the disturbed nest of insects from climbing up my boots and inside my jungle fatigues.

The man behind us said, "Your dog is going to get eaten up out here."

"No shit, Sherlock!" I called back to him.

I moved to the side and let the others pass. One soldier stopped to help me get the pests off Clipper, who eventually calmed down, so we were able to catch up to the man with the machete. *If Clipper could talk, he would not say, "I don't have time for pain, John. Let's just keep going."* I once again wished that the military would make boots for war dogs, because their paws sure took a beating.

For most of the morning, we walked at a turtle's pace behind the machete man. The rain calmed down and finally stopped. Again, the sounds of birds and flying insects filled the jungle air. We could easily see and walk around the large wet spider webs. I'd never seen so many huge spiders in

189

my life. Everyone steered clear of them. When someone spotted a snake, each man quickly passed on its location and the word, '*snake*.' Everywhere in the jungle, weird-looking critters crawled on the ground and through the leaves and branches around us.

Getting bit was part of life but leeches were the most disgusting of creatures. They clung to you and sucked your blood until they were bloated sacks hanging from your skin. You didn't feel them until they had their way with you. To get them to fall off, you'd have to put a lighted match to them.

So far, there were no signs of Charlie. The only noises that the troops made were the sounds of men slapping attacking bugs and mosquitoes. The machete's sound as it cut through vegetation was heard less frequently as the jungle thinned out. The platoon leader decided to halt and give the platoon a short lunch break while he posted flank guards. He positioned machine gun teams in front and to the rear of our column, keeping the entire platoon on the ready.

I sat on the wet jungle floor against a big tree. Clipper didn't seem to mind me examining him for bugs and bites. He had a lot of bite marks on his paws' tender areas. I brushed my fingers through his furry back and neck, and Clipper enjoyed the grooming. I felt bloated, bloody, purple, peanut-size wood ticks attached to Clipper's skin. I lit a cigarette, got it red-hot, and burned off the ticks with it. Clipper was happy to have me get rid of his little pests. *Besides,* I thought, *this is what best friends are supposed to do.*

I expressed my love for Clipper by hugging him. I told my dog he was doing a good job and that he was brave. I gave him some fresh water and a package of dog food. Clipper showed his appreciation by licking my filthy, sweating face. After Clipper nourished himself, he lay down on his side and leaned against me while he licked his paws. I ate a jungle-temperature can of ham and lima beans and washed it down with some cool water from my canteen. While we relaxed, the smell of American cigarette smoke filled the air. I wondered if letting Clipper breathe in this smoke might dull his extremely sensitive sense of smell. When American soldiers took a break, they relaxed by smoking. They wouldn't be inclined to stop that habit to keep a dog's nose in better working condition.

As I looked around, I saw steam rising from damp jungle fatigues. Squad leaders quietly moved around to make sure everyone was okay and to remind us to bury our trash. I spotted the radio telephone operator next to a tree talking into the handset and radioing a situation report to someone. After he finished, I asked him if I could start using Clipper to scout, since the jungle wasn't as dense as it had been. He said that it would be okay for us to take the point.

The lieutenant was a West Point graduate. I was impressed with his leadership skills. He walked and talked with the confidence of an organized and well-trained man. I noticed that when he spoke, his squad leaders listened and obeyed his instructions. I preferred being with a disciplined unit like this. Working with many units was the nature of my job and though a different units' group dynamics varied little, some were more disciplined and better-trained than others.

As a scout dog handler, my job made it more difficult for me to get to know anyone in the field very well. I was working with this platoon for first time so I didn't know anyone's names. I didn't mind too much because it could be painful to get attached to people.

Kenny Mook had been my last human buddy, before I became a scout dog handler. Clipper was my new best friend, and we were getting to know each other very well. We'd been together longer than I'd been with Kenny. Sure, I had a lot of scout dog handler friends back in base camp, but we never traveled together on the same missions. I had no idea how they worked in the field or reacted under fire. I assumed that they managed things the same way I did in the bush.

After the lieutenant approved my request, I took the point and told the flank guards not to get ahead of Clipper. I explained that they'd diminish his scouting effectiveness. Clipper started forward and slowly picked his way through the jungle. I watched his head and ears for any signs of an alert.

Soon, Clipper alerted with his ears up high. The platoon leader sent a fire team to investigate, as the rest of the platoon got down and covered us. The fire team came back and reported that they didn't find anything. Clipper and I continued forward. About fifty yards later, Clipper alerted a second time. The platoon leader sent out a fire team. They returned and again reported that they saw nothing. The platoon leader came up to me and asked why I thought Clipper was alerting. I told him that I wasn't sure what was out there. Maybe Charlie had left a fresh scent or was hiding up ahead. A base camp could also be nearby. I admitted that I didn't know exactly why Clipper was alerting.

Suddenly, something came dashing and crashing through the low brush on Clipper's right. It crossed in front of us at a super fast speed. Clipper's head moved sharply from right to left. Clipper looked as amazed and spooked as the rest of us. Before I knew it, whatever had crossed our path disappeared quickly.

The lieutenant came up and asked what we'd seen. I told him that I thought it had been a small animal moving low and fast under the vegetation and close to the ground. All any of us could see was the vegetation moving, as it blew by us in high gear.

The platoon leader decided to send out a patrol to sweep the area another fifty yards to the front. When the fire team came back, they reported finding a base camp with trails directly ahead. The platoon leader assembled his squad leaders to check out the report. He assumed that since Charlie hadn't engaged the fire team in battle, the enemy had either left or was hiding in wait.

The platoon leader told us we were doing a good job. He leaned down and gave Clipper a pat on the head and thanked him for the alert. He told me to go into the base camp with the first squad and an M60 machine gun team from the weapons squad. The first squad spread out and cautiously began to step through the jungle at the edge of the base camp with the second squad behind us. The rest of the platoon remained in reserve.

I had a flashback to the time I'd followed the platoon leader to check out a bunker. The results were deadly; the lieutenant had been killed in front of me. This wasn't a good thing to be thinking about now, so I quickly erased it from my mind. Clipper and I slowly followed the squad. Not long into our forward progress, everyone in front of me promptly got down. I knelt, ready to fire my CAR15. This time I hadn't forgotten to pack my grenades. I wasn't going to ever get caught again without a few grenades.

A soldier up front signaled me to move up. Clipper led the way. By this time, it was only a short walk to the inside of the Viet Cong base camp. The first squad spread out and carefully moved around, checking for signs of danger.

VC base camps varied in size, depending on their purpose and how much of a force they housed. The VC used some base camps as training sites for local guerrillas. For the most part, everything in a Viet Cong base camp was underground, leaving only a few ground-level signs of their existence with carefully cleared-away vegetation and beaten paths nearby. Recently disturbed vegetation on the jungle floor was a good sign that someone had been using the camp.

Clipper alerted wildly, but since there was an entire squad of ten American soldiers moving about inside, I thought that he must be alerting on Americans. Then another squad of the platoon moved in.

The VC base camp, which was about one acre in size, had tiny bunkers and well-worn paths throughout. We had to be careful, because Charlie could spring up at any time. The camp appeared to be empty but well-used. It probably accommodated a company-size VC unit. When the rest of the platoon joined us, Clipper and I carefully searched the base camp with two other soldiers following us for security.

Inside one of the bunkers, someone found a pile of Chinese Communist grenades. I knew from past experience never to touch a pile of enemy grenades that were lying around, because they might be booby-trapped. Someone used C-ration toilet paper to mark the bunker with the grenades to warn others to leave them alone. Those primitive grenades were filled with black powder. They had a cast-iron head, shaped like a tiny pineapple, attached to a hollow wooden handle with a string that hung out of it. Pull the string, throw the grenade by the handle, and *boom!* These grenades worked well, but the American grenades had a more complex design and were a lot deadlier.

Clipper alerted to something on the ground and sniffed at a clump of cut branches. I recognized it as a cover for something hidden below. I pulled Clipper away in case this area might be booby-trapped. I motioned everyone nearby to get back behind something. From behind a tree, I used a bamboo stick to move the brush away. I didn't trigger an explosion. Lucky for us the lid wasn't booby-trapped. As I peered from behind the tree into what Clipper had found, I realized it was a fifty-gallon drum full of what looked like dried and crushed green weeds. As I got closer, I smelled marijuana. I couldn't believe it. Clipper had found Charlie's stash of Mary Jane!

Word quickly spread throughout the platoon about the great marijuana find. No one said anything when some fellows stuffed weed into their pockets. Everybody who came by wanted to know who had found the stash. Clipper was once again a hero.

It didn't take much to excite a bunch of teen-aged grunts.

The platoon leader got on the radio and reported the findings and ordered the marijuana burned. One of the squad leaders stuck a flare down inside the drum of marijuana and ignited it. The scent of marijuana smoke carried throughout the base camp. I knew I should get out of there before I got high inhaling the smoke from the marijuana. Besides, I wasn't sure that getting loaded wouldn't impair Clipper's abilities.

We blew up the small cache of grenades that we'd found inside the bunker. The explosion's force blew the bunker's top sky high and scattered debris all around, but no one was hurt.

After we completed our search, the lieutenant called for a spotter round of artillery, so we could try to pinpoint our location. A minute or so later, an artillery round whistled through the air and exploded a few hundred yards away. The spotter round satisfied the platoon leader and he marked his map. The map coordinates could be used later to destroy the VC base camp by an artillery or a bombing run.

Late in the afternoon, our platoon left the base camp. I stayed on as pointman, since Clipper wasn't finding the jungle difficult to navigate. Flank guards were posted about ten yards on either side of the column formation. We departed without incident and reached a small clearing.

It was getting too late to travel any further. The lieutenant decided that we should set up camp for the evening inside the small clearing. Clipper and I took a position inside the platoon perimeter near the platoon leader's command post (CP). We hoped the VC would pass our way when they returned to their base camp, so fifty percent of the platoon had to be awake throughout the night. Clipper remained alert, but nothing out of the ordinary happened.

The next morning, Clipper assumed the point position. We slowly moved through a heavily wooded area with knee-high vegetation. Clipper stopped at the edge of a tiny clearing with ankle-high grass. It was about half the size of a basketball court with a small tree nearly centered in it. I followed Clipper as he crossed the clearing. When Clipper reached the tree, he sprang up and over me as if he was jumping from a trampoline. He let out a loud yelp. I hit the ground, thinking that Clipper must have been hit.

As I lay on the ground, Clipper stood on his hind legs, howled, and stretched his front paw high above him. He twisted and turned, trying to get loose from something that was suspending him. No shots had been fired. I was completely confused until I noticed that something on the tree held one of Clipper's paws. Then I realized that Clipper had been caught in an animal snare. I released his right paw and checked him for injury. He was shaken but okay. I turned around and saw two soldiers, lying on the ground, shaking their heads in disgust but not saying anything. I felt embarrassed that Clipper hadn't sensed the animal trap and avoided it. I hurried to the other side of the clearing to continue the mission.

As we walked, I kept wondering what had happened back there. Thoughts hurried through my mind:

How could Clipper step into an animal snare? He'd had so much tripwire training. Maybe, I should have trained him to detect animal snares too.

Had my dog lost his instinctive edge?

Perhaps, the effects of the marijuana smoke he inhaled impaired his sense of smell.

Maybe, Clipper was tired of the bush and getting lackadaisical. Had he had enough rest, food, and water? How could he need anything, when we'd been on the move for only a short time?

Finally, I concluded that Clipper had made a mistake. *So what?* I thought. *It happens to everyone.*

More importantly, no one had been hurt. I realized that I couldn't blame Clipper. I needed to clear my mind of all these thoughts and doubts and stay focused. A lot of people were depending on us. I was grateful when

Clipper and I made it to the edge of the rubber tree plantation without further incident.

Then the platoon leader stopped us and reset the tactical formation for movement through the open area. I felt relieved when no one said anything to me about what had happened to Clipper. The squad leaders spread their men out. They moved flank guards out to the far right and left wings of the main element.

After the platoon leader changed the formation, Clipper and I continued to walk point. We passed row after row of rubber trees. It was quiet and we didn't spot any Vietnamese while we worked through the next sector. The age and thickness of vegetation between and around the rubber trees told us whether the Vietnamese had worked a particular sector. Within this rubber tree plantation, the hamlets were considered to be unfriendly territory. However, we were under orders not to fire inside a hamlet for fear of wounding or killing noncombatants.

One hundred yards into the advancement, we heard several explosions echoing in the near distance, followed by small-arms fire. The platoon leader halted us in place. I looked back and saw him talking on the radio. The platoon leader started running and passed me. His pumped his fist up and down over his head and yelled, "Double time! Double time!"

The entire platoon started running to keep up. The fast pace didn't last long, because of the weight of our heavy packs. The platoon leader stayed in the lead with his radio/telephone operator (RTO) and finally slowed to a quick-step. Clipper and I were right behind him, trying to keep up. The rest of the platoon spread out behind us to maintain the formation's pace and discipline through this open area.

The sound of small-arms fire stopped. I waited for shooting to start again, but it didn't. Minutes continued to pass, and still I heard no rifle fire. I assumed the attack was over, and Charlie had broken off contact. I heard choppers in the distance, but couldn't see them through the rubber trees. It sounded as if we were still several hundred yards from the action. The squad leaders shouted to their troops to stay alert. We began to move more easily at a brisk pace through the tall grass and weeds between the rubber trees.

196

We abruptly halted our forward progress when Clipper came upon a steep ravine with a creek below. A narrow footpath led to a log that bridged over to the other side of the creek. The Vietnamese must use this bridge to cross the creek, I thought. The platoon leader directed two riflemen to cross the creek first—a distance of about thirty feet—while the rest of us provided cover. After the advance team reached and secured the other side, one-by-one, we carefully crossed over the thick log with no handrails, and hovered over the slow moving stream twenty feet below.

Clipper cautiously stepped onto the log. He crouched so low it looked as if he were hugging it. Step-by-step, he cautiously and steadily picked his way across the log. I was careful to give him enough slack in the leash as I followed behind him. It took us a little longer to get across, but we made it. I was glad I had him in a harness. With a collar or choke chain on, the leash would have snapped his neck, if he fell from the log. I had no doubt that our base camp training, crossing-the-log, had helped to prepare Clipper for this real-life obstacle. When we got to the other side, I gave Clipper a big hug and praised him for a job well-done. He crossed the log so well that it made it easy to forget his mishap with the animal snare.

Fortunately, we reached the other side without anyone losing balance and falling into the creek. The platoon leader motioned the lead squad to move out quickly. Clipper and I assumed the pointman position. The platoon leader, his RTO, and two riflemen were directly behind us. The rest of the platoon spread out in a tactical formation to the left, right, and behind. The platoon leader kept instructing me to move faster, so Clipper and I quickened our pace.

Clipper gave a strong alert to the right front. He stopped and stood rigidly with his head and ears pointing to the right. I turned in the direction that Clipper was pointing and spotted troop movement about one hundred yards away through the rubber trees. I hit the ground and pointed to alert the men behind. The platoon leader got flat on the ground directly behind me.

I heard the platoon leader talking on the radio. He learned that we must be on the backside of a sister platoon ahead of us. The platoon leader directed me to move in the direction where Clipper had spotted the troop movement. I got up, tapped the bottom of the twenty-round clip to ensure it was properly seated in my CAR15, and made sure that the safety lever was on. I yanked on Clipper's leash to motion him to move out.

It was quiet as we penetrated further into the rubber trees toward the American lines. Even though Clipper kept alerting directly ahead, I didn't stop until we spotted an American soldier waving for us come forward. When I reached the first American soldier, the platoon leader stopped me from going any farther. I knelt on one knee and Clipper got down on all fours.

We'd arrived twenty minutes after we'd first heard the sound of shooting. The platoon leader headed for our sister platoon's command post (CP). He told us to stay in place until he returned.

I sat quietly next to a soldier from the other platoon. Then I asked him what had happened. He told me that the platoon had spread out and moved through the rubber trees. Then command-detonated mines struck down the front of his platoon. The VC had planted the mines in the rubber trees. When the platoon got into the killing zone, the VC had detonated the mines. A few men had been killed instantly, and several others were wounded. He said the rest of the platoon had fired in the direction of the explosions, but Charlie never returned their fire. The platoon's advancement halted, while they waited for reinforcements.

I saw gunships and choppers in the air. Several choppers landed on a road nearby to pick up the dead and wounded. When the platoon leader returned to where we waited, he changed our mission. He said that our platoon was to merge with the platoon ahead and sweep through the hamlet area. There was a possibility that the VC who had detonated the mines might be hiding in the hamlet along with women and children. He told us that we were not to shoot while inside the hamlet, unless we had a clear target of aggression. As he talked, I noticed that the nearby area of rubber trees had been well-worked by the Vietnamese. There was little to no grass or weeds between the rows.

We cautiously moved out in a spread-out formation with weapons ready. I was asked to take point for the sister platoon because I had the only scout dog. Well in the lead, I stepped on something that felt weird and rubbery under my boot. I looked down and saw a human hand, but I didn't stop to think about it. I had to keep moving until I reached the outer perimeter of the lead platoon.

American soldiers spread throughout the rubber trees and waited for orders to move out. When the order was given, they moved forward. We weren't far from the hamlet, when Clipper's ears perked up. I didn't stop because I assumed that Clipper was alerting on the hamlet's inhabitants.

A soldier to my right said, "Hey, dog handler, check out the bomb lying against the trunk of that rubber tree."

I glanced at the tree trunk and saw a huge warhead at its base. The soldier told me that his platoon had discovered it after they were hit by the mines. He explained that the VC mustn't have had time to rig it as a booby trap or they would have already detonated it. Instead, an American soldier had booby-trapped it for the VC. If anyone tried to move or tamper with it, the bomb would explode. Clipper couldn't stop alerting on that booby trap until he had completely lost sight of it.

When we arrived at the hamlet, Vietnamese women and children quickly came out of their huts to greet the American troops. Clipper became agitated and growled as they approached. I held him back, as the other soldiers entered the hamlet. I also held my finger on the safety of my weapon. I was ready to flick it to automatic if I had to shoot. More soldiers entered the village and started searching the huts one-by-one. They looked for the VC who had detonated the mines and killed and wounded our comrades.

As they searched, I heard someone shout inside one of the huts, "You, VC? You kill Americans? Where VC? Bullshit! You lie!"

A thorough search of the hamlet, inside and out, revealed only the hiding places of women, children, and old men. We couldn't figure out where the VC were hiding. We knew that they couldn't have vanished. We began to think that one of these women, an old man, or even a child had detonated the mines.

I watched the hamlet fill with a lot of commotion and confusion as the soldiers completely surrounded them. Several squads searched inside each hut. The Americans were having major communication problems with the Vietnamese. After several hours, a few Vietnamese interpreters flew in to help translate and interrogate every adult in the hamlet.

The Vietnamese were afraid of Clipper, so I stayed outside and didn't participate in the search for fear that Clipper might bite someone. If I let Clipper loose, he'd attack the first Vietnamese he found. I decided to take advantage of Clipper's aggressive behavior and use him as my guard.

When the situation calmed down in the village, Vietnamese women, moving quickly past Clipper, roamed around the hamlet with baskets of bananas and offered them to the American troops.

We took several Vietnamese into custody and later loaded them into choppers that waited on the nearby road. I was part of the first group of soldiers ordered to move out of the village. I headed across the dirt road, up the bank on the other side, and into the rubber trees.

Now we were on the last leg of our mission and approximately one mile east to Dau Tieng. Our final objective was to form a long, on-line, sweeping formation to cover a lot of ground and hunt for VC hideouts. After Clipper and I moved past a few rows of rubber trees, we were ordered to stop. As we waited for instructions, soldiers spread out and positioned themselves among the rubber trees.

We waited for several minutes for the rest of the platoon to leave the hamlet and join the main element. Finally, the signal was given to move out again. As Clipper and I passed between a row of trees, we heard a shattering explosion to our immediate right. I hit the ground and dragged Clipper down beside me. We didn't hear any shots being fired. Then I heard the sounds of a hurt soldier two trees away from me. I quickly crawled over to him as several others soldiers arrived at the same time. The wounded soldier was lying on his back, rocking in pain, with his legs and boots covered in blood.

Almost at once, several of us cried, "Medic! Medic!"

When the medic arrived, he cut the young soldier's boots off and treated the wounds on his legs and feet. Looking around on the ground, I discovered a broken tripwire attached to a short stick that was stuck in the ground. The other end of the wire was tied to a rubber tree.

I realized that could have been me if I'd moved one more tree over before I stopped. Would Clipper have alerted on this booby trap? I'd never know the answer to that question.

I decided that it was time to put to the test all the training that Clipper and I had gone through. Clipper had shown in our recent training sessions that he knew how to detect booby trap tripwires. He'd have to do it for real now, or more of these men would be injured or killed.

After the helicopter removed the soldier, I told the platoon leader that I'd take the lead. I asked him to move the rest of the platoon into a column and to follow me and my dog. I didn't give the platoon leader a chance to respond as I turned away. Then I slowly moved forward and began to follow Clipper's lead. As I glanced behind, I noticed that the platoon leader had ordered the troops to form a single column.

I thought, *Clipper is in charge now, even if he doesn't realize it. If anyone can do it, Clipper can get us through this area and safely home to Dau Tieng.*

With the outer perimeter of our Dau Tieng base camp less than a half-mile away, I kept my attention glued to Clipper's head and ears while he guided me forward. Clipper gave a faint alert to the left, briefly hesitated, and then moved right. I glanced in that direction and saw nothing, so I didn't stop. My field of vision was only clear at eye level. The ground below was overgrown with knee-high weeds and grass below Clipper's head. It was easy to walk through, and Clipper didn't have a problem negotiating a path. I had to trust Clipper's training and natural instincts for danger.

Clipper gave another weak alert to his right and then moved left. He performed this maneuver again and again without much hesitation or stopping. A short time later, a voice from behind ordered me to stop. As I looked back, I saw a long column of American troops snaked through the rubber trees behind me. We stopped only briefly and then moved out again. This stop-and-go situation occurred several times during the journey. I wasn't completely sure why we were stopping. No one behind me said anything about it. I didn't ask because I was too far forward. They could have been checking something out or reviewing the map for direction of travel. Someone may have spotted tripwires or booby traps, but I was guessing.

I didn't think Clipper's alerts were strong enough for me to worry about danger. The way he was moving, it looked as if he was deliberately going around things that could be tripwires or booby traps. Clipper had performed this kind of maneuver during our training sessions in base camp, but now when he'd move from one direction to another, I couldn't see anything out of the ordinary. I decided to keep my eyes on Clipper instead of trying to figure out why he was walking from left or right so much. I was grateful that there were no more explosions. I assumed that Clipper was leading us on a safe path.

We finally reached the outskirts of Dau Tieng's base camp. I stopped short of the concertina wire and spotted soldiers staring at us and standing on the other side next to their sand-bagged bunkers. I dropped to one knee and waited for the rest of the platoon to catch up. My right knee was aching again, but I knew that I'd soon be safe inside the K-9 compound.

While I knelt and rubbed my right knee, several soldiers caught up with us. One of them stopped and told me to wait for the platoon leader. Another soldier smiled as he passed by. The soldiers formed a column and walked along the fence of concertina wire toward the base camp's entrance gate.

The platoon leader, the lieutenant I had talked with when this mission began, finally showed up. I stood up to greet him. He smiled and thanked me for getting his men through all the other booby traps.

I was puzzled, so I asked, "What booby traps?"

The platoon leader looked at me, as though I should have known the answer to that question. He told me that when Clipper had changed directions for the first time, one of his men had spotted a grenade tied to the base of a rubber tree, right where the dog had changed directions.

He pointed out, "After you and your dog changed directions several times, my men got wise to what was going on, so they started searching for booby traps. The times we stopped were to mark the ones we discovered. They will be detonated after the entire company is safely out of the area."

The lieutenant knelt and gave Clipper a hug and told him what a great dog he was. The lieutenant put his hand out and said, "Shake!" To my surprise, Clipper lifted his paw up and put it into the Lieutenant's hand.

I was happy to hear that I had been right! Clipper deliberately went around the booby traps and tripwires. I didn't spot them because I didn't stop to search.

Playfully, Clipper lies in the grass after locating the booby traps (1967).

The platoon leader praised me for taking the lead. He said that if it hadn't been for Clipper, some of his men would be on stretchers. He told me that he was going to recommend us for the Bronze Star Medal. We shook hands and parted company. As the lieutenant walked away, he turned and said, "I'm going to ask for you the next time I need a scout." I smiled, waved, and gave the lieutenant a thumbs up signal.

That was the finest compliment I'd ever received for doing my job.

I looked down at Clipper and tapped my chest. Clipper jumped up and rested his front paws on my shoulders. I looked into Clipper's eyes and then gave him a bear hug. I told him what a great warrior he was and how proud I was to have him as a partner and scout.

I thought about the lieutenant's words. This was the first time anyone had ever wanted to recommend me for a medal. I felt honored, but I knew that all the credit belonged to my dog. He'd been the meritorious hero that day. I was just the lucky guy behind the leash, and grateful to have such a wonderful companion to lead us to safety. I felt that there was nothing more valuable or rewarding than knowing that others had lived because of my dog. My trust and confidence in Clipper dramatically increased that day.

Clipper and I moved out behind the rest of the troops through the gate entrance. I walked with my head up and shoulders back, and smiled all the way home.

The trip-wire training paid off. Lives were saved, and another mission was over.

Chapter 15

The Capture

Clipper and I were assigned to support Company A, 2ⁿᵈ Battalion, 12ᵗʰ Infantry. Brigade S-2 intelligence reported that an NVA courier sometimes traveled alone between the provinces of Tay Ninh and Dau Tieng. They wanted him captured.

Army intelligence had mapped out some possible places where we could set up a trap. Our mission was to capture the courier and bring him back alive for interrogation. This type of mission is normally reserved for Long Range Reconnaissance Patrol (LRRP) teams, but the teams must have been too busy at the time, so the regular infantry had been assigned the job.

It was a two-day mission. Choppers were to lift us off at the crack of dawn and head to the base of the majestic Black Virgin mountain, an inactive volcano. Nui Ba Den, as the Vietnamese called it, jutted up from the ground about 3000 feet, and towered above the Tay Ninh Province about eighty miles west of Saigon. Its summit was shrouded by clouds and mist and covered in a thick green blanket of dense rugged jungle. Nui Ba Den could easily be seen from miles around. Below and around the inactive volcano were trails, clearings, and flatland jungle terrain.

The peak had been captured by the U.S. Army 5ᵗʰ Special Forces Group in 1964. From the air, it was a beautiful site. When we flew close to Nui Ba Den, we could see the 25ᵗʰ Infantry Division signal corps's VHF and FM relay station, tall radio tower and antennas. This station relayed communication between the 25ᵗʰ Infantry Division and its subordinate commands located in Cu Chi, Tay Ninh, and Dau Tieng. The peak of Nui Ba Den was heavily fortified and appeared impossible to reach by foot from below.

Black Virgin Mountain as seen from atop the lookout tower.

The VC used the lower slopes of Nui Ba Den for observation and their own radio relay. They constantly harassed the American troops stationed on top with sniper fire and mortar attacks.

Four combat infantry platoons were assigned to this mission to capture the enemy courier. Each had separate areas to reconnoiter ambush sites. I didn't know why I'd been the only dog handler assigned to the mission. We could have used four scout dog teams, one attached to each combat platoon.

When we saw the green smoke signaling that it was safe, the chopper landed in a small clearing less than a mile from the base of Nui Ba Den. We quickly moved away from the aircraft under cover of the surrounding jungle. The patrol leader signaled me to take the lead. Clipper and I headed into the jungle, which wasn't too thick to walk through. We distanced ourselves about one hundred feet ahead of everyone else.

The patrol leader frequently signaled me to stop while he checked the map and distance to a trail we were trying to reach. We cautiously moved parallel to Nui Ba Den for several hours. Clipper eventually gave a strong alert with his ears and head held high. I stopped, dropped to one knee, and motioned the nearest man forward. After a brief discussion, a fire team of three men moved ahead to check it out. They reported a well-used trail less than two hundred feet ahead. The patrol leader moved up to my position and evaluated his map coordinates. We were on target and near the trails the enemy courier was expected to be using.

Clipper and I approached the trail beneath the jungle cover. The platoon didn't want to get on the trail and risk exposure. We moved quietly and undetected by using savvy patrol discipline—radio silence, camouflage, concealment, and quiet movement. We set up an ambush alongside a natural fork where two trails intersected. The location provided excellent vision in either direction. The platoon leader strategically positioned each man about five feet inside the jungle overlooking the narrow pathways. The natural surroundings helped to camouflage us. Clipper and I were positioned at one end of the ambush. This gave Clipper the best chance to alert if someone came bopping down the trail. The other platoons supporting this operation were within a mile radius of our position.

The plan was to surprise and capture the courier, not kill him. The ambush platoon waited for several hours, quietly swatting mosquitoes and killing bugs, ants, and spiders. Some men catnapped during the long wait, but most stayed vigilant. It reminded me of a spider in a web awaiting its prey. As the hours went by, the sky grew darker until nothing within a few feet remained visible. The men stayed alert in stationary positions all night, but nothing happened.

As early morning light chased the long shadows away, men stirred. No one was allowed to smoke cigarettes because the smoke might alert the enemy to our presence. This type of situation was always a crapshoot, because we didn't know if Charlie already knew we were there, or if we were going to succeed in ambushing him.

Early in the morning Clipper alerted toward the trail. I immediately informed the man next to me. He passed the warning signal down the line. Even though the early morning light was dim, I spotted the target of Clipper's alert—an NVA soldier in khaki uniform riding a bicycle, wearing a straw hat, and a rifle slung over his back. I got a major rush of adrenaline as I watched the enemy come closer. I realized that I'd be the first man he'd reach. Clipper remained silent, but ready to pounce. The enemy soldier appeared to be alone and relaxed. He had two canvas bags draped over his bicycle's back fender.

This must be our man, I thought.

When the courier was right in front of me, I turned Clipper loose and he darted into the road, lunged, and knocked the NVA soldier off his bicycle. The man hit the ground and landed on his back. I gave Clipper the command, "Watch him!" Clipper growled and showed his teeth but didn't attack. The enemy soldier looked so completely surprised, that I thought his eyeballs were going to pop out of his head. Immediately, the rest of the patrol surrounded the soldier at gunpoint. Clipper's growling and barking kept the frightened man squirming on his back in the dirt. Someone took away his rifle.

I handed my CAR15 and Clipper's leash to the nearest soldier and told him to hold back the dog. As a former high school wrestling champion, I had no doubt I could contain this prisoner without using a weapon. I reached down and rolled the prisoner over to his stomach, straddled his body, and spread his arms and legs. The prisoner was shaking and so scared that he pissed in his pants while I searched him.

In the prisoner's pocket, I found a worn American Zippo cigarette lighter that was engraved with a 1st Infantry Division shoulder patch and the slogan, *Big Red One.* The Big Red One didn't operate near the Tay Ninh province, but was stationed in the north. The canvas bags attached to the bicycle were filled with Vietnamese currency and documents. This led me to believe we had the NVA courier Army intelligence was so eager to capture.

I didn't want to think how that North Vietnamese soldier had gotten this lighter. I thought, *The bastard must have taken it from a dead American.*

It is honorable for a soldier to die on the field of battle. Normal procedure is to take weapons, ammunition, and military documents from a dead man. But it is immoral and disgraceful to rob a dead body of valuables. The soldier's personal effects should be returned to his surviving family and not stolen by the enemy, no matter which side he's on. But the war in

The author takes a break at the ambush site near the Black Virgin Mountain.

Vietnam wasn't a gentleman's war. It was as brutal and ugly as the death it left in its wake.

I was in complete control of this prisoner now. If he'd tried to escape, I'd tackle and pin him in a wrestling hold that he couldn't wiggle away from. Using the right pressure hold, I could easily break his arms. I could also command Clipper to attack him. *There's no damn way this prisoner is going to get away,* I thought, as my blood boiled. I began almost hoping that he'd try to resist or escape. If he did, I'd have an excuse to vent my anger. But the prisoner was too scared to move a muscle.

After I completed the body search, two soldiers took over from me. They tied the prisoner's hands behind his back, taped his mouth shut, and blindfolded him. The patrol leader radioed for a chopper to get us out of the area immediately. We quickly moved under jungle cover to the pickup point.

Later that morning several choppers arrived. They flew the prisoner and platoon back to Dau Tieng. I felt grateful that we'd accomplished our mission and had no American casualties. I hoped that the rest of my missions in Vietnam would be this successful, but safety was never a guarantee in this *undeclared war.*

Chapter 16

Life between Missions

It was always a welcome comfort to return to base camp after a mission, like coming home from work and spending time relaxing with your friends. Our K-9 club was the best place for us to unwind and try to forget our troubles on the job.

The K-9 club, huddled within the wooden buildings of our sleeping area, served as the mailroom and lounge. It was modestly furnished with tables, chairs, a refrigerator, a bar, and portable air-conditioners. Screened-in windows, covered with scrapped sheets of clear plastic, kept cool air inside. The club was even wired for electricity to accommodate these modest, but important morale-lifting conveniences.

The talk of good and bad times with family and friends back home was always a hot topic of conversation. Some guys bragged about all the girls that were waiting for them back home. Others talked of going to college, getting a job, and starting a business. Nobody had aspirations of making Army life into a career.

The local *Stars and Stripes* newspaper reported the war's current events throughout Vietnam. Many of the dog handlers passed time reading books, magazines, and hometown newspapers. They played cards and drank soda pop and Ballantine and Pabst Blue Ribbon beer. They especially enjoyed drinking Kool-Aid, because it spiced up the nasty taste of the local water supply.

News of our fellow dog handlers, who were in hospitals recovering from wounds, was always a major topic. Kentucky, wounded during the kennel attack, was wounded a second time in the buttocks by a VC sniper during

Lieutenant Robert Fenner, Sergeant Shelton, and the author outside their living quarters in Dau Tieng base camp.

a search-and-destroy mission. Another dog handler, Randy Cox, was severely burned with his dog while inside an armored personnel carrier that got hit by an enemy rocket. Randy was evacuated to a hospital burn unit in the States and did not return to active military service. His dog died of burns.

In May 1967, I read a story in the 3rd Brigade's newspaper about Mike Phillips and his scout dog, Beau. Mike was a twenty-year old, curly-haired redhead from Cleveland. Beau was a large German shepherd with an aggressive attitude. They trained together in the States and arrived in Vietnam with the original 44th IPSD in January. Both had tasted the bitterness of war for five months.

According to the story, Beau had been wounded two different times, first while Beau was on a three-day mission. Phillips and Beau scouting for

212

an infantry unit near a large clearing when Beau alerted. Phillips immediately recognized the danger, signaled the platoon behind him, and dove for cover. The Viet Cong opened fire, but Beau had thwarted their surprise ambush on the Americans.

During the ensuing firefight, a bullet from an enemy AK-47 rifle had struck Beau in the front leg. Phillips protected his dog by covering him with his body while he returned fire. The Americans suffered only light casualties in that battle and defeated the enemy. If it hadn't been for Beau's alert, American casualties could have been greater. Beau's wound turned out not to be too serious, and Doc Glydon patched him up.

Mike and Beau were back in action for operation Junction City in a rugged area of War Zone C. Mike and Beau were sitting in a clearing preparing to move out when enemy mortar rounds began piercing the air and exploding all around them. During the mortar attack, Beau and Phillips were wounded. A piece of shrapnel passed completely through Beau's middle, breaking part of his backbone. Phillips right arm was pierced with a piece of shrapnel. Beau's wound was so serious that he was evacuated to a hospital in Saigon. A death certificate was filed at Dau Tieng because no one expected Beau to survive, let alone rejoin his platoon. Beau was a tough dog, however, and refused to give up. He made it through surgery and was rehabilitated back to health.

A month later, Beau returned to duty with the 44th and his death certificate was torn up and thrown away.

Ollie, Mac, Scott, Durback, and other dog handlers worked their dogs off-leash without problems. However, I preferred to work Timber and Clipper on-leash. Roger Jones was no exception. Roger had won the Trainee-of-the-Cycle award at the scout dog school in Fort Benning, Georgia.

In June 1967, Roger was supporting a platoon on a mission when they got into a firefight with the enemy. His unleashed dog, Ringo, bolted from the scene. Lt. Fenner and Doc Bob Glydon felt accountable for every scout dog and handler and were furious that Roger had lost Ringo. They filed a Report of Survey form that charged Roger with suspicion of negligence.

Members of the 44th Scout Dog Platoon: (left to right) Mike Phillips, Wiggins, "Mac" McClellen (sitting), Sergeant Shelton, Cecil, Dan Barnett, Lieutenant Robert Fenner, Unknown, Unknown, Al Walters (kneeling), Bill Zantos, John Burnam, Ollie Whetstone (1967).

This could have resulted in court-martial proceedings, but Roger was never punished further for the incident.

A few weeks after Roger lost Ringo, the local *Stars and Stripes* newspaper carried the story of a wounded German shepherd who had followed an American combat patrol into the Cu Chi base camp. According to the story, the dog had been badly wounded in the jaw, dehydrated, and hungry. The wounded dog had survived several days hiding in the jungle.

The German shepherd had been taken to the 38th IPSD for medical attention. The 38th was a sister scout dog platoon based at Cu Chi. Because each dog had a serial number tattooed in his left ear, it was learned that this dog did not belong to the 38th. The platoon leader contacted Lt. Fenner of the 44th to see if he was one of their dogs. Doc Glydon was able to verify that the wounded dog's serial number matched that of Roger's missing scout dog.

Ringo had suffered from a close-range gunshot wound in the face. The bullet had entered one side of his jaw and exited the other side. Ringo was evacuated to Saigon where he underwent a special surgical operation performed by a well-known military dental surgeon. Roger flew to Saigon to accompany his dog. The surgical procedure was a success, and a month later, the handler and his dog returned to the 44th IPSD. Ringo eventually recovered from his wounds, except for his tongue. When it hung from his mouth, it was evident that part of his tongue was missing.

For surviving his wounds, hiding in the bush, and finding an American patrol to follow home, Ringo was our hero. We admired his courage and strength to escape and evade being killed by the enemy.

Sergeant Dan Barnett and Scout dog Ringo after Ringo returned from surgery in Saigon. Note that part of Ringo's tongue is missing.

Dog handlers have their own personalities and ways of expressing their individuality. For example, my hooch-mate Dan Scott always seemed to have a book sticking out of his back pocket and he liked to read every chance he could. After dropping out of Officer Candidate School, Scott was reassigned to scout dog training. When he graduated, Scott was shipped to Vietnam and assigned to the 44th IPSD in March 1967, the same month that I returned to Vietnam.

Somehow Scott had acquired a World War II, twenty-five inch long forty-five caliber machine gun we called a *grease gun*. Although .45 caliber ammunition was a standard item within the Dau Tieng supply channels, Dan had also bought several thirty-round ammunition clips to go along with his weapon. The gun was designed to be slung from a shoulder strap and fired waist-high with one hand.

Lt. Fenner didn't seem to care that some of his men preferred weapons other than the standard-issue CAR15 or M16. Mac for one insisted on carrying his M1 rifle to the field and wouldn't trade for anything else. Scott toted his grease gun on every mission and swore it never jammed when fired. It didn't have a semi-automatic selector switch like the CAR15 because it was designed to fire only on full automatic. I didn't think the grease gun could hit the broad side of a barn beyond twenty feet, but everyone agreed that if the bullets didn't kill the enemy, the noise would scare him to death.

One day Scott stood outside my hooch and called, "Hey, Burnam! Get out here! I have something to show you!"

I went out to see what he wanted and found Scott holding two jars in his hands. Inside one jar was the biggest and longest centipede I'd ever seen. In the other jar was a large scorpion. Before long, several other dog handlers gathered around while Scott placed the two jars on the ground. We started placing bets on which of the critters would survive in a fight. I bet on the scorpion because it looked meaner. When all the bets were in— about fifty-fifty on the scorpion and the centipede—Scott emptied the jars and forced the critters into a fight that didn't last long. Less than a minute into the first round, the centipede killed the scorpion, and I lost my bet.

The author poses with "44," the mascot of the 44th IPSD. "44" came over with the original platoon from Fort Benning, Georgia in January of 1967.

A sense of humor was not only a way of expressing ourselves but of staying mentally healthy in Vietnam, so we often looked for ways to have some fun.

One day, Dan Scott, Mike Phillips, and I found a torn camouflage parachute from a logistics sergeant and decided to liven up our hooch with it. Onto the ceiling, we centered the parachute's apex, which Scott painted black. He glued strands of steel wool around it. We spread out and nailed the rest of the parachute material to the rafters and walls and called our creative decoration *The Pussy That Swallowed Vietnam.*

While Dan, Mike, and I fantasized about women, Bill Zantos, a fellow scout dog handler found a unique way of meeting a girlfriend. Two local Vietnamese women we called Mama San operated a laundry and boot shine service inside a large military canvas tent across the road from the K-9 compound. A black chalkboard listed the prices they charged for each laundry item as well as the cost of boot-polishing services. We used Military Pay Currency, or *paper money,* to pay for these services.

One of the older Vietnamese women who worked in the laundry tent took a shining to Bill Zantos. Compared to the rest of us, Bill had a robust body, which quickly earned him the nickname, *Heavy.* When the dog handlers found out that Heavy was doing the *boom boom* thing with a Mama San in the back of the laundry tent, they had a great time poking fun at him. Fortunately, Bill had a good sense of humor and he laughed right along with us.

The 44th IPSD set up a volleyball net between two rubber trees inside the K-9 compound. Playing volleyball gave us some exercise and helped take our minds off our troubles. There always seemed to be plenty of dog handlers who wanted to play a game. We'd play for hours without shirts under cover of the fully-leafed rubber trees.

About once a week, from a small range of mountains north of our K-9 compound, Charlie launched mortar rounds at the airstrip. We quickly learned that the maximum range of Charlie's mortar rounds was about 200 yards short of the volleyball court. So whenever we heard mortars exploding on the airstrip, we'd stop the volleyball game and watch.

Since the shrapnel from the mortar rounds never reached us during those random daytime mortar attacks, we didn't need to run and seek shelter in the bunkers. The players would stand on the volleyball court and watch the fireworks. Most of the shells exploded in and around the airfield's runway. Then the helicopters would scramble to get airborne. During each mortar attack, Dau Tieng sounded a siren, like the one used for an air raid. The mortar attacks never lasted long. It was Charlie's way of saying hello!

Occasionally, Charlie would get lucky and blow up a helicopter or a vehicle, or hit a building near the runway. American retaliatory artillery strikes were immediate and our gunships airborne. With a vengeance, the Americans would fire volley after volley of artillery rounds. The infantry would patrol on foot and search through the rugged and difficult mountainous terrain. Scout dog teams would also be sent out to locate Charlie's mortar squads. Once in a while we got lucky and surprised Charlie, killing him and capturing some of his mortar tubes. For the most part, however, this was a cat-and-mouse game. Charlie was too smart and usually got away in time only to return another day and launch more shells. We learned to respect the tenacious little bastards, because they were so good at this type of warfare.

It became a challenge to keep our skills and exercise levels high in between missions.

On September 2, 1967, a beautiful, hot and humid morning with not a cloud in the sky, Lt. Fenner decided that we should go on a road march because he thought we weren't getting enough exercise in base camp. He directed the entire platoon of fifteen or so scout dog teams to assemble. They were to march around the entire perimeter of Dau Tieng. The dog handlers decided to travel light with only their helmets, weapons, one canteen of water, and their dogs on leashes. With the hot sun and balmy air, none of us were too happy with the idea of a road march. But shortly after lunch, we formed up in single file for the march.

As we headed out of the K-9 compound, we must have made a magnificent sight, with German shepherds and scout dog handlers stretched out for a quarter mile. When the platoon moved along the shoulder of the road, I realized that it was the first time I'd seen this type of organized activity since my assignment with the sentry dog platoon in Okinawa. Back then, it was routine to march around in formations. In Vietnam, emphasis wasn't placed on organized training activities. Usually, we rested while in base camp, and we trained at our individual discretion.

Because our base camp wasn't very large, the dogs drew immediate attention as we passed infantry company areas, battalion and brigade headquarters, the field hospital, motor pools, the airstrip, maintenance hangers, and trucks and jeeps that were driving down the road. We figured that we'd be gone for only a short time. It must have been 110 degrees that afternoon, and the dusty road offered no cover or protection from the sun and heat. We marched at a slow pace. In about two hours, the column of scout dog teams had made a complete non-stop loop around the entire base camp of Dau Tieng. Everyone was out of water and the dogs' tongues were dragging the dirt.

We were within a few hundred yards of walking through the entrance of our K-9 compound when the worst possible thing happened. Tony Pettingill's scout dog, Prince, gasped for air and collapsed near the entrance to the K-9 compound. Doc Glydon wasn't able to revive Prince, so he died of dehydration. I watched as Tony cradled Prince in his arms and sobbed. There was nothing anyone could do for him. Prince was the only casualty of that road march, just another tragic accident that took the life of a war dog.

Tony was devastated over the needless death of his dog. We buried Prince in the cemetery inside the K-9 compound next to the dogs who had died before him — Erik, Shadow, Sergeant, Buckshot, 44, Hardcore, and others. The grave markers were starting to add up.

The Army never let a grunt rest for very long. Even when we were back at base camp between jungle missions and assignments, we had to go on duty with the 3rd Brigade, 25th Infantry Division Military Police detachment. This served to keep us occupied and useful.

The Military Police detachment was responsible for law and order as well as a ton of other jobs in and around Dau Tieng. The town of Dau Tieng was

A dead 44th scout dog believed to be Prince, after having been placed on a stretcher by handler Bob Pettingill (1967).

off-limits to American grunts at all times. The MPs had complete military jurisdiction wherever they went in this Vietnamese district. No liberty passes were ever issued for American infantry troops to enter the town. Besides, there was really nothing to see or anything worth buying there.

The primary reason American troops occupied Dau Tieng was because the rubber tree plantations happened to be strategically located for military use as a forward fire base, and as a buffer between Cambodia and Saigon. The Vietnamese used the Saigon River, which ran right through the village, for fishing, bathing, and transport.

Somehow, the 44th IPSD got involved supporting MP night patrols in the Dau Tieng village. Lt. Fenner maintained the duty roster and made sure that every scout dog handler was on his list. When we weren't in the field, dog handlers were expected to go on what was dubbed *Rat Patrol.*

Rat Patrol was never conducted during daylight hours. It was performed after midnight and lasted for several hours. Mainly a show of force, a scout dog team would accompany a small detachment of MPs into the village several nights during the week. A dog handler traveled light, carrying a CAR15, a bandoleer of ammunition, a flashlight, and a few canteens of water for the dog. We wore a soft flop hat instead of a steel pot. The MPs carried M16s and .45 caliber pistols as sidearms. One member of the MP team carried the PRC/25 radio for use in getting help and providing situation reports.

The local whorehouse, off-limits to Americans, was one of the village's checkpoints. An ARVN and an American Military Assistance Command Vietnam (MACV) command post, near the center of town was heavily guarded and surrounded by barbed wire and sandbags. The Rat Patrol used it as a pit stop for a cup of coffee and as a place to hang out and talk with the American advisors who were on duty there.

Rat patrol was conducted with clockwork precision and didn't surprise any of the locals. Every villager knew where we went and how many of us were on the team. The patrol walked the main road and beaten paths of the village. Every now and then they had to chase some assholes through the darkness, but the perpetrators always seemed to get away. The Rat Patrol never surprised a lone Viet Cong, never snuck up on a squad of North Vietnamese Regulars sitting around smoking pot or setting up a mortar tube. Charlie was too slick for that.

Dau Tieng didn't have street lamps, traffic signals, or a town square with a huge lit-up clock. It was a poor town where people didn't drive cars or have fancy houses. They lived in small huts and mostly traveled on foot or by bicycle. No white picket fences and green lawns surrounded the homes of these Vietnamese. Instead, their dirt yards had chickens, oxen, pigs, and tiny dogs hanging around. There were no paved roads. Everything was dirt, including most of the floors inside the homes. Some of the businesses in town had a more permanent look, heavily influenced by the French style of architecture. Permanent-looking structures were far and few between in the village of Dau Tieng.

Sergeant Way and an American Red Cross volunteer enter the K-9 Club.

We enjoyed going on Rat Patrol for one reason—we could visit the local bakery. Dau Tieng's Vietnamese baker used a primitive brick oven with a cast iron door to bake small loaves of bread. What a treat it was to smell and taste hot baked bread rolls at two o'clock in the morning! The baker gave us hot bread and never charged us for it. He said the rat patrol kept away the VC.

Part of a scout dog handler's mission on Rat Patrol was to bring back some bread rolls for his friends. I found it amusing that the Military Police were like the local police back home. Instead of free donuts and coffee at the local late-night store, they enjoyed free bread rolls at the local Vietnamese bakery. The only redeeming value of going on Rat Patrol was bringing home these hot bread roles, which was just another way of relieving some of the tension of serving as a scout dog handler.

What I didn't know was that my old right knee injury would force me to leave Dau Tieng and my best friend, Clipper.

Chapter 17

Becoming a Short-Timer

On Christmas Day, December 25, 1967, the battalion mess hall served turkey with all the trimmings for lunch. The past week had seen a major increase in incoming mail and packages from the States.

I woke up early that Christmas morning and felt great, even though it was hot and muggy outside. Everyone I ran into seemed to be in a good mood. The dogs were barking and hungry. It was a day like any other in Vietnam for Clipper and his pals in the kennel. Same old dog food, same old rubber tree, same old water pail, same old kennel run, and the same old mutts as neighbors. Clipper must view his life as a war dog as a pathetic existence, I thought. He didn't even know that he had no chance in hell of ever going back to the States to become a pet in my back yard. This was too depressing a thought, so dog handlers didn't talk about it much.

This Christmas, I thought about the three previous ones.

On Christmas in 1965, I'd been in Littleton, Colorado living it up on a week's furlough from infantry recruit training. I had no idea that the Army would be shipping my butt off to Vietnam in March 1966.

On Christmas Day in 1966. I was a sentry dog handler with the 267th Chemical Company in Okinawa. Guarding chemical weapons of mass destruction was one of the many reasons I chose to return to Vietnam.

On this, my first Christmas in South Vietnam, the radio played Christmas music, courtesy of the armed services radio station. Since the Asian culture was Buddhist, not Christian, there were no colored lights or Christmas trees in town. Cold weather and snow was unheard of in Vietnam.

225

Separated from families and friends on the other side of the planet, no children surrounded us and shared their excitement about Santa Claus or a special Christmas toy. We couldn't shop for Christmas gifts, because there were no real stores nearby. Civilian life seemed a distant memory, even though many of us had been civilian teenagers less than a year earlier. Although we felt light years away from the comforts and traditions of a civilian Christmas, we enjoyed each other's company, and shared Christmas packages of food from home.

The nearby chapel offered a variety of religious services throughout the day. Catholics could go to confession, attend mass, and receive communion. I still felt bitter over the sermon the chaplain had given for Ed Hughes, so I'd stopped attending church services. However, I was truly thankful that I was well and had been spared from falling sick with malaria, dysentery, or Asian Flu, or that I wasn't lying in some hospital bed suffering from another combat wound.

We shared care packages of food from home that usually contained various types of fruitcakes.

I hated fruitcake! In this, I wasn't alone. In fact, many of the dog handlers disliked the taste of fruitcake. We refused to feed it to our dogs, because we thought they'd puke from the taste. Nonetheless, we were grateful to receive it, and there was always someone who'd eat the fruitcakes we received. Our fellow dog handler, Coonrod, would eat about anything. Coonrod was known to swallow large chunks of cooked hog fat just to gross people out.

People back home figured that fruitcake wouldn't spoil on the long and slow journey to South Vietnam. A fellow wouldn't think of writing home to complain about the contents of a care package, not even if it contained fruitcake. Homemade chocolate chip, oatmeal and raisin cookies, and chocolate cakes were our favorites. They arrived in cardboard boxes, wrapped and taped in plastic and tin foil, and packed in popcorn. Those goodies never lasted long, because you couldn't eat one cookie without eating another and another. We even ate the stale popcorn used for packing. Sometimes, the packages took a beating during the long trip. Many times the cookies arrived broken and crumbled, and the cakes were mashed, but they still tasted great. We ate all the crumbs.

Rumor had it that if the United States declared war on North Vietnam, we would all be in Vietnam for the duration. The war could go on for several years, which would've been the biggest of all bummers. I didn't figure I'd last the duration of a full-blown war with North Vietnam. I truly believed that my line of work, walking point and being the first exposed to the enemy, would get me killed sooner or later. It was taboo to allow yourself to think too much about death, so I dwelled on surviving in Vietnam.

I believed the Americans could kick ass and take names all the way to Hanoi, if the Army unchained us from all the war restrictions, and let us take and keep the ground we fought so hard to capture. As it stood, we operated out of base camps, fought the enemy, and returned to base camps, only to go out another day to the same places and do the same things over again. That was like continuously mopping up the water from a leaking pipe, but never fixing the plumbing problem.

A Christmas cease-fire to last a few days into the New Year of 1968 was announced throughout Vietnam. There would be no major offensive, no search-and-destroy operations. They called this *standing down.* However, the defensive perimeter circling the Dau Tieng base camp still had to be manned around the clock. Patrols were scheduled, as a minimum security, to probe right outside the perimeter during the cease-fire period. This was our only insurance against one of Charlie's surprises. No one wanted to get caught with his pants down. Even though the 3rd Brigade's infantry units were standing down, they remained on a one-hour alert status.

All the scout dog teams were in base camp for the week but ready for deployment if needed. Charlie was supposed to honor the holiday cease-fire and we didn't expect him to attack our base camp with mortars, rockets, or snipers, but there was no telling if all of Charlie's units hiding in the jungle had gotten the message or would obey a cease-fire.

The Vietnamese, in general, didn't recognize or honor Christian holidays. For me, the Christmas holiday was just another day off from the war, which was a good thing. Any day I didn't have to expose Clipper and me to the enemy was a good day. I couldn't believe I was only 2½ months away from ending my tour of duty in Vietnam. My rotation month was the

227

middle of March 1968 and my twelve-month stint would soon be over. Soon, I would have accomplished my mission, even though the Army had reneged on my promised assignment when I volunteered to return to this hellhole. I didn't want to think about that broken agreement, because it still upset me.

My hope was that the Army would get me home in time to celebrate my twenty-first birthday on March 16, 1968.

In Vietnam, there was no such thing as a travel agent at headquarters who took advance requests for plane reservations and a window seat. I knew exactly how the Army operated. I was just another number, a man without a face who'd be processed out when my time was up. I had grown used to expecting the hurry-up-and-wait for the unknown routine. I couldn't understand how lifers, career soldiers, dealt with the Army for five, ten, and even fifteen years.

The combat missions, combined with walking, running, jumping, and carrying a loaded backpack, had taken a heavy toll on my right knee. Over the last few months, I'd been feeling more and more discomfort as if my knee was wearing out on me. After a mission, it stayed inflamed, puffy, and red for days. Every now and then, it would lock up, and I'd walk stiff-legged until it unlocked. After the swelling went down, I'd feel okay, but then I'd have to get ready for another mission. I began walking with a noticeable limp, but I wasn't a complainer, slacker, ghost, or skater, when it came to pulling my load.

When I talked to Lt. Fenner about my knee injury, he agreed that I should see a doctor. After an initial medical evaluation at the local field hospital, the news the doctor gave me wasn't good. I had damaged ligaments around the fleshy area of my old bamboo punji stick wound. I also had degenerative arthritis developing in the joint. The doctor told me that this condition could worsen with age.

Age? I thought. *I'm only 20 years old!* I wondered what my knee would be like when I became an old man of thirty.

The doctor said that further aggravation of my knee would cause even more discomfort or permanent damage, and then I'd need another operation to repair the ligaments. For at least a year since my operation, I'd been pounding on this knee hard. I didn't want to go under the knife again. The recuperation period was too long, and I was almost through with my tour. I knew that I had to hang in here for a few more months before I went home.

The doctor at the Dau Tieng field hospital scheduled an appointment for me to see an orthopedic specialist in Cu Chi, the home of the 25th Infantry Division. The 3rd Brigade in Dau Tieng was a subordinate command of the 25th Infantry Division. The medical facilities at Cu Chi were more permanent and better-staffed than the small field hospital in dusty old Dau Tieng.

In the middle of January 1968, I flew in a supply chopper to visit an orthopedic specialist in Cu Chi. I expected to be gone from Clipper for only a few days.

Boy, was I wrong!

When I met with the doctor, I underwent another complete medical examination, including a blood work-up. The doctor told me that he was going to put a cast on my leg to immobilize it for one month. He asked me how much time I had left in Vietnam. I told him that I was scheduled to rotate back to the States in two months. Based on the condition of my knee, he said that I wouldn't be leaving Cu Chi. He placed me under medical observation and care in the Cu Chi hospital for my remaining time in Vietnam.

I thought that this news was fine and dandy, but I really needed to get back to Dau Tieng to collect my personal effects and see Clipper. I'd always been bothered by this kind of quick decision-making that was so typical in the Army.

The hospital issued me a temporary physical profile, signed by the doctor who performed the examination. It stipulated that I was to do no more strenuous physical activity. I was restricted from running, jumping crawling, prolonged standing, or marching. The term of the temporary physical profile was three months, which would carry past my rotation date in March. I had to carry the document in my pocket at all times. It was my special-duty pass.

Not having to hump the boonies anymore was great, but I really missed

Clipper. My only comfort was that I knew my hooch buddy, Dan Scott would take good care of Clipper while I was gone.

The doctor told me that he was obligated to properly look after and ensure my health and welfare. My knee would get better only if I quit abusing it. In his eyes, I was "just a kid," and he told me so. I decided to educate the doctor on my idea of a man.

I said, "I resent being called a kid or a boy. If I'm old enough to fight a war and spill blood for my country, I'm old enough to be called a man."

The graying old guy smiled and told me that he had boys my age, but they were in school. I told him that his sons would probably be drafted for Vietnam duty, if the war continued. I had the impression that the doctor was trying to give me the gift of a valid medical reason for staying out of a combat unit. I decided not to push the "man" point with him. My health was important to me, too. I may have been a little crazy in the head to return to Vietnam for more punishment, but I sure as hell wasn't so stupid as to pass up an opportunity not to get shot at anymore.

Because I never discussed with a military doctor how he felt about war, I'd been forming my opinions about doctors' attitudes by observing them. I remembered the kindness of Dr. George Bogumill, the physician in Japan who had performed surgery on my knee. I concluded that doctors were truly a breed apart from the military infantry world, where I lived and breathed. They weren't motivated by war like a field commander in constant need of warm, fresh, and healthy bodies to fight the enemy. Field commanders expected a certain amount of casualties and considered infantrymen replaceable. I'd experienced that scenario many times over during my short time in the service. Doctors, on the other hand, had more caring and sensitive natures. They didn't see or experience the battle, they dealt with the aftermath. They helped mend the bloody young bodies toted in on stretchers fresh from the battlefield. Sadly, many times a doctor and his medical staff weren't able to save these young lives.

Because it meant having to watch my fellow soldiers' suffering, I didn't like being in a field hospital. When I milled around the tents of the Cu Chi hospital, I saw naked men sitting inside ice-filled metal bathtubs on dirt floors. These men were burning up with fever caused by malaria. I was glad I'd taken my malaria pills regularly. I'd heard that some of those men would die if the doctors couldn't break their fevers in time. What a way to go out of this lousy war—shaking all over, high temperature, sitting in ice water, and then dying. It was so easy for me to sense the pain those young guys must have been going through. We could only watch, wait, and hope.

For me, though, the most depressing aspect of being a patient in the hospital at Cu Chi was that I wouldn't get a chance to say good-bye to Clipper or my dog handler friends. Everything was more complicated, now that I was in a different base camp. Because of the distance between base camps, communication had to be done by some kind of operator patching system. I felt a little uncomfortable going into some unit's headquarters and asking if I could make a long distance call to check on my dog. I felt helpless to do anything out of the ordinary, since I was a stranger in these surroundings. The hospital personnel clerk told me that he'd contact the 44th IPSD and forward the paperwork authorizing my reassignment to the hospital.

The doctor decided not to cover my leg in a cast. Instead, he wrapped it in a large flexible bandage. He told me not to overdue physical activity. I was to see him for checkups every few days until the swelling went down. If my knee continued to swell with fluid, it would have to be drained with a syringe. I've hated needles ever since a doctor back in Littleton, Colorado stuck one in my left ear to drain fluid.

My ear had frequently puffed up with fluid during my glory days as a high school wrestler—a result of my not wearing protective headgear. After a few times having my ear drained with a needle, the doctor had decided to lance it with a scalpel and squeeze the fluid out. That little procedure had hurt like hell. After the scalpel visit, I never went back. Over time, the fluid had hardened. My left ear became deformed, but it didn't hurt anymore. Wrestlers called this condition *cauliflower ear.*

I was assigned to living quarters at Headquarters Company, 25th Supply and Transportation Battalion (S&T). I reported to First Sergeant Milanoski. When he noticed the CIB and Jump Wings sewn above my left breast pocket, he smiled and said, "Welcome, Sergeant Burnam!" (Oh yes, I'd finally been promoted to Sergeant, E5 in December 1967. My scout dog platoon sergeant, *Sergeant D,* had pinned my stripes on me in the K-9 club.) Rear echelon guys couldn't earn a CIB unless they were in the infantry, but they respected anyone who wore it.

I'd been promoted a few weeks after Private First Class Ed Hughes had been killed in action. The timing of the promotion and celebration was poor, but to ease the memories of Ed, I had a few beers with my fellow dog handlers. However, my promotion hadn't been the result of *blood stripes*—when a sergeant gets killed in battle and his stripes are given to the next person in line for a promotion. I wore my new three-stripe chevrons on my sleeve with pride. I felt pretty cool and cocky to be a sergeant—equivalent to a squad leader in rank and authority—especially when I was addressed as *Sarge.*

The first sergeant at my new base camp, Top, was trim, short, and about the same build and height as me. He sported a typical military haircut with his head covered in a clean military OD baseball hat. He wore properly fitting and pressed jungle fatigues and brush-shined jungle boots. He was the perfect example of a professional career soldier or Lifer. I liked him, and he seemed to like me, too.

Since I was a sergeant, Top assigned me to the non-commissioned officers' (NCO) quarters. No one below the rank of sergeant was allowed to live there. NCOs were separated from the lower enlisted men and not allowed to fraternize. I violated the hell out of that military rule of protocol. My new NCO quarters were nothing more than an army green canvas tent with no special accouterments. I had better quarters in Dau Tieng.

After I settled into my new digs, a runner came by to tell me to report to First Sergeant Milanowski. I hustled my butt over to Top's office in the head shed—the headquarters building. Top informed me that I had been assigned to work at the Post Exchange. I was to report to Sergeant Major Kelly. With a smile, Top told me that it was the best job he could find for me, and I believed him. I thanked Top and headed out in search of SGM Kelly. High ranking soldiers always made me nervous.

The PX was about a mile away from the 25th S&T. I walked along the dirt road, which wound its way around the entire inside perimeter of Cu Chi. My knee was wrapped tightly and I limped a little, but at least I no longer had to carry a sixty-pound pack and rifle.

SGM (E-9) was the highest enlisted rank in the army. I'd never served under a SGM before. I found SGM Kelly's office behind the PX and saw him through the screen door. He was seated in a chair at a desk with his back to the door. I knocked lightly on the wooden screen door. Without looking, he told me to enter. I walked in, removed my head gear, stood at attention, and announced myself: "Sergeant Burnam reporting as directed, Sergeant Major!"

The SGM faced me by swiveling his chair around. "Do you have any experience working in a store, Buck Sergeant?" he asked. (Buck Sergeant was a common nickname of a three-striper.)

"No, Sergeant Major!"

"Well, you'll learn."

He told me to stand at ease and tell him about myself. I recognized the SGM had a Combat Infantry Badge with two stars connecting the top of the wreath, which meant that he'd been awarded the CIB three times—in W.W.II, Korea, and Vietnam. He looked old and wrinkled around his eyes and cheeks, and obviously well-traveled in this man's Army. *One war is enough for me,* I thought. I couldn't imagine serving in three wars as an infantryman. That old soldier must have been triple crazy, but he deserved my ultimate respect. I wasn't about to ask him how he ended up as the SGM for the PX. SGM Kelly assigned me to new quarters near the PX. He told me that when he needed me he didn't like waiting.

My new accommodations were in a wooden building with a wooden floor. I had a metal bunk bed with a mosquito net rigged above it. The hooch was equipped with a refrigerator stocked with food, soft drinks, and beer. It had tables, floor lamps, chairs, and a small bookshelf stocked with paperbacks. This was the nicest place I'd lived since entering the Army!

By this time, I'd been in Cu Chi for two weeks. When I asked the SGM for a chance to visit Clipper in Dau Tieng, he denied my request. Officially, I was no longer a scout dog handler assigned to the 44th IPSD. The SGM told me that I hadn't worked long enough to earn time off, but he promised me a convoy trip or chopper ride to Dau Tieng before I left Vietnam in March.

I'd heard Army promises before, though, so I wasn't sure if this one would be kept. I hoped it would be. I sure did miss Clipper and my buddies.

My new job was to drive a tractor and trailer rig to the infantry units throughout the base camp's inside perimeter. My fully enclosed trailer was stocked with assorted sundries such as candy, peanuts, canned finger-food, canned soda, beer, writing utensils, cigarettes, and Zippo cigarette lighters. The truck was really a mobile store and a morale-booster for the troops.

What a job! I thought. *To have all the food and drink I could handle.*

When I pulled up to an infantry company area and opened the doors for business, I had no problem selling the stocked items and collecting money. I had to turn in all the money to SGM Kelly at the end of the day. He didn't require an inventory of stock. He left that up to me. My job was to keep the truck re-supplied. Needless to say, it was tempting to take whatever and as much as I wanted. If I got caught stealing, however, I'd probably end up in LBJ (Long Bin Jail). I wasn't about to mess up this job for some petty theft rap, especially with only a month-and-a-half left to serve in Vietnam. I knew that I could do this PX job standing on my head. Any infantryman would have loved to trade places with me.

When I parked the rig within the compound of an infantry company, it was like the Good Humor Man had arrived. After opening the large metal door and lowering the stairs for business, a line would quickly form to come aboard. I'd position myself at the small cash register near the entrance, which also served as the exit. Due to the cramped space inside, I could only let in a handful of soldiers at a time. As the troops entered, their eyes would light up when they saw the rows of metal baskets filled with packaged candy, canned food, and drinks.

Infantrymen were very special to me, and I knew how hard they worked in South Vietnam. I'd always smile and welcome each of them as they entered the store. I liked to make up my own rules for them. When I serviced an infantry unit smelling of fresh muck from the field, I'd yell, "It's a two-for-one sale today, men!" They'd smile and go crazy, buying all they could carry.

I knew that some of those young guys would never make it home to their families alive or in good health. Many of them looked as greenhorn as I did when I first got to Vietnam two years earlier. The officers and non-commissioned officers would always be the last group to climb aboard to buy goodies. I'd see a bunch of different units each day, seven days a week. Although sometimes I'd have a day off, I liked staying busy, because it helped me to keep my mind away from missing Clipper and my friends in the 44th IPSD.

I couldn't believe my time in Vietnam would be coming to an end. However, one month and a half seemed like an eternity, and anything could happen before I went home. I certainly didn't want to become a casualty during my last month. If I dwelled on these thoughts, I knew each day would take forever to go by. I tried not to worry about things I had no control over. I had to remain positive and do my job. I knew that there'd be plenty of time to reflect on my experiences after I left and was safely back in the United States.

A soldier with thirty days or less to serve was called a *short-timer*. Some field commanders did their best to keep short-timers out of harm's way. Some guys still humped the boonies, getting killed or wounded weeks or days before they were scheduled to leave Vietnam. The goal of an infantry short-timer was to become an REMF (Rear-Echelon-Mother-Fucker). This was the nickname for guys who stayed in base camp and never went into the jungle to hunt Charlie. Some examples of REMFs were truck drivers, supply clerks, vehicle mechanics, hospital technicians, personnel and finance clerks, cooks, and engineers. They manned the base camp perimeter when the infantry was out looking for a fight. After an infantryman became a short-timer, he started hunting for a job as a REMF to justify staying away from combat until he left Vietnam.

It was also tradition, once a guy reached short-timer status, to carry around a short-timer-stick. Some short-timers carved fancy sticks from tree branches and notched them to show how many days they had left in Vietnam. As each day went by, they cut the stick off a notch until only a stub was left. A short-timer also marked a big X on his calendar as each day passed. Many of them spent much of their free time writing letters and sending stuff home.

You'd be surprised at some of the things short-timers tried to mail home. I thought their attempts at mailing keepsakes of their time in Vietnam were more funny than shocking. For example, there was the story of a soldier who sent home an M60 machine gun. He broke it down into little pieces and mailed each piece in a separate package. The recipient wrote back to report what had arrived and what didn't. The operation took several months, but the man was finally successful. The military postal system had so many packages coming in and out of Vietnam, that it was impossible to check each one for illegal contents. Weapons were reported lost or stolen all the time. The military police investigated, and the unit reporting the loss had to complete a lengthy Report of Survey. Sometimes, the weapons were recovered but many times they weren't.

Some short-timers became superstitious. They acted weird and would only do things they believed wouldn't put them in danger. They'd avoid walking too close to the perimeter, for fear of getting shot by a sniper. If they walked around base camp with several other men, they'd refuse to take the lead or bring up the rear. They ate with their backs to the wall, so they could keep an eye on everything. Some wore a flack vest every day while they were in base camp. Others had been known to live and sleep inside a bunker during the last thirty days. The list goes on and on.

One short-timer told me, "I'm so short and bold that I can look a fire ant in the eye and still kick his ass!"

No one wanted to hang around short-timers, especially an FNG (Fucking New Guy) who had twelve months ahead of him to serve. It was tough enough for the veterans to have to listen to short-timer bullshit.

I hoped that I wouldn't develop any superstitions when I had only thirty days left to serve in Vietnam. I believed that if it was my time to meet my Maker, nothing on earth was going to save me. Period.

I also knew this fact to be true: Somehow, I had to find a way to see Clipper and my fellow scout dog handlers before I left Vietnam.

Chapter 18

The Tet Offensive

On January 31, 1968, the Chinese Lunar New Year, the North Vietnamese Army launched an all-out attack on Saigon's military district, the U.S. Embassy, and almost every military fire base throughout South Vietnam, including Cu Chi, Tay Ninh, and Dau Tieng. The history books called this massive attack, "The Tet Offensive," because Tet is the name for the Chinese Lunar New Year celebration. We had a truce in place at the time and the enemy violated it by attacking. The enemy thought they could win a major victory in the process. With my departure approaching in March, the Tet Offensive couldn't have come at a worse time.

Fucking Charlie! I thought. *Why can't he wait until after March to do this, when I'm safe at home?*

Early on the morning of the Tet Offensive, I heard mortar rounds and rockets exploding. My hooch and the PX were deep inside the perimeter, but the mortars and rockets were exploding nearby.

I jumped out of my bunk, grabbed an M16 and a bandoleer of magazines, and headed outside for the bunker. I'd never heard so many explosions all at once. Enemy B-40 rockets whistled through the air past the bunker. I began to realize that this storm was shaping up to be much more intense than the mortar attack on our kennel back in November. The only thing any of us could do was to stay inside and look for VC who might breach the base camp's perimeter of defense.

Minutes went by, and all I heard was explosion after explosion outside the bunker. From what we could see through the portholes, it looked as if stacked sandbags, around the bunker and hooches, were absorbing shrapnel. At one point, a huge explosion rocked the walls and shook dust from the sandbags. My ears were ringing from the loud sounds.

We had no radio inside the bunker, so we couldn't contact anyone to get a status report. Machine gun and artillery fired in the distance. I assumed that the perimeter must be under heavy attack. Several men in the bunker were scared shitless at being there without their weapons. They sat on the dirt floor, curled up against the sandbagged walls, and covered their bare heads with their hands. I guessed they'd never had the war this close to them. They looked and acted like REMFs and FNGs.

Thank goodness, we were far enough away from the action going on around the perimeter. Cu Chi contained countless numbers of men and women. I thought of the helpless hospital patients and hoped they'd be okay.

A nearby ammunition dump took a direct hit, and there was no way to put out the fire. As each wooden crate of ammunition, rockets, artillery, and grenades exploded, it set off another crate until the entire stockpile of munitions went up in smoke. The Army's own rockets and artillery rounds whistled through the air and exploded. Several ammunition dumps were strategically located throughout the division's base camp. They'd definitely be on Charlie's list of critical targets to destroy. Some bunkers held strategic and tactical communication systems, so Charlie would have a hard time taking out those targets using only rockets and mortars.

The ammunition dump finally burned out, but we could hear sporadic small-arms fire in the distance. It was late in the afternoon before I came out of the bunker to check the damage to my hooch. I hadn't fired one round from my M16. None of the nearby hooches were destroyed by shrapnel, and damage inside them was minimal. My personal items were unharmed.

That night, the sky lit brightly with flares carried by small parachutes that slowly descended to the ground. An artillery battery launched flares into the air with howitzers to light up the perimeter, allowing the men in the bunkers to better see their targets. The flares also made Charlie visible, so he couldn't amass a sneak attack at night.

In the morning, the base camp buzzed with activity. I reported to work as usual. The PX and surrounding buildings had sustained minor damage. A few days after the all-out attack on our base camp, SGM Kelly summoned me. He told me that General William Westmoreland, Commanding General of the Vietnam Armed Forces was scheduled to give a speech over the armed forces radio. It was to be broadcast for all the troops stationed throughout South Vietnam.

General Westmoreland's speech was long and motivational. He said that the Tet Offensive, with an estimated 70,000 enemy troops involved in the attacks, had been a major military defeat for the Viet Cong and the North Vietnamese Army. They'd been repelled overwhelmingly. The American embassy had been secured, and law and order was restored on the streets of Saigon. Many military base camps throughout Vietnam had been attacked simultaneously, but none were in the hands of the enemy. American casualties were reported as minimal, but the VC and NVA had suffered thousands of dead and wounded. General Westmoreland called the Tet Offensive a great victory for South Vietnam and the American and allied forces. I waited for the general to say that all orders to leave Vietnam for the States were canceled, but he didn't and I breathed a sigh of relief.

I could think only of Dau Tieng and wondered how Clipper and the rest of my pals were getting along. Getting news from there was especially difficult now. I went to see SGM Kelly and pleaded with him to find out what was going on in Dau Tieng. SGM Kelly put me in contact with a SGM buddy of his who worked at Division operations. I found the SGM and he took me to the communications shed—a heavily fortified bunker with a bunch of antennas sticking out of it. The shed buzzed with radio communication. The SGM got on a radio and patched me through to the 44th Scout Dog Platoon's landline.

Through some static, I could hear Sergeant Barnett on the other end of the handset. He told me that everything was okay: there had been no dog or handler casualties. I felt relieved. The VC had hit Dau Tieng hard but didn't realize that most of the infantry units were in base camp at the time of the attack. They'd easily driven back Charlie, and he hadn't penetrated the camp. He told me that all the original dog handlers and Lieutenant Fenner had rotated back to the States already, but he extended for six months.

Sergeant Barnett asked how my knee was doing. He explained that most of the dog teams were out on patrol supporting Tet counteroffensive operations. He told me that Clipper had not been assigned to another handler and assured me that he was my dog until I left Vietnam. He told me that Dan Scott was taking good care of Clipper for me. Sergeant Barnett asked if I was going to get a chance to come back to Dau Tieng before I rotated to the States in March. I told him I was trying all the time, and not to give up on my return. That was the end of the transmission.

By the middle of February 1968, the 25th Infantry Division was continuing Tet offensive counter-operations throughout Cu Chi's surrounding base camp.

One day, I was ordered to report to Sergeant Major Kelly. I thought he would be giving me a butt-chewing and I didn't know why. Instead, the SGM told me that with all the hell going on with the Tet Offensive, he needed experienced combat infantryman to ride shotgun on his re-supply convoy to Saigon. He'd requested support from the infantry units, but they told him to go blow. They couldn't spare infantry troops for that kind of task. They'd told him to use REMF's for the job—cooks, mechanics, supply clerks, and administrative personnel. Considering the circumstances, SGM Kelly was uncomfortable with this idea. In the past, he'd always had infantry troop support. Several infantry combat veterans were already assigned to PX jobs, but they were all recovering wounded short-timers.

SGM Kelly said that he needed a good sergeant like me, who had combat experience, to be his convoy master. My job would be to honcho an empty convoy into Saigon and Bien Hoa to pick up supplies for the division. If I accepted the mission, SMG Kelly promised that when I returned, he'd make sure I got a chopper ride to Dau Tieng to see my dog.

Those were exactly the words I wanted to hear. Without hesitation, I volunteered. To be able to see my dog again outweighed the risks of that mission. I had a good feeling that the SGM wouldn't fuck me on this deal, so I trusted him.

What I missed most about Clipper was his loving companionship. I wanted to roll around in the dirt with him one more time, I longed to have him sit next to me and lean against my leg when he was tired. I wanted to watch him get excited to hear me call his name. I missed the simple pleasure of having Clipper with me all the time. It was tormenting not to be able to see my dog.

After I told him my decision, SGM Kelly leaned close to my face, looked me in the eye, smiled, and told me that I'd separated myself from all the boys in Vietnam. I figured that was a compliment from a man who'd earned three Combat Infantry Badges. To me, the incentives outweighed the risk of a trip outside base camp. I didn't have to walk, so I wouldn't be violating my medical profile restrictions, but I decided that I'd better not tell my doctor about the mission. He might find a way to keep me from going and ruin my chance for a trip to see Clipper and my other K-9 brothers.

My orders were to leave at first light. The convoy would be fueled with engines running and waiting at the staging area on the roadside near the PX. That night, I had as visitors some new pals I'd met —Freddie and a soldier I'll call Red. Both worked in the PX for SGM Kelly. Red was supposed to ride shotgun in one of the convoy's trucks. I soon learned that Red also had another reason for wanting to go to Saigon. He said that he needed to see his Vietnamese dentist about a tooth problem.

I liked Red and Freddie, but Freddie wasn't scheduled to ride shotgun, so he stayed behind. The trip was designed to be a three-day mission. One day to get there, one day to load up, and one day to get back. After a long bullshit session with those guys, I turned in for the evening.

The next morning, I rode in a jeep at the head of the convoy. We were escorted by Military Police who rode in several fully equipped jeeps. If we needed them, gunships, artillery, and infantry troops were within immediate striking distance of us. My jeep was equipped with a driver, a mounted M60 machine gun, several thousand rounds of ammunition, a machine gunner, two radios, and a radio operator who could communicate with SGM Kelly, and call for air-strikes if needed. I was responsible for coordinating all tactical decisions with the experienced convoy escort MPs who were in charge. I felt more comfortable knowing that I'd be working with military police who had worked outside the perimeter of a base camp. I considered them to be as highly respectable and capable as infantrymen.

SGM Kelly issued me the SOI (Signal Operating Instructions)—a tiny booklet with "Secret" printed on each page. The SOI contained all the call signs and frequencies to get military support. The SOI was attached to a chain I wore inside my shirt. I was responsible for this highly classified military document, and if I was in imminent danger of being captured by the enemy, destroying this book would become my highest priority.

The day long convoy trip to Saigon took us on a road that went through the middle of the fiercest fighting in our war zone. Cu Chi was near Hobo Woods, where the Viet Cong were heavily concentrated. Because they fought like hell to keep Hobo Woods, many Americans and some 38th IPSD scout dog teams had lost their lives in that dreadful place.

The road from Cu Chi to Saigon was damaged but clear. The distance between the two places was about seventy miles east on a narrow road called Highway 13. Infantry foot soldiers and mechanized and armored tank squadrons had secured the most dangerous sections of the road. Highway 13 was a vital link to our supply lines and had to stay open during all daylight hours. For obvious reasons, no convoys traveled outside base camp at night.

By the time the convoy of flatbed trailers attached to diesel tractors was assembled and prepared to leave, I was also ready to go. I didn't have enough time to check over everything carefully, so I relied on the drivers to ensure their vehicles were serviceable enough to make the three-day journey. But, what the hell, I've learned to live without ever having enough time.

I put my M16 and backpack in the back of the jeep. Each truck had one man riding shotgun inside a canvas-covered cab. I walked down the line of ten or so flatbed trucks. Motors ran, and smokestacks filled the air with the stinking smell of diesel fuel. One MP jeep rode ahead of me and another one brought up the rear. I sat in the second vehicle behind the lead jeep. Since we didn't know what kind of road conditions we'd meet, we planned to keep the column moving together tightly.

Everybody was ready. I sat in the jeep waiting for the MPs to signal and start rolling. The machine-gunner handed me a set of goggles and said that I'd need them to keep the dust out of my eyes. Red rode shotgun in the first truck behind my jeep.

My radio squawked with chatters of call signs for radio checks. After we were assured that everyone was on the net and right frequency, it was time to go. One-by-one, we rolled out of the gate and into no-man's land.

I remembered that President Roosevelt once said, "We have nothing to fear, but fear itself." I was feeling fear at first, but my stomach soon settled down as we continued on the slow and bumpy ride.

Several miles into the trip, I saw a few burned-out military trucks tipped over on the roadside. They'd apparently been pushed there by bulldozers. Helicopters followed overhead and infantry troops were positioned alongside us near the tree lines.

It looked as if the Americans had broken Charlie's back when he'd tried his all-out attack a few weeks earlier. I figured that he was probably licking his wounds and regrouping, so this was good timing to run a convoy. So far, I felt okay about this mission.

About twenty miles into the trip and several hours later the convoy still hadn't been attacked. We were going at a snail's pace but making steady progress. We needed to get into Saigon before dark. We passed another tank and several wheeled vehicles that had been burned out and were rusting on the roadsides.

Every bridge we needed to use had been damaged, but the engineers had made paths around them where we could cross. About fifteen miles from Saigon, not a shot had been fired at the convoy and all of our trucks were accounted for. During some stretches, the jungle was thick and close to the road. If Charlie was going to hit the convoy, that was where we'd be the most vulnerable. Maybe Charlie had already seen us and decided not to attack, because he saw that the convoy was empty. Or maybe, this was our lucky day.

Sections of the road were dry and dusty. The goggles came in handy as dust caked around my face. It was a long hot ride, but I still had plenty of water and snack food. The radios stayed on, but remained silent, except for the sounds of occasional situation reports.

At last, the convoy was closing in on the outskirts of Saigon and heading for a secure staging area within the Cholon District. In Cholon, we were scheduled to park in a fenced and guarded compound and spend the night in a hotel across the street. The next morning the convoy was to roll from the city of Saigon and into the Ben Hoa beer-and-soda yard.

As we entered Saigon's Cholon district, I could see signs of recent fighting. Direct hits from tank and artillery rounds had made gaping holes in some of the buildings, and war debris littered the roadsides. Several civilian cars were burned and overturned on the shoulders of the road we traveled. Very few pedestrians walked the streets. Martial law had been declared, and roadblocks were set up all over the place. The MP jeep ahead of mine was doing a good job leading the way. So far, we'd kept all the trucks intact and didn't have to stop along the way for emergencies or maintenance problems.

At about six o'clock in the evening, the convoy reached a large parking lot surrounded by a ten-foot triple barbed wire fence. South Vietnamese Army troops, wearing burgundy berets, opened the fenced gate to let us pass though. All of the trucks and jeeps fit inside with plenty of room to spare. The South Vietnamese military would handle the vehicles' security, and our hotel expense had already been paid. We only had to check in and get a room for the night.

Many of the troops left their vehicles carrying their gear and weapons, and headed for the hotel. I wanted one of those burgundy berets as a souvenir, so I approached a Vietnamese guard and offered a trade. He couldn't speak English, so I took a dollar out of my pocket and used hand gestures to bargain for his beret. The soldier smiled, took the money and gave me his beret. I didn't realize it would be that easy. I was prepared to give more if he demanded.

I put the beret away and Red and I walked to the hotel, carrying our M16s, bandoleers of fully loaded magazines, lightly packed backpacks, and .45 caliber pistols. The trucks were under the security and protection of the Vietnamese Army.

The hotel Mama San greeted us and assigned us to rooms. She recognized my stripes and offered me a special room. The hotel was about three stories high and wasn't fancy by any stretch of the imagination. My room had only a single metal frame bed and a beat-up dresser with a small dirty mirror. I had a window view of the vehicles that were parked across the street. When I looked outside, I noticed that a few Vietnamese troops guarded our vehicles and patrolled the street. Curfew was in effect for everyone except the military.

Later that night, Red came to my room to talk. I knew from previous conversations with him that he spoke excellent Vietnamese and had served as interpreter, working for military intelligence in Saigon, before being transferred to Cu Chi several months earlier. Red had less than thirty days before he'd be going home. When he became a short-timer, he'd talked his way into a rear area job in the PX, which was where we met.

Red told me he'd broken a tooth two days earlier, and it was getting infected. After he'd heard about the convoy run to Saigon, he'd volunteered to ride shotgun because he refused to see a military doctor or dentist. Instead, he insisted on seeing his Vietnamese dentist in Saigon.

Because he could speak Vietnamese and had been well-established in Saigon before coming to Cu Chi, he had a lot of friends there. He didn't have approval from any military medical personnel to see a dentist in Saigon. I could see that Red was using the excuse that he didn't want to see an American dentist, so he could see a Saigon dentist that he preferred.

Red told me so many stories about Saigon, that I trusted him to know how to get around the city. I reminded him that we were restricted to the hotel for the night, but Red insisted on going to see his dentist. I told him that he knew the city was under martial law and he was out of his fucking mind to leave the hotel's safety.

Red argued that there was nothing to worry about. He said his dentist worked only a few blocks from the hotel. I told Red that he had to stay put in this shitty little hotel, because it was going to be my ass in trouble if I lost a man due to my own negligence.

Red said that he had to at least get some painkillers. He said he'd be back before I could miss him. With those words, Red left my room and headed downstairs to the hotel lobby. After he left, I paced back and forth for a few seconds.

Ah, shit, I thought. *I can't let him go by himself and I can't keep his ass here, either. He's a fucking bone-head.*

I quickly grabbed my rifle and bandoleer of ammunition, and followed after Red. I caught him on the street as he was about to climb into a black-covered rickshaw being pulled by a horse.

"Red!" I yelled.

Red turned around and broke into an ear-to-ear grin. He waved and told me to hurry. I caught up with him and climbed into the rickshaw driven by a smiling Vietnamese man. Red spoke in Vietnamese as he gave the driver directions to the dentist's office. I looked at him, shook my head, and told him that I couldn't let him go alone. So off we went like a couple of war-zone tourists.

The driver headed toward the first Vietnamese-manned roadblock where soldiers stood, holding machine guns. When we arrived at the roadblock, Red spoke Vietnamese to the guards who immediately smiled and let us pass by.

"Shit, your dentist isn't just down the street from our hotel, is he, Red? Do you know where you're fucking going?"

"Sure, I do. We're almost there," he assured me with a big grin.

We turned down some side streets that had no pedestrians on them. Eventually, we pulled over and stopped in front of a row of small buildings. Several Vietnamese citizens walked around on these streets, and I noticed that there were no military personnel in sight.

I checked my watch and saw that it was a little after seven o'clock. I advised Red that if his dentist wasn't there, we were going back to the hotel before it got dark. Red said nothing as he stepped out of the rickshaw, walked to the entrance of a building, and knocked on the door. A Vietnamese woman opened it, smiled, and greeted Red as if he'd been a long-lost friend. They talked in Vietnamese and laughed, when Red showed her his tooth.

I was getting nervous, sitting outside in the rickshaw. Red finally came back to tell me that his doctor had left, but would be back at six o'clock in the morning. He also said that we had plenty of time for him to get his tooth fixed and get back to lead the convoy by nine o'clock the next morning.

"Trust me," Red said. "The beer-and-soda yard at Ben Hoa is less than an hour away."

"Why did I let myself get into this shit?" I asked myself.

Red told me that this building was a hotel and a dentist office. After I climbed out of the rickshaw, the well-dressed Vietnamese woman greeted me with a smile. She spoke broken English as she bowed and motioned for me to come inside. I didn't smile back, but gave Red a dirty look. I told him to call our hotel to let a member of our convoy team know where we were and when we'd be back. Red made the call, using the Vietnamese woman's phone, and spoke in Vietnamese to someone back at our hotel.

After the phone call, he looked at me and said, "John, we're set, and they expect us back by nine o'clock tomorrow morning. Hey, buddy, I'll take care of you. Isn't this a nicer place to sleep than that rat hole we were in?"

"Uh huh, this is great," I agreed. "But we're only two people here and I feel safer being in numbers, especially American numbers."

Red was right about one thing, though. The inside of this hotel was upscale compared to where we'd been assigned to spend the night. Aside from the Vietnamese woman and her family, no one else was staying in the hotel. I thought that seemed to be a little too strange. Also, the dentist's office was locked. I wondered how Red would get the painkillers he said he needed, unless he planned to break into it.

The Vietnamese woman asked if we were hungry. She said that the recent fighting in the streets had chased away her customers. She gave us a bowl of steamed rice with chunks of egg and meat mixed in it.

"Hey, Red, this is pretty good," I said. "It's the first hot meal we've had. The meat tastes a little like beef. Ask her what kind it is."

Red looked at me and said, "It's dog! That's a delicacy within the Vietnamese culture."

I spit out a mouthful on the table.

"I can't eat this shit if it's dog! Why the hell didn't you tell me that before I ate it? You know I'm a dog handler for chrissake! What the fuck is wrong with you, Red?"

Red smiled and said, "I think it tastes great!"

After we ate, Red decided that he wanted to visit a female friend he used to stay with when he lived in Saigon. He told me that she was a beautiful

Vietnamese/French girl with round eyes. I opposed leaving the hotel, especially to see a woman. Red was really pressing his luck with me.

Before I knew it, a small black car pulled up in front of the hotel. Red already had a plan he was putting into action. He told me to bring my weapons and get into the car to take a short ride. He promised that we'd be back in a half-hour. We were going to pick up the woman.

It was late and dark outside. I wasn't excited about going for a car ride that time of night. Red, on the other hand, was totally calm and relaxed, as if there was no martial law or war going on in Vietnam. When he walked to the car, I couldn't see myself staying behind, so I followed. Splitting up now would be an even worse idea.

I didn't like it that Red had placed me in a totally reactionary mode since we'd arrived in Saigon. He was driving me nuts with his complete disregard for all the danger signs around us. Although we hadn't heard any shooting since we came to Saigon, we had no way of knowing what could happen.

We sat in the back seat of the little black car, and Red spoke Vietnamese to the driver and off we went. The driver headed down a dark and quiet side road several blocks from the hotel/dentist office. Then the driver turned left onto another side street which looked more like an alleyway. Red began to look nervous. He spoke to the driver in a louder than normal tone. The driver turned his lights off and kept driving slowly down the alleyway while he talked to Red. Up ahead, several figures suddenly appeared out of the darkness. They slowly approached the car. It looked as if they were armed with rifles. Red quickly jumped into the front seat of the car. He pointed his .45 caliber pistol at the driver's temple. He was talking fast in Vietnamese. The car's tires screeched to a sudden stop.

The armed figures in dark clothes continued to walk in our direction with their weapons at the ready. From a distance, I could see that they didn't look friendly. I chambered a round into my M16, moved to the window, and quickly rolled it down. I stuck the barrel out and awkwardly pointed it in the direction of the approaching figures. Red screamed in Vietnamese at the driver.

All of a sudden, Red's pistol went off. I flinched and ducked. My ears were ringing like crazy. I looked up quickly to see what had happened. Red hadn't hit the driver, but had fired and blew out the driver's side window.

The driver threw his car into reverse and put his lights back on. The men started firing on us. Several bullets hit the front of the car. I awkwardly fired my M16 in the direction of the men who were shooting at us. Because the car was bouncing; my aim was terrible, but I squeezed off one round after another.

Finally, we were out of the alleyway. The car screeched on the pavement as the driver spun the steering wheel to straighten it out. Through this entire time, Red was still pointing the barrel of the .45 caliber pistol at the driver's temple.

The car sped down the street. It made another turn onto a different road. I was totally lost and didn't know where we were. My adrenaline was up. My heart pumped hard inside my chest. I was relieved to see that we weren't being chased or fired at anymore.

Red's face was dripping in sweat and his eyes bulged out of their sockets. He looked like an enraged madman. He kept talking to the driver who answered him with terror in his voice. To my surprise, the driver stopped the car suddenly.

I was scared. All I could think of was that we needed to get out of there. The city of Saigon at night was an unfamiliar battleground for me. I knew we weren't safe and wondered if we could survive on these streets. We had to make it back to that hotel quickly. The Tet Offensive had brought the war to every nook and cranny throughout Vietnam. We weren't safe anywhere.

Then I heard Red shout, "John! Get the fuck out!"

I didn't hesitate or ask any questions. Once I was outside the car, I nervously looked up and down the street, but saw only darkness and no sign of activity. Red scooted over to the door. I pointed my weapon through the windshield to cover the driver. The driver froze with both hands on the steering wheel. I was afraid Red would shoot the driver as he frantically shouted in Vietnamese. Then he came flying out of the car door. He told me to follow him and not to look back.

My heart pounded fast. I followed Red. He turned the corner and ran across the street. To my amazement, we were only a block away from the hotel. The streets were bare and totally dark. I ran behind Red until I almost knocked him over. He suddenly stopped, turned, and banged a clenched fist on the hotel door, which opened to let us inside. By this time, we were al-most completely out of breath. Red reached into his pocket and pulled out some keys. He said he took them so the driver couldn't run us down.

The nicely dressed Vietnamese woman who managed the hotel, looked bewildered as she and Red chattered in Vietnamese. After they finished talking, Red told me the woman wouldn't be letting anyone else come into the hotel that evening. I knew that she'd said more. He wasn't telling me the whole story. Since it was late in the evening, I didn't feel like asking any more questions.

One thing was for certain. My right knee was killing me. I hoped that it wouldn't swell up after I rested it. I didn't want to have to see the doctor when I got back to base camp with my knee in this bad of condition. All I needed was for the doctor to tell me that he was putting a cast on my knee, or worse, scheduling me for surgery.

We locked the door, barricaded ourselves inside the room, and took turns pulling guard duty until the sun came up. Throughout the night, I heard vehicle noises and voices on the street outside the hotel. I was sweat-ing that someone may have spotted us and knew where we were. I was scared to death and felt trapped.

Neither Red nor I caught a wink of sleep that night. Finally, it was light outside. I heard a man's voice downstairs. Red quickly sat up and smiled. He told me the male voice was his Vietnamese dentist. I looked at my watch and saw that the dentist had arrived on his usual schedule, promptly at six o'clock. Red moved the barricade, unlocked the door, and went down-stairs. I was still stunned by the events of the night before. I stayed behind the dresser with my M-16 at the ready. From downstairs, I heard the sounds of laughter and friendly voices.

I cautiously made my way to the bottom of the carpeted stairs. Red was already sitting in the dentist's chair and getting his tooth looked over.

When the dentist finished, Red got up from the chair, pocketed some pills, and paid the man. All I wanted to do was to get the fuck out of there and safely back to the hotel where we were supposed to be staying.

As we left, I saw few people on the street outside. Red flagged a rickshaw and we headed back to our hotel. I got real nervous as we approached the first manned roadblock. Red instructed me not to say anything, but to look tough and hold my weapon, so the Vietnamese could see it. I did as he instructed and to my surprise the soldiers lifted the arm of the road-block and let us pass easily. We crossed through three more roadblocks the same way before we reached the hotel.

We made it back before nine o'clock. Neither of us talked about our near-fatal encounter with the enemy. I grabbed a can of spaghetti and meatballs from my pack and gulped it down as if I hadn't eaten in a week. Red disappeared somewhere. After I ate, I washed my face and shaved. Through the window, I saw troops milling around the parked trucks inside the fenced yard. I grabbed my gear and walked out of the hotel to my jeep. Red was already sitting inside the first truck behind my jeep. He waved at me with a smile on his face.

I was fuming and thinking, *How could that fucker smile at me after putting us through all that shit? The bastard has a death wish and I blame myself for becoming part of it.*

That morning, I walked past each vehicle and checked inside for a head count, two men per truck. Every man was accounted for and ready to go. After a radio check, the MP jeep slowly led us into the street. We drove to the Ben Hoa beer-and-soda yard as our convoy wound its way through the narrow streets of Saigon.

I noticed that Red had been right about one thing—Bien Hoa was only an hour from the hotel. And what an incredible sight it was to see so many piled pallets of beer and soda. Vietnamese civilians operated forklifts, lifting pallet after pallet and loading them onto the trucks' flatbeds. The Vietnamese civilians tied down the pallets with hand-held metal banding machines, while the Americans watched and directed the loading procedure. It took about five hours for the trucks to be fully loaded. Then the convoy maneuvered back through the streets of Saigon without having any incidents or trouble.

The fully loaded convoy pulled into the staging area at Cholon before six o'clock that evening. The same as the night before, we stayed at the hotel across the street for our last evening in Saigon. The second leg of the trip was now over.

Back in the same hotel room, Red and I had a long talk over a few beers. We discussed the details of the incident that we'd barely survived the night before. According to Red, the Vietnamese driver had been a North Vietnamese Officer posing as a cab driver, and was trained to capture unsuspecting Americans.

"If it wasn't for my background in military intelligence and the fact that I could speak Vietnamese, we'd both be prisoners of war right now," Red blurted out with a serious look on his face.

I quickly replied in anger, "You're full of shit! You almost got us both captured or killed."

I wasn't too happy with myself because I could have prevented the whole situation from happening. I'd made two bad decisions. First, I let Red leave the hotel where we were supposed to stay. Secondly, I foolishly went with him. I couldn't figure out why we'd taken such risks when we had only a month left to serve in Vietnam. I told Red that we were both out of our fucking minds and that I wanted to forget about this entire trip. Red didn't say another word.

The next morning we cranked up the engines and headed down the road for the long trip back to Cu Chi. I could hardly wait for this mission to be completed.

When we arrived back at Cu Chi, SGM Kelly was standing on the side of the road watching his convoy pull up to the PX. After I reported to him that all the men and trucks were accounted for, and that the goods were intact, SGM Kelly smiled at me for the first time since we met.

"Job well done, Buck Sergeant. Give me the SOI and I'll have these trucks unloaded. Anything happen on this mission that I need to know about?"

No Sergeant Major, just the same old bullshit!"

Now I intended to take up Sergeant Major Kelly on his promise. I was going to see Clipper. And after I returned from Dau Tieng, I didn't plan to leave base until it was time for me to catch a ride on a commercial airliner back to the United States.

Chapter 19

Good-bye, Clipper

A s SGM Kelly promised, he personally coordinated a spot for me on a re-supply chopper to Dau Tieng. I packed a bunch of goodies for my dog handler friends.

When I arrived at the Dau Tieng airstrip, I had to walk for about ten minutes to get to the K-9 compound. With thoughts of seeing Clipper again, the limp in my step seemed unimportant. When I arrived at the base camp, I first stopped at the kennel and met Dan Scott at the entrance. He was walking around shirtless, as usual. We shook hands and I gave him a bear hug. It had been a long time since we'd seen each other. I told Dan that I'd come to see Clipper, give out some free stuff, and then I had go back to Cu Chi first thing in the morning.

Dan knew that I couldn't leave Vietnam without coming back to say good-bye. It felt like Christmas when I handed him a brand new Zippo lighter with flints and lighter fluid. I showed him a copy of my orders to leave Vietnam on March 14—a mere two weeks away. Dan was really excited for me. He asked how my gimpy knee was healing and what Cu Chi was like. After a short bullshit session, I decided to spend some time with Clipper. Dan and I planned to party in the K-9 club later that night.

I headed into the kennel, but Clipper wasn't in his run. I should have known that he'd be out under his tree during the day. As I walked through the kennel, it was great seeing all the other scout dogs and listening to them bark like crazy for attention.

I walked to the rubber trees to find Clipper. In the distance, I spotted my dog, lying on the ground and taking a nap. I quietly called his name.

253

Goodbye, Clipper

Clipper's ears popped up, and he canted his head. He looked in my direction, rose to his feet, and turned his head slightly to the left and then to the right. I could tell that he was trying to figure out who had called him.

I walked closer without saying another word. When Clipper recognized me, he went crazy. He charged toward me until his leash fully extended and stopped him in his tracks. I rushed over to Clipper and he jumped up on my chest with his front paws. He licked all over my face and wagged his tail joyfully. Clipper was so excited that he piddled on my leg and boots. It felt great being with Clipper again. I hugged his soft furry body again.

Joy and excitement bubbled up inside me and came bursting out uncontrollably. What an exhilarating moment! Words can't begin to describe the emotions that poured out of me for this dog. He was my best friend and at last we were together again.

I clipped Clipper's choke chain to the leather leash and took him for a walk to calm us both down. I gave Clipper no commands but let him be free. Clipper automatically moved to my left side and walked at a slow pace while constantly staring up at me with love and happiness on his face. He remembered exactly what my walking pace was and didn't once pull ahead or cross over my path. After awhile, I slowly worked Clipper through some basic commands and scouting positions. It was as if we'd never been separated.

How am I ever going to leave this dog after seeing him again? I wondered.

Clipper thought I was back to stay. He didn't realize I'd only be visiting him for a short time. We spent the entire afternoon together outside in the shade of the rubber trees.

Later that night, I joined the rest of the scout dog handlers in the K-9 club. Some new guys had arrived since my departure. It was the end of February 1968 and all my old friends from the original 44th had returned to the States. Their twelve-month tour had passed and I didn't get a chance to say goodbye. Dan Scott was due for rotation in March, so he was a short-timer like me. After we said our parting farewells, I crashed in an empty cot inside my old hooch to sleep one last night in Dau Tieng.

I got up early the next morning to say my last goodbye to a dog that didn't deserve the fate in store for him.

I walked into the kennel to see Clipper. I opened his run and he ran off non-stop to wait under his tree until I caught up and hooked his collar to the twenty-five-foot leash. I filled his water bucket with fresh water and cleaned his run for the last time. Afterwards, I sat with him under his tree and stroked his head and back. My mind flashed back to the many combat missions we'd gone on as a team. Clipper had alerted me to danger and saved countless lives on so many occasions. It was hard to believe I was going to have to leave him behind. He was a real American hero, but he'd never get to go home and receive the hero's welcome he deserved.

Clipper couldn't speak for himself. He was at the mercy of the people who had recruited him for military life, indoctrinated him for war, shipped him off to Vietnam, and teamed him with a handler. As Clipper's handler, I was the only one who had truly developed an allegiance with this dog.

Because our government had classified Clipper as expendable equipment, I had to leave him behind. I felt as if I was abandoning a brother who was condemned to the dangerous job of walking point for the rest of the war. How can my country weigh me down with the burden of this lifelong memory? Clipper deserved to live the rest of his life in a peaceful environment away from this war. I wanted Clipper to be treated with the same dignity and appreciation as I expected for myself.

Dogs that served in WWII and Korea were repatriated with their devoted handlers. It was not to be so for the valiant animals that fought in Vietnam. For their service, their heroism, their bravery under fire, they were disposed of, killed, buried, and all but forgotten.

It had always been my dream to bring Clipper home. He'd have made a great pet in my back yard. By this time, Clipper had served in Vietnam for almost fifteen months. How many more missions or months would he survive? I feared that Clipper's death would be violent, especially after the Tet Offensive had agitated the war into such a frenzy. I could only hope that when Clipper finally did fall, he'd die quickly and painlessly.

I knew, as I sat under the tree with my dog leaning against my leg that I'd never see him again in this lifetime. The tragedy of it all haunted me like a nightmare.

I noticed that the sign I'd placed above Clipper's tree was still there. I'd written, "*War is good business. Invest your dog.*" Now that sign disgusted me. I got up, ripped it down and broke it into pieces.

At last, the time came for me to go. I tried to hold back my tears. I didn't know how to say goodbye to my best friend, so I looked into Clipper's eyes and gave him one last farewell bear hug. Afterwards, I turned and walked away with the bitter and sad knowledge that Vietnam would become my dog's final resting place.

Clipper stood erect with ears pointed high like the champion he'd always been. I sensed that he was watching me as I eventually vanished down the dirt road away from the 44th IPSD.

Now I knew that I truly had no more reason to stay in Vietnam.

Chapter 20

Leaving Vietnam

I left Cu Chi for Saigon to hop on a commercial flight to the States on March 14, 1968. My departure couldn't have come at a worse time. Because the Americans were in the middle of a fierce counteroffensive with the North Vietnamese Army near the surrounding areas of Cu Chi and Tay Ninh Province, I was fortunate not to have my exit orders rescinded.

Before I left, Sergeant Major Kelly summoned me to his office. He promised me another stripe if I'd stayed on for six more months. I politely declined his offer by saying, "No fucking way, Sergeant Major!

I knew it was time for me to leave the war behind, go home to Colorado, and have a big party with my family and friends. Two years was a long enough time for me to spend fighting in Southeast Asia.

Under a heavily armed convoy, escorted by tanks and helicopter gunships, I made it out of Cu Chi base camp in the back of a troop truck. The road to Saigon was still littered with burned-out vehicles cleared to the side of the road. Along the way, infantry troops were positioned off the road to protect the convoy from attack and to keep the road open. Without incident, the convoy reached the city limits of Saigon. It reeked of the devastation brought about by the Tet Offensive and the American counteroffensive.

Homeless pedestrians walked on the roadways and filled crowded busses. Armed American Military Police and South Vietnamese Army troops barricaded and manned the major intersections of the dilapidated roads.

My convoy stopped along the road next to Camp Alpha, the U.S. Army Replacement Center, where I'd first entered Vietnam. I climbed out of the back of the truck, grabbed my duffel bag, and handed my M16 rifle and bandoleer of ammunition to a sergeant who had been riding shotgun. As I entered the gates of Camp Alpha, I handed a copy of my orders to a soldier who stood at the gate with a clipboard in his hand. Each step was bringing me closer to returning to the world outside of Vietnam.

While I in-processed, I tried to locate the faces of the sergeant and the major that changed my orders a year ago. They were nowhere to be seen, so I suspected that they must have rotated back to the States.

I stayed in Camp Alpha for several days to out-process. My name was placed on a manifest and I was assigned a group number. When I heard my group number called, I reported to a numbered building where we were strip-searched. The Military Police looked for and confiscated any pistols, grenades, knives, and other items that weren't allowed to be brought onboard a commercial plane.

I hadn't tried to bring souvenirs like those out of Vietnam. Clipper was all I had wanted to take back home with me.

When the strip-search was finished, I boarded a bus to Ton San Nut airfield. During the ride, I sat on a bench seat next to the window and thought about my Vietnam experience, Clipper, and the friends I was leaving behind. Before I realized it, the bus ride ended and I was standing on the runway of Ton San Nut airfield. Military guards in jeeps surrounded a commercial jetliner waiting in the near distance to receive its passengers. In single file, we walked to the plane where a military attendant with a manifest checked off our names as we climbed up the steps and into the passenger cabin. I found an empty seat next to a window and sat down. To my amazement, I spotted a Sentry dog team just off the runway. I waved and the handler waved back.

When everyone was on board, the doors closed and the plane wasted no time moving down the runway. As soon as it lifted off, a roaring cheer broke the silence. I settled back into the soft seat and looked out of the window. During takeoff, I watched the airfield and city of Saigon grow smaller and smaller as the plane climbed higher and higher. After several minutes, only the South China Sea was visible below us.

Enjoying a Pabst Blue Ribbon beer with Jeff Einbinder at Camp Alpha before leaving Vietnam for good on March 14, 1968.

Our next stop would be to set foot again on American soil in San Francisco.

The timing and process to get everyone out of Vietnam had been impeccable. I was impressed by the terrific job the Army did of not wasting time getting us out safely. I only wished they would apply this same sense of urgency to rescuing our four-legged brothers. I figured that the Tet Offensive must have lit a spark under their butts. In a matter of only twenty-four hours, I was out of harm's way and heading away from Vietnam forever.

During the long flight, cute round-eyed American female stewardesses smiled and waited on the passengers. They served coffee, tea, soda, snacks and hot meals but no alcohol.

I had a lot of time on that flight to think about going home. I couldn't

259

wait to once again be part of the American culture I'd left behind two years earlier.

I wondered: *How will the new cars look? Will clothes be different from when I left? I'll see a lot of American girls again; will they like me? Will my family and friends be different from how I remember them? Who will pick me up at the airport in Denver?*

My only fear was that I'd heard some of the new guys talk about the people back home starting to reject the war. I didn't remember reading anything about this in the letters I'd received from family and friends. Everyone was always wishing me well and saying how they couldn't wait to see me. I didn't understand how people could reject what we were doing in Vietnam when they hadn't been there.

I thought about some of the first things I'd do when I returned. I wanted to get a new car. I'd heard that the 1968 Dodge Charger, 440 RT had a 300 horsepower engine and ram-air, and that it could clock thirteen seconds in a quarter mile. I had to have that car. My plan was to find a date one night, drive up to a lookout point in the Colorado Rocky Mountains, and peer down on the city lights of Denver.

I still had my tiny red address book that listed the names and addresses of family and friends with whom I'd corresponded while I was in Vietnam. I hoped that they hadn't moved or changed their phone numbers because I wanted to call and see them again.

I thought that it would be so nice to finally be living halfway around the world away from the sounds of explosions, machine guns, helicopters, fighter jets, armored vehicles, infantry talk, and the stinking smell of fish. I felt full of excitement to be finally going home and getting away from everything. I turned nineteen when I first got to Vietnam and in a few days, I'd be twenty one.

As the wheels touched down on San Francisco International Airport's runway, a chorus of cheers reverberated throughout the plane. When I touched the runway's pavement with the bottom of my shoe, I bent down and kissed the ground. I was so grateful to be home.

Military policemen greeted and escorted us to several military buses parked on the runway. They took us directly to Oakland Army Base. We didn't have to go through U.S. Customs. After we arrived at the base, we were confined to a warehouse holding area for in-processing, reassignments, and discharging personnel. There were no marching bands or welcome-home parades. It was all quiet on the western front, so to speak. However, we were treated to steak dinners in the warehouse mess hall.

At last, I was on American soil, and that was all that mattered to me. During out-processing, I was paid in American greenbacks. I reached into my pocket and felt a coin. When I pulled it out, I saw that it was a South Vietnamese five dong, silver-plated coin, dated 1966. I decided to hold onto it as a keepsake always to remind me of the year that I arrived in Vietnam.

Within eight hours after I arrived in Oakland, I was released on furlough. The personnel sergeant told me that I'd soon be receiving a stateside unit of assignment in the mail at my home of record. And that was it. I was now cleared to leave Oakland Army Base.

Taxicabs lined up outside the gate to take us wherever we wanted to go. Several of us shared a ride to the San Francisco Airport, so we could continue our journeys home. However, when the cab pulled up in front of the airport, I hooked up with George Johnson, another infantryman I sat next to on the plane. We'd met during out-processing in Camp Alpha. George was going home to Alabama.

George and I couldn't believe that in as little as a day-and-a-half, we were out of the jungles of Vietnam and walking on the streets of San Francisco. We agreed that things were happening a little too fast. We decided not to book a flight home right away. We wanted to go into San Francisco, clear our heads a bit, and get used to American soil. So we put our baggage in lockers inside the terminal and took off.

On this day, March 15, 1968, we proudly walked around San Francisco, wearing our Class A Khaki uniforms, combat infantry badges, and Vietnam combat service ribbons. The next day would be my twenty-first birthday. I felt so peaceful to be walking on San Francisco's downtown sidewalks.

George wanted to buy our first beers in an American bar, so we stopped at local downtown bar and sat down to enjoy the scenery. I began to notice that we were the only soldiers in the place. It wasn't crowded and the bartender was friendly to us. I ordered a bottle of Coors beer, but they didn't have any. I figured that I'd have to wait until I got to Denver to get a cold Coors. We ended up ordering bottles of PBR (Pabst Blue Ribbon).

Suddenly, our uniforms became targets of some angry Americans who were protesting against the Vietnam war. One of the bar's patrons blurted out, "Hey, baby killers! Did you enjoy burning down villages?"

I was outraged by this man's taunts. I gnashed my teeth and held back my anger. Having gone through what I had in Vietnam taught me how to control my emotions in a heated situation. I realized that the consequences of getting into a bar fight would mean police and jail time.

I felt perplexed because I didn't understand why this man was so fired up against soldiers who had served in Vietnam. I wondered if the people who had been writing to me while I was over there held back the truth about how they really felt about the war. It made me feel apprehensive about what unexpected attitudes I might be confronted with when I finally got home to Colorado.

George raised up from his barstool in anger, but I put my hand on his shoulder and told him that fighting this guy wouldn't be worth the consequences. George agreed, so we decided to ignore his remarks. A few other men sitting in the bar joined him in taunting us. This caught us by surprise and the longer we stayed there, the more uncomfortable and upset we became. We decided to keep our mouths shut and get away from there. George paid the tab and we walked out without finishing our beers.

After we left the bar, George suggested that it would be a good idea if we got out of uniform. We found the closest men's clothing store, bought civilian clothes and shoes, changed in the store's dressing room, and walked away with our uniforms in paper bags. Only our military haircuts distinguished us from rest of the American male public. God, how we wished we had long hair, so we could blend into the crowd. I felt completely depressed and constantly looked around, trying not to appear so military. My dream of coming home and being welcome had been shattered in only one afternoon.

I'd be back in Colorado on furlough for forty-five days. The plans and dreams I had while flying home on the plane were already crumbling. I no longer felt enthusiastic about buying a car, having a big party, or hanging out in public places with my friends. I had been in the military for two and a half years, and now I felt like an outsider in my own country for the first time in my life. Soon the Army would send me orders to report to another military duty station. It surprised me to realize that, because of the attitudes of my fellow American citizens, I was now feeling more safe and comfortable around military people than civilians.

My brother Tom picked me up at Stapleton Airport in Denver. He was very happy to see me and we talked all the way home. I clued him in on the incident in San Francisco. Tom told me I should kicked their asses. Tom was a no nonsense, short-tempered type of guy. If he had been with me, he would've gone after those men in the bar.

At first I wanted to believe the incident in San Francisco had been an isolated one, but it wasn't. I was soon to learn that many people my age around the country were protesting against the Vietnam War.

From this point on, even in my hometown, I had to fight a war of words with people who didn't have any idea what we'd been through over there. Occasionally, I got pushed around and wound up in fights. The television news covered the war every day. Protesters were everywhere and flower-power was in; draft-dodging was acceptable; and "Hell, no, I won't go," was the chant of the day. I felt as if I no longer fit in my own country. I began to believe that it was safer to be in the military, where people like me understood one another.

After the initial shock of my homecoming, I worked hard to re-acclimate myself to the American way of life and to appreciate the fact that we all had freedom of speech. I eventually overcame my fear of having some Vietnam protester bust my head wide open.

I endured many nightmares about my war experiences and often woke up from them unable to go back to sleep. I'd sit up and stare into the darkness of my room. I worried about my inability to adjust to a normal life. The feelings and emotions I was confronting at home reminded me of the enemy I'd faced so many times in the Vietnam jungles.

My return home shocked me with how badly the tables had turned in a direction I hadn't expected. I felt that the people, who I thought were sup-

porting me while I was fighting in Vietnam, now viewed me as their enemy. In my own backyard, I was having to fight a *little Vietnam* conflict.
However, it would be a cold day in hell before I'd let anyone drive me out
of the country I loved or to deprive me of the freedom I'd fought to pre-
serve.

Saigon fell on April 30, 1975, two years after the American military forces
pulled out the last American troops on March 29, 1973. In Paris, on January 27, 1973, America signed a peace agreement with the North Vietnamese. It called for release of all U.S. prisoners, withdrawal of U.S. forces,
limitation of both sides' forces inside South Vietnam, and a commitment
to the peaceful reunification of North and South Vietnam.

Chapter 21

Years Later — A Dream Fulfilled

W hen I left Vietnam in March 1968, I went on with my life and learned to deal with the memories of my war experiences. Many times over the years, I told stories of the sacrifices made by the soldiers and war dogs I had known. Two questions continued to linger in my mind: Would I ever heal from grieving over the loss of my fellow soldiers and war dogs? How were the other men I served with in Vietnam handling their past experiences?

I often wondered what I could do to keep alive the memories of these soldiers, dogs, and events.

By the 1990s, American citizens had finally established many local and national monuments and memorials, honoring the men and women who had served and died in Vietnam. However, there were no national memorials recognizing the bravery of the Vietnam war dogs who had given our country their unconditional loyalty and honor.

In 1991, I accepted an invitation to spend Memorial Day weekend with my good friend Mark Hart and his family at their summer home near Lake Pymatuming in northern Pennsylvania. I mentioned to Mark that I had a Vietnam buddy, Kenny Mook, whose last known residence was Meadeville, Pennsylvania. Mark assured me that his family would help me find Kenny, if he still lived in Meadeville. It was a nice gesture, but I didn't think there would be much of a chance of reuniting with Kenny. After all, twenty-five years had passed, and I hadn't met a single person with whom I'd personally served alongside in Vietnam.

Shortly after we settled in for our holiday weekend in Pennsylvania, Mark's sister Barbara got on the phone and located a Kenneth Mook in Saegertown. After she handed me the phone, my joy and excitement escalated when the man on the other end of the line confirmed that he was the same Kenny Mook who had been severely wounded by the enemy in Bong Son on May 6, 1966. We arranged to meet at Mark's place that Memorial Day weekend.

After we talked on the phone, I kept recalling incidents of our time together. Anticipating seeing Kenny after all this time was making me feel nervous, even though I eagerly looked forward to it. When we finally met face-to-face, our eyes focused on one another like magnifying glasses, looking for hidden clues to our past. Although we were older, Kenny's face, eyes, and physical stature looked the same as I remembered them.

When I saw Kenny, I quickly spoke the first words between us and asked, "How's the arm?"

"Fine," he replied. He smiled and rolled back his shirtsleeve to show me the old wound had healed. He also pulled up his shirt, so I could see the bullet hole scars on his belly. Kenny now wore, on a chain hanging from his neck, the bullets that had been extracted from his body.

We shook hands and hugged. Neither of us could believe it had taken us so long to finally get together. At the start of our visit, I was doing most of the talking while Kenny stared at me and listened. I suddenly remembered that I had always been the talker, and Kenny the listener. It was funny to notice that this one thing hadn't changed in 25 years.

Next, Kenny introduced me to his charming wife Judy and their two teenage children, Carter and Amy. Then I met Kenny's mother and father. They remembered the letter I'd sent to them about their son that had arrived before the official military mail. I choked up with tears when Kenny's father shook my hand in a firm grip and said, "Thank you for saving my son!"

Kenny and I continued our reunion by talking about our past relationship, the places we'd traveled to together, and the soldiers we'd served alongside. I was amazed at how accurately our memories teamed up on similar details of our experiences. Even though many years had separated us, we were still closely bonded by our vivid memories. Kenny told me that seeing me again was like finding a long lost brother. I don't know if anyone else could have understood how deep a bond there was between us.

This was the most remarkable Memorial Day Sunday I'd ever experienced. It became the catalyst for my decision to write a story about our experiences in Vietnam. I figured the project would be completed in about ten pages. Several months and eighty pages later, I ended my story by writing, *"I returned to Vietnam for a second tour as a scout dog handler. But that's another story."*

In 1996, I contacted retired Lieutenant General (LTG) Harold K. Moore, my former battalion commander. He was the Army officer who had given me a drink of water in the Ia Drang Valley in April 1966.

LTG Moore and Joseph L. Galloway had co-authored the book, *We Were Soldier's Once and Young: Ia Drang, The Battle that Changed the War in Vietnam.* As I read their book, I was often moved to tears, but couldn't put it down until I finished it. I had served with some of the survivors mentioned in the book. Reading the story of the lost platoon reminded me of my first squad leader, Sergeant Dorman. He'd told me that story thirty years earlier, just as these authors had written about in their book.

After reading the book, I mailed LTG Moore a copy of the story I'd written in 1991 following my reunion with Kenny Mook. LTG Moore's comment back to me was that I'd left him hanging by not finishing my stories about being a scout dog handler in Vietnam. He encouraged me to complete the book for my family. Not to complete it, he warned, would be a tragedy. I heeded his advice and over the next couple of years, I slowly pecked away at piecing together the remaining stories.

After I connected with LTG Moore again, he invited me to the 7th Cavalry's 30th Reunion of the battle of the Ia Drang. When I arrived at the reunion, I searched for the men I'd served with and found my former platoon sergeant, Sergeant Ernie Savage. We talked about the battles of Ia Drang and Bong Son. I was a little disappointed that Sergeant Doreman, my former squad leader, was unable to make this reunion.

LTG Moore introduced me to his co-author, Joseph L. Galloway, a civilian correspondent and author. He had been the only American civilian on

The author and Charlie Cargo, Military Technical Advisors on location for the filming of *War Dogs,* October 1998. Note original beret worn by 44th IPSD.

the ground with the 7th Cavalry during the battle of Ia Drang. Mr. Galloway has since been awarded the Bronze Star Medal for valor for his participation in that battle. I believe he should have also been awarded the coveted Combat Infantry Badge (CIB).

There were hundreds of men and family members in attendance at this reunion. Part of the evening's ceremony was for the former soldiers to stand up and be recognized. Each survivor of the battle of Ia Drang stood up, stated his name, unit of assignment, and said a few words about being a survivor. I was moved as I listened.

Although I wasn't a survivor of the Ia Drang battle in November 1965, I felt the need to be recognized at this reunion because I'd been to Ia Drang after the battle and fought alongside some of those survivors in Bong Son, where Kenny Mook had been wounded.

When the introductions reached my table, I stood up and said, "My name is John Burnam. I served as a rifleman with the 2nd Platoon, Company B, 1st Battalion, 7th Cavalry from March to July 1966. Although I didn't participate in the battle of Ia Drang, I served as a member of Sergeant Doreman's weapons squad when the 2nd platoon returned there in April 1966 for the first time since your battle. I came here to thank LTG Moore publicly and in person for giving me water from his canteen to keep me from dehydrating in the Ia Drang. It was my first combat mission."

After I sat down, LTG Moore stepped up to the podium and said, "I remember that incident. You can drink from my canteen anytime, soldier. Gary Owen!"

In August 1997, my neighbor gave me an article about Vietnam War dogs. It had been published in a popular dog magazine. The article included the Internet address of the Vietnam Dog Handlers Association (VDHA), a registered non-profit organization (http://www.vdhaonline. org/). I had no idea that such an organization existed. I was electrified with excitement to find Dan Scott and Oliver "Ollie" Whetstone, two scout dog handlers I'd served with in the 44th Scout Dog Platoon, listed as members. By this time, I had written a lot about them in my ongoing book project, especially the story of the mortar attack on the kennel. These men were the only members of the 44th listed as members, so I decided to join the VDHA—the first Vietnam organization I'd ever joined.

In June 1998, Ollie and I reunited in his hometown of Kenosha, Wisconsin. It was like old times. He had photos of scout dogs and handlers I hadn't seen since 1967. We talked at length about that painful night Ollie's scout dog, Erik, had to be put down. We spent several days together going over the details of the stories I'd written about in my manuscript. Ollie and I had rekindled our relationship.

My next reunion was with Dan Scott. He was surprised when I called him, because it had been thirty years since we'd heard each other's voices. The first thing Dan said was, "You sound the same, Burnam." This greeting sounded familiar because we'd always called one another by our last names.

269

As we reflected on our memories, Scott finished sentences that I started. He seemed to know exactly what I'd say next. Scott and I talked about his dog, Shadow, the night of the mortar attack, and Sergeant Barnett's decision to put Shadow down. Dan was still emotionally affected by the events of that dreadful night. One of the few pictures he still had was a faded one of Shadow's grave marker. The rest of his pictures of Shadow and other Vietnam memories had been stolen from his wall locker shortly after he returned home in 1968.

A fellow scout dog handler from the 44th Scout Dog Platoon, Dan Barnett, surprised me with a phone call in June 1999. We hadn't talked or seen one another in 31 years. We talked for an hour on the telephone about how all the main characters in my book suddenly came into my life. Dan remembered many things about our relationship, including serving with the 1st Air Cavalry Division, the attack on the kennel and shooting Dan Scott's dog, Shadow, to put him out of his misery. Dan told me that he was with fellow scout dog handler Sergeant Robert Hartsock the night Robert won the nation's highest military award for valor, the Congressional Medal of Honor — posthumously. Hartsock died of his wounds and was the only war dog handler to receive such an award during the Vietnam war.

I found it very strange that, after thirty years, the only two dog handlers with whom I'd reunited had lost their scout dogs the night the Viet Cong attacked our base camp. Furthermore, I was the only member of the 44th they had contact with since returning from Vietnam.

In June 1998, I decided to consult an orthopedic doctor because my right knee had been in severe pain for several weeks. It had been ten years since I went to see a doctor about this injury. During the examination, the doctor evaluated the scar tissue, the deformity of the knee joint, my restricted range of motion, and the smaller circumference of the thigh muscle compared to the left leg. I explained that in 1966 I'd been injured by a bamboo spear in Vietnam and was sent to a hospital in Japan. I told the doctor that Dr. Bogumill had performed my surgery.

With a surprised look, the doctor smiled and said, "You know Dr. Bogumill?"

"I know a Dr. Bogumill," I replied.

"Did you know he's now a famous hand surgeon practicing at Georgetown University Hospital?"

"But the Dr. Bogumill I knew worked on limbs. I'm sure it's not the same guy."

The doctor continued to examine my knee and then recommended that I try physical therapy to build up my thigh muscle. She warned that a knee replacement would be necessary when I decided I couldn't stand the pain anymore. I opted to live with the pain for a few more years.

After the examination, I was given Dr. Bogumill's office phone number. As soon as I got home, I called his office, but he wasn't there to take my call. I left a message to have him call me only if he had served in the Army as an orthopedic surgeon in Japan in 1966.

A few hours later, I received a phone call from Dr. George Bogumill. He confirmed that he'd been in the Army and had worked as an orthopedic surgeon at the 106th General Hospital in Japan in 1966. He informed me that I was only the second patient he'd made contact with since he departed from Japan in 1967.

I marveled at this timely and coincidental connection from the past concerning another story I had already written about in my book.

In July 1998, I was contacted by Tom Mitchell, President of the Vietnam Dog Handlers Association (VDHA). He explained that the VDHA, GRB Entertainment, and Nature's Recipe Pet Foods had teamed together to create the first documentary about the war dogs of Vietnam. He also said that there would be a national fund-raising effort to establish a war dogs memorial. Tom explained that the film could not be done without the members giving up their stories.

I granted Tom permission to release my name and phone number to the War Dogs research team of GRB Entertainment in Hollywood. I became excited and told everyone I knew about the documentary on war dogs. It was all I could think about as I passed each day waiting for a call from Hollywood.

Many questions from members of the VDHA, their families, and friends

War Dogs director Arthur Albert and actor Jeff Boland with the author on location (October 1998).

flew around the Internet: What will *War Dogs* actually be about? Who's going to be in it? When is it going to be released? Will it be accurate? What is the War Dogs Memorial going to look like and where is it going to be placed? My telephone bills skyrocketed as I placed calls to people around the country seeking information and answers.

I finally got a call from GRB Entertainment in Hollywood, California. I was so excited that I didn't know where to begin or which story to tell. After calming down, I told GRB that it would be better if they could read some of my unpublished scout dog stories rather than have me try to tell them over the phone. GRB agreed, so I mailed the stories and figured that if they were still interested, I would be contacted again.

In late July, GRB called and made me an offer I couldn't refuse—an all expense paid trip to Hollywood for an on-camera interview. I was warned that doing the interview did not guarantee that my story would be part of the finished documentary.

I arrived in Hollywood on August 20, 1998. When I arrived at the hotel, I was greeted by Tom Mitchell, President of the VDHA. Tom was on hand to help coordinate the live interviews, greet the dog handlers, and oversee the entire film production process. I was impressed to see that the VDHA was an integral part of this operation and Tom was the perfect man for the job.

The next day, Tim Prokop, head writer for *War Dogs*, conducted the interview. The two stories Tim selected for me to tell was the kennel attack and saying good-bye to Clipper. These were sad stories and I never told them with a camera in my face or microphone boom over my head.

For the interview, I sat in an armless, straight-back chair in front of a dimly lit jungle scenery set. Tiny fans, hidden from view, blew on the leaves ever so slightly to give the impression of being outdoors. Tim sat a few feet in front of me with a huge camera lens over his left shoulder. I sat erect in my chair, feeling nervous and not knowing what to expect. Tim smiled and asked me to relax and try to concentrate throughout the interview by talking directly to him without looking into the camera. Several people stood quietly in the shadows and stared at me.

First, Tim asked me several practice questions: "How old are you? Where are you from? What years did you serve in Vietnam?

Tim told me that the audience wouldn't hear or see him; they would only hear and see me. I wasn't to repeat the question, just answer it. As I listened to Tim's instructions, my mouth got really dry.

Then I heard, "Three, two, one, action. We're live. John, tell us what happened on the night of November 9, 1967, when your kennel was hit with mortars?"

I began to talk about the events that led up to the attack, the attack itself and what happened afterwards. As the interview progressed, I eventually relaxed and settled into a one-on-one storytelling mode.

I had a difficult time controlling my emotions while I described what I'd seen when I went into the kennel after the mortar attack. My emotions continued to pour out, as I talked about saying good-bye to Clipper.

273

When the interview was over and I stood up from the chair, I felt physically and emotionally drained. I looked around and was surprised to see the film crew weeping and wiping tears from their eyes. The interviewer, cameramen, executive producer, makeup artist, and many others came over to shake my hand and pat me on the back for telling such emotionally charged stories.

After the interview, I decided to stay and listen to other Vietnam war dog handlers tell their stories. John Flannelley was scheduled after my interview. He told how his scout dog, Bruiser, had saved his life by dragging him into a bomb crater. Next up was Mike Bailey, a Navy Seal. He shared the incredible story of when his scout dog, Prince, had alerted and saved his patrol from getting pounded by a huge enemy force. After Mike, Judy Dale told a heart-warming story about donating her German shepherd dog, Toro, for military service, and how she kept in touch with Toro and his handler, Carl Dobbins, while they were in Vietnam.

I got choked up on emotion and tears during these interviews. As an onlooker, it was impossible not to be touched by the power of the stories and the love these people still had for their long gone, four-footed companions. When all of the interviews were over at six o'clock that evening, we'd used up every available tissue wiping our tears. It was the first time I'd met so many Vietnam dog handlers who had such important stories to tell.

GRB had already completed a bunch of interviews before that day and had many more to go. I overheard Tom Mitchell ask John Drimmer, the supervising producer, how they were going to edit all that material into a one hour show. John responded by saying it was going to be tough to decide what segments would stay or be cut. I was glad that I didn't have to make that decision.

In early September 1998, I received a phone call from GRB advising me that my story made the cut and would be a part of the one-hour documentary. I was both excited and nervous at the same time. I'd never been on television before, and soon millions of people would see and hear me tell my story.

In late September 1998, I received an e-mail from Michael (Mac) McClellan's daughter, Kristin Ashby. She was searching for dog handlers who had served with her father in the 44th Scout Dog Platoon in 1967. She had located me through the VDHA. I remembered Mac very well. He was the dog handler who had taken Ollie's dog, Erik, behind the kennel and put him down to relieve his pain and suffering after the enemy mortar attack.

I couldn't believe the timing of Kristin's message, since GRB had just picked the one story in my manuscript in which the characters (Ollie, Scott, and Mac) had miraculously popped into my life at the very time the story was about to be filmed and released for television. I found this entire scenario to be very strange, as if there was an unseen force working some kind of magic on me. I had a hard time sleeping after Kristen's e-mail. I reflected on the momentum and frequency of these *coincidental* events and encounters that were having a startling impact on my life.

In October, John Drimmer, GRB supervising producer, invited me to observe and help with the staging of the reenactment scenes of War Dogs. The film site was Soledad Canyon, northeast of Los Angeles, California. I decided to take a leave of absence from work to participate in this once-in-a-lifetime project.

When I arrived at the set, I met another Vietnam scout dog handler, Charlie Cargo, from Southern California. Charlie and I became instant friends. Charlie had donated his personal time to this project for the same reason I did. Charlie's story was also part of documentary. Charlie described how his scout dog, Wolf, had saved him and many other men from tripping a wire connected to a bomb. We met at the film site at six o'clock in the morning each day, and left when it grew dark. We were dubbed military technical advisors, so we worked with wardrobe people and actors and helped to stage the combat reenactment scenes. We tried to make them as realistic as possible.

At the film location, there were about fifty or sixty people—including security personnel, a fire marshal, a representative from the animal protection agency, cameramen, wardrobe people, the director, props and spe-

Supervising Producer John Drimmer stages a reenactment scene from *War Dogs*.

cial effects staff, food catering personnel, stuntmen, the art director, producer, electrician, actors, extras, etc. — and tons of equipment. Charlie and I got acquainted with the film director, Arthur Albert, who had worked on the television series, "Wonder Years." We met Carl Miller, a famous animal actor coordinator whose German shepherd dogs had performed in many Hollywood movies. We were treated like royalty and overwhelmed far beyond our wildest expectations.

The night they filmed the mortar attack on the kennel, I met and coached actor Jeff Boland who played the younger me. He looked almost exactly as I had when I was his age, but he was taller, thinner, and had a full head of hair. I thought he was a handsome devil. We got along great. I even gave him a replica of my Purple Heart as a gift for acting in this role. I told him that the Purple Heart really belonged to Timber and Clipper, but they would be proud if he kept it for them.

Charlie and I met the co-producers of *War Dogs*, Gary Benz, CEO of GRB Entertainment, and Jeffrey Bennett, President of Nature's Recipe Pet

Foods. Mr. Bennett informed us of the plans to market the documentary and the fund-raising campaign for building national War Dogs memorials at Riverside, California and in the Washington D.C. area.

Tim Prokop, the documentary's head writer, interviewed Charlie and me on-camera, recording our impressions of the production and what it had been like to watch our stories reenacted. Charlie and I felt alike about watching the filming of scenes that reenacted our stories: The actors, dogs, uniforms, weapons, shooting, and explosions were all too real. It had been surreal to watch part of our past staged and acted out in detail before our very eyes. There were moments when I felt instantly transported back to Vietnam. This had been a scary experience and it reminded me of the horrible nightmares I'd left behind many years ago. Charlie and I walked away from the set several times to regain our composure.

Many questions came to mind as I watched some of my life's most painful experiences in Vietnam being reenacted: "Why am I doing this? Why am I exposing to the public what has, until now, been known to only my family, personal friends, and me?"

The answers came to me. In my heart, I believed Timber and Clipper had given their lives to save mine, so I could live to tell their story after our country had cooled down from that unpopular war.

I had brought a journal with me to the production set, so I could record my experiences there. Towards the end of my stay, I asked the people who had been involved with producing *War Dogs,* to write in this journal. Before I left the set, I had collected over thirty entries.

Although the following comments from my journal were made to me, they apply to everyone who served as Vietnam war dog handlers.

I want to thank you for the relentless expertise, concern, and creativity you've brought to your role as technical advisor for our production of *War Dogs.* When we invited you to play this special role, we knew we were getting someone who could ensure verisimilitude in myriad ways. What we didn't fully appreciate is how compassionately you would guide us all — the director, writer, actors, and crew — to a deep resonant un-

Left to right: Joanne Worley, John Flanelley, Loretta Switt, John Burnam, Jan Bennett, and Jeff Bennett at Nature's Recipe *Show Dogs of the Year* Awards Dinner in New York, February 6, 1999.

derstanding of the bond between animal and man and the experience of being a young soldier in Vietnam.

— *John Drimmer, Supervising Producer*

It has been a very long time since I've had a chance to work on stories that moved me as these have. Thank you so much for telling this story and sharing it with people. I've always felt that you guys, who went over to Vietnam, have never gotten the recognition you deserve. I hope this documentary makes a small step toward changing that. Your presence here has been an inspiration to the whole crew, especially to the actors, who are too young to know what happened over there. I'll always remember you and the stories you shared with me.

— *Arthur Albert, Director*

I'd like to thank you and your fellow veterans for taking the time, interest, effort, and having the confidence in us to put this thing together for you. This is the first of many documentaries for me, and I can say that it's one of the best, because of the personal satisfaction I've gotten from working with you. You're genuine, personable, and above all, a good storyteller. Your story needs and deserves to be seen and heard by the American public.

— *James Gordon, GRB*

I sincerely thank you for all your participation in the making of *War Dogs.* Your willingness to tell us your story touches my heart, because I realize how difficult it must have been in Vietnam. The telling of these truths will make all the difference in the show and in how the public receives it. Your dedication and hard work to such a worthwhile subject has truly made a difference. Thank you for your strength and positive attitude. We really couldn't have done it without all of you. My prayers are for you, Clipper, and your safety as you continue your journey.

— *Scottie Guinn, GRB*

Here's what you have meant to the production:
- You gave the writer a story
- You gave the director inspiration
- You helped everyone understand why this is important
- You taught the actor how to be real.

— *Tim Prokop, Writer/Producer*

I have a great appreciation for what you and Clipper did in Vietnam. After meeting you, I will never take for granted the freedoms I enjoy that you served to protect. Your stories fascinated and touched me. You are a true inspiration. I was proud and honored to portray a living hero on film. I only hope I did you justice. You are truly a veteran in every sense of the word.

— *Jeff Boland, Actor*

In November 1998, I attended the VDHA Reunion in San Diego, California. This meeting was the mother lode of Vietnam war dog handlers. It included scout, sentry, tracker, mine, tunnel, and booby trap handlers from all the military services. I had a great time making new friends and enjoying the stories everyone shared. The highlight of the reunion was the much-anticipated viewing of a demonstration video tape of the *War Dogs* documentary, prepared by GRB Entertainment and funded by Nature's Recipe Pet Foods.

The tape featured a sampling of interviews with fellow war dog handlers and associated reenactment scenes. We watched as our untold story finally came to the big screen.

The video lasted for about five minutes; enough to whet our appetites. When the lights came on, there wasn't a dry eye in the hotel ballroom. We knew that if the rest of the show was anything like what we'd sampled, we were going to need bigger boxes of tissues. The *War Dogs* video tape instantly became our main topic of conversation for the rest of the reunion.

To get word out about the documentary, Laura Benge, Nature's Recipe Pet Foods organized a media blitz. Meanwhile, GRB worked hard to complete the film before its Hollywood premiere on February 10th and the television premiere on the Discovery channel on February 15th.

Many newspapers, radio shows, and television news stations picked up on the *War Dogs* story. Vietnam veteran dog handlers were interviewed by local and national press and some made it into morning and evening news reports. Newspapers from California to New York printed stories about their local war dog handlers and the brave dogs they loved, but forced to leave behind in Vietnam. The public's focus on our great untold story was growing. *War Dogs, America's Forgotten Heroes* was the perfect title for this historical project.

Thanksgiving, Christmas, and New Years came and went while my emotions and excitement built toward the Hollywood premiere and television broadcast of *War Dogs*.

On February 6, 1999, John Flannelley and I were in New York for a *War Dogs* media promotion. We interviewed with a few New York radio stations. Jeffrey Bennett and I teamed up for an interview with the *Osgood File* radio show and toured the CBS Studios. The same night as that interview, John and I attended the Nature's Recipe Show Dogs of the Year Awards, with Laura Benge as our escort.

After dinner, Mr. Bennett introduced an audience of 500 dog lovers to a sample viewing of *War Dogs*. Afterwards, John and I got to meet two famous dog lovers and Hollywood icons, Loretta Switt and Joanne Worely.

Years Later — A Dream Fulfilled

On February 10, 1999, about thirty-five Vietnam veteran dog handlers, their families, and friends attended the Hollywood premiere at the Leonard H. Goldenson Theatre in Los Angeles. The 600-seat theater was filled to capacity.

Watching *War Dogs* on a huge theater screen with my fellow Vietnam war dog handlers made all the difference in the world. We felt as if we were being transported back in time, reliving our own personal stories, and saying goodbye to our dogs. It was difficult for us all to hold back our tears.

What I appreciated most was the fact that the film maximized on the storytelling of the dog handlers, which gave the film its incredible life and emotion, and caused tears to run down the cheeks of the audience. The reenactment scenes were blended into each story with sensitivity and gripping power. The real-life dog training and actual Vietnam film footage added more authenticity. Martin Sheen's narration was clear and concise. The music score by David Eisley added a poetic touch that blended beautifully with the theme.

But the evening wasn't over yet. People crowded around autograph tables to get the signatures of dog handlers on their *War Dogs* posters, hats, and T-shirts. Cameras flashed and video tapes rolled. Many people shook our hands and thanked our dogs through us. It was a wonderful feeling and a public welcome we never got for our service in Vietnam.

After *War Dogs* aired on national television, the Internet Web sites of the Vietnam Dog Handlers Association and Nature's Recipe overflowed with electronic mail from people all over the United States and abroad. The telephone lines lit up as people spread the word about what they'd seen on television. The documentary had served as a wake-up call for dog lovers across America. With each passing day, more messages stormed the Web sites and telephone answering machines.

The documentary's impact was far beyond any dog handlers' expectation. For two magnificent nights, the memories of our Vietnam war dogs finally got recognized by the public, and these courageous animal heroes had been elevated to star status.

The author and John Flannelley show off the jackets they were presented for their service as scout dog handlers in Vietnam.

Every day after I came home from work, I sat at my computer reading and answering electronic mail and placing and receiving phone calls around the country. The words in each message cried out the senders' heartfelt emotions and pain for the war dogs who had been left behind, and the handlers who still carried in their hearts, the loving memories of their four-footed partners .

The following are extracts from some of the electronic mail and letters I have received since the airing of War Dogs:

I want to thank you and Mr. Mitchell for assisting in finding my uncle, Dan Scott, whom I never met, and my mom hasn't seen in thirty years. I watched War Dogs on television and I was glad to see your story about Clipper. It touched my mom when, in your story, the actor who played you said good-night to Shadow, Dan's scout dog. She was also touched

282

by another actor, who we think was playing Dan, because he was yelling out for Shadow from inside the bunker. I loved the documentary and my mother has watched it four times already.

My mother and my uncle, Dan, have talked at least once a week since the documentary aired, and they have traded pictures. I have the utmost respect for all Vietnam vets and I'm eternally grateful to you, Mr. Burnam, and Mr. Mitchell for bringing happiness to my mother and her brother."

— *Timothy Bolde*

You and Clipper were so brave. God gave you a wonderful friend for a little while — someone you will never forget. I hate how the country abandoned those heroes, but Clipper's memory lives on in you and especially in the War Dogs program. Thanks for being a part of this program, so that the American public can know more about the war dogs.

— *Harold Wood*

I was an RTO (Radio Telephone Operator) and team leader on a combat tracker team, 75th Infantry Detachment, 173rd Airborne Brigade. Even though I didn't have a dog for my own, each of us became close to our two tracker dogs, Bryn & Moose. Thank you for sharing your story. Thank you for sharing your life. I cried right along with you. I think my wife and son understand me a little bit better now. Thank you, brother!"

— *Bob Baker*

First, I thank you for going over to Vietnam for us. I've never personally thanked a war veteran before. By chance, I came across War Dogs and was riveted. As I watched, I kept pulling my dogs closer to me. I'm writing to let you know how profoundly that show, specifically your story, has affected me. I didn't sleep the night after I watched it. I was stunned to learn that man's best friend had been left behind.

The scene, where you had to walk away from Clipper, keeps replaying over in my mind like a continuous loop. The bond you had with Clipper must have been extremely intense, as if he were an extension of yourself. To leave Clipper behind must have been the toughest thing you've ever had to do. I know it was hard for you to tell your story, but you have profoundly affected this thirty-three-year-old grown man who can't get it out of his mind. I thank you for telling us what happened. May you find your peace.

— *James Eiden*

Thank you and all the other Vietnam dog handlers for your courageous dedication to duty. Without you and your dogs, so many, including
my Dad, might not have come back home. I especially want to thank you
for reopening an old wound by telling your story. It went a long way to
help educate those of us who had no idea the role of the dog handlers and
their war dogs. This country owes a great debt to those who fought, par-
ticularly the K9 corps. I am proud of you John, you paid quite a tribute to
Clipper. I know that he continues to look after you from above.

— *Joanie Kyle*

I have nothing but the utmost respect for you and your fellow war dog
handlers. Over the years I've been fortunate to train with some military
working dog handlers and have always been impressed by their skills.
My partner, K-9 Starko, retired after seven years of service as a patrol
dog and now lives with my family and me. Working with him was the
best seven years of my career.

When I watched your story I found it hard to hold back the tears in
front of my family, but fortunately, being a K-9 family, they more than
understood. Although my partner and I fought our battles on the streets,
you guys fought yours in a far more frightening place and did it with
honor, courage, and loyalty. People, who aren't dog handlers, will never
understand the bond that exists between a handler and his dog. They
might cry while watching the documentary, but only another handler
understands the loss. I can only hope that Starko lived up to the standards that Clipper set so many years ago in the jungle. From one handler to another, thanks for a job well done.

— *Rick Dietz*

Please don't stop telling your story. The dogs can't speak for themselves. People need to understand what happened, so no government
can again use and then cast off such courageous animals. After watching *War Dogs*, I was amazed and, of course, cried a lot. I watched the
movie with my trusty assistance dog, Clancy. He has been my companion, day-in-and-day-out, for almost five years.

You are the only person who really understands how I feel about
Clancy. People always say, "I know how you must feel." No, they don't!!
You can't understand unless you have been there. And you've been there
and back!

You and I know on an intimate level what it means to have a canine partner, to listen to their language and what they're trying to tell us. And to receive the unconditional love and devotion only a good dog can offer.

We'd also like to take this opportunity to personally thank you from the bottom of our hearts for your service in the military during such a dangerous time.

— Darla and Paul Purguson

The Vietnam *War Dogs* documentary is an accurate portrayal of what our dogs accomplished to save lives and it shows how much we loved them. Leaving Clipper in Vietnam was like leaving a brother behind to be executed by the same government that had trained him to save lives, but had classified him as expendable equipment. My government has weighed me down with the burden of that memory for the rest of my life.

I hope that *Dog Tags of Courage* will help my fellow Vietnam veterans, Vietnam war dog handlers, and their families to heal from the lingering pain of the Vietnam war experience. I also hope that my story will help other people better understand what it was like to have been a teenager who served in one of the most unpopular wars in the history of our great country.

My heart soars with the joy that comes from knowing our war dogs will finally have memorials dedicated to honor them at Riverside, California and Washington D.C. All of us will now have a special place to pay our respects to the war dogs of all wars.

Appendix

Gone but Not Forgotten

The Vietnam Dog Handlers Association (VDHA) supplied the following names and supporting data for each dog handler and war dog who died during the war in South Vietnam. The VDHA web site is at **www.vdhaonline.org**.

Congressional Medal Of Honor

The Congressional Medal of Honor is the highest military decoration for bravery that can be bestowed upon a military service member by our great country.

Staff Sergeant Robert W. Hartsock, 44th Infantry Platoon Scout Dogs, 3d Brigade, 25th Infantry Division was the only war dog handler to receive such an award during the Vietnam War. Staff Sergeant Hartsock was born on January 24, 1945 in Cumberland, Maryland. He entered the service at Fairmont, West Virginia.

Staff Sergeant Hartsock earned the Congressional Medal Of Honor for extraordinary heroism in the Hau Nghia Province, Republic of Vietnam on February 23, 1969.

Citation: "For conspicuous gallantry and intrepidity in action at the risk of his life above and beyond the call of duty. Staff Sergeant Hartsock distinguished himself in action while serving as section leader with the 44th Infantry Platoon Scout Dogs. When the Dau Tieng Base Camp came under a heavy enemy rocket and mortar attack, Staff Sergeant Hartsock and his platoon commander spotted an enemy sapper squad which had infiltrated the camp undetected.

Sergeant Robert Hartsock in his hooch with CAR15 and machete (1968).

Realizing the enemy squad was heading for the brigade tactical operations center and nearby prisoner compound, they concealed themselves and, although heavily outnumbered, awaited the approach of the hostile soldiers. When the enemy was almost upon them, Staff Sergeant Hartsock and his platoon commander opened fire on the squad. As a wounded enemy soldier fell, he managed to detonate a satchel charge he was carrying.

Staff Sergeant Hartsock, with complete disregard for his life, threw himself on the charge and was gravely wounded. In spite of his wounds, Staff Sergeant Hartsock crawled about 5 meters to a ditch and provided heavy suppressive fire, completely pinning down the enemy and allowing his commander to seek shelter. Staff Sergeant Hartsock continued his deadly stream of fire until he succumbed to his wounds. Staff Sergeant Hartsock's extraordinary heroism and profound concern for the lives of his fellow soldiers were in keeping with the highest traditions of the military service and reflect great credit on him, his unit, and the United States Army."

Dog Handlers and Visual Trackers Killed in Action
1965-1975

Last Name	First Name & Middle Initial	Date of Death & Age	Branch/Unit	Home Town	State
Ahern	Robert P.	3/30/69, 26	Army 37th	ScoutLaconia	NH
Alcorn, Jr.	Dale R.	9/06/69, 19	Army 60th Mine	Redondo Beach	CA
Amick	Richard M.	5/12/69, 20	Army Scout	Nashville	TN
Anderson	William A.	11/06/69, 21	Army Visual	Mt. Vernon	AL
Anderson	Wayne M.	12/03/69, 20	Army Scout	Pullman	WA
Armstrong	Robert D.	1/16/69, 20	USMC Scout	Fayetteville	TN
Atkins III	Joshua, A.	4/26/67, 19	Army Scout	Washington	DC
Baker	Donald L.	9/06/67, 20	USMC Sentry	Huntington Park	CA
Baker	Gary P.	5/11/70, 21	Army Scout	Monroe City	MO
Baldoni	Lindsay D.	8/22/67, 21	Army 39th Scout	Detroit	MI
Banaszynski	Richard M.	10/25/68, 22	Army 59th Scout	Pulaski	WI
Barkley	Earl D.	11/09/71, 21	Army Scout	Indian Head	PA
Beauregard	Richard M.	4/24/71, 19	Army Scout	Woonsocket	RI
Beck	Terrance D.	12/20/67, 18	USMC Scout	Ft. Atkinson	WI
Beesley	Gary E.	6/22/67, 21	Army Scout	St. Louis	MO
Behrens	Peter C.	12/04/70, 26	Army Scout	Newburg	MO
Belcher	Robert W.	4/11/68, 22	USMC Scout	Winthrop	MA
Bell	Mark W.	6/09/69, 19	USMC Scout	Redondo Beach	CA
Bennett	John W.	10/14/69, 20	Army Scout	Columbus	OH
Best	Billy H.	3/03/69, 18	USMC Scout	Baltimore	MD
Beuke	Dennis A.	10/11/67, 21	Army Tracker 8	Chicago	IL
Bevich, Jr.	George M.	12/04/66, 22	USAF 377th SPS	Summit Hill	PA
Blaauw	James E.	3/22/68, 21	Army Scout	Grayling	MI
Blair	Charles D.	5/14/70, 20	AR 64th Tracker	Orlando	FL
Bost	Michael, J.	5/14/67, 20	Army 42nd Scout	Grand Rapids	MI
Bowman	Stephen W.	6/02/68, 18	Army 49th Scout	Alta Loma	CA
Boyer	James R.	9/22/67, 20	Army Visual	St. Louis	MO
Bozier, Jr.	Willie	7/09/70, 21	Army Scout	New York	NY
Brede	Robert W.	11/16/67, 23	Army Visual	Alexandria	MN
Brophy	Martin E.	5/05/68, 24	Army 41st Scout	Buffalo	NY
Brown	Charles P.	3/09/67, 21	Army Scout	South Amboy	NJ
Buckingham	Keith C.	2/25/69, 22	Army 43rd Scout	Minneapolis	MN
Burdette, Jr.	Hilburn M.	7/12/70, 20	Army Scout	Simpsonville	SC
Burk	Jimmy R.	11/30/69, 21	Army 43rd Scout	Littlefield	TX
Burlock, Jr.	Kenneth G.	9/17/69, 23	Army Scout	Jacksonville	NC
Burnette, Jr.	Archie	1/31/68, 20	Army Scout	Aberdeen	WA
Cabarubio	James	6/18/69, 20	USMC Scout	Odessa	TX
Cain	Douglas M.	7/14/68, 23	Army 43rd Scout	Sioux City	IA

Appendix

Last Name	First Name & Middle Initial	Date of Death & Age	Branch/Unit	Home Town	State
Camp	Anthony L.	6/04/69, 21	USMC Scout	Dallas	GA
Campbell	William L.	3/03/67, 21	Army 49th Scout	Silver Hill	MO
Carinici	Joseph A.	12/12/70, 28	USMC Scout	Derby	CT
Carrillo	Melvin	3/03/68, 19	Army Scout	Roswell	NM
Carter	Merle K.	10/22/67, 20	Navy Sentry	Sapulpa	OK
Castle	Russell L.	7/02/67, 24	Army 40th Scout	Woodbridge	VA
Chisholm	Ronald. L.	5/11/67, 22	USMC Sentry	Jacksonville	FL
Clark	Walter L.	10/29/67, 20	Army 46th Scout	Roseville	MI
Clokes	Robert	12/04/68, 21	Army Scout	New York	NY
Colford	Darrell L.	11/08/70, 25	Army 38th Scout	West Chicago	IL
Collier	Steven E.	10/27/68, 19	Army Scout	Branford	CT
Conklin	Michael L.	6/24/70, 22	Army Scout	Midland	MI
Conners, Jr.	Ralph W.	5/22/69, 22	Army 41st Scout	Washington	DC
Connors	Jack L.	8/21/69, 23	Army 557th Tracker	Filion	MI
Cox, Jr.	Edward E.	2/15/69, 20	Army 43rd Scout	Shreveport	LA
Crawford	Bobby D.	1/10/68, 22	Army 43rd Scout	Buncombe	IL
Crawford	Gordon L.	2/01/71, 24	Army Scout	Ft. Wayne	IN
Cumbie	William T.	2/09/69, 20	USMC Scout	Jacksonville	FL
Currier, Jr.	Gordon L.	1/31/68, 22	Army 212th MP	Independence	MO
Czarnota	Chris Z.	3/22/71, 20	Army Scout	Perth Amboy	NJ
Davis	Abron E.	1/11/69, 20	USMC Scout	Youngstown	OH
Davis	Eligah L.	4/05/70, 19	USMC Mine	Cecil	GA
Davis	Alan E.	3/21/71, 21	Army Scout	Tulare	CA
Dell	Kenneth J.	11/05/68, 21	Army 49th Scout	E. Vandergrift	PA
Detrick	Gary G.	4/13/69, 20	Army 47th Scout	Wapakoneta	OH
Dillinder	Randy E.	12/10/67, 19	Army 34th Scout	Dearborn	MI
Doria	Richard A.	8/19/69, 21	Army Scout	White Plains	NY
Doyle	John F.	8/25/66, 19	Army 59th Scout	Prospect	CT
Drobena	Michael J.	2/23/69, 23	USMC Scout	Temple	TX
Drum	Thomas	3/04/70, 21	Army 62nd Visual	Johnson City	NY
Drysdale	Charles D.	1/26/69, 22	USMC Scout	Birmingham	AL
Ducote, Jr.	Lonnie J.	8/13/67, 22	Army 34th Scout	Corpus Christi	TX
Duff	Phillip R.	7/07/72, 20	Army Scout	Cornelia	GA
Duke	Douglas O.	12/20/68, 23	Army Vet Tech	Rush Springs	OK
Dunning	William M.	6/22/70, 24	Army 66th Tracker	Bridgeport	CT
Elliott	Robert W.	8/09/70, 24	USMC Mine	Woodbury	NJ
Erickson	Russell M.	7/24/68, 24	Army 59th Scout	Franklin Park	IL
Esterly	Lawrence A.	7/18/69, 20	USMC Scout	Lisbon	OH
Eubanks	George F.	12/07/67, 21	Army 25th Scout	Barboursville	WV
Evans	Ronald L.	4/29/71, 24	Army 42nd Scout	Morrow	OH
Farley	Marshall C.	9/19/67, 20	Army 42nd Scout	Folsom	CA

Last Name	First Name & Middle Initial	Date of Death & Age	Branch/Unit	Home Town	State
Fisher	Thomas W.	9/04/67, 19	USMC Sentry	Allentown	PA
Ford	Richard E.	1/18/70, 22	Army 35th Scout	Surf City	NJ
Fraley	Eugene T.	1/21/68, 28	Navy Seal Team 2	Lansing	MI
Freeman	David M.	8/11/69, 20	Army Scout	Putnam	CT
Freeman	Jeffrey A.	4/08/70, 19	Army 39th Scout	Lakewood	OH
Freppon	John D.	2/02/69, 20	Army Scout	Cincinnati	OH
Fritz	Gerald W.	5/13/75, 20	USAF 56th SPS	Junction	TX
Fuller	Gary L.	2/27/67, 21	USAF Sentry	The Plains	OH
Fuller	Stanley C.	12/12/68, 21	Army 45th Scout	Fullerton	CA
Gaspard, Jr.	Claude J.	5/20/68, 21	Army Scout	Short Hills	NJ
Giberson	Jerry G.	6/20/70, 21	Army Scout	Donnellson	IA
Glenn	Livingston	12/09/67, 28	Army 57th Scout	Boston	GA
Goudelock	William R.	3/18/68, 19	Army 57th Scout	Meridian	CA
Green	Billy M.	6/24/66, 22	Army Scout	Los Angeles	CA
Grieve	Michael A.	1/31/68, 21	Army Scout	Hazel Park	MI
Grifasi	James A.	3/26/70, 22	Army Scout	Tonawanda	NY
Griffin II	William D.	12/15/70, 23	Army 63rd Tracker	Pontiac	MI
Groves	William E.	11/30/67, 20	Army Scout	Seattle	WA
Grundy	Dallas G.	11/05/66, 23	Army Scout	San Jose	CA
Gyulveszi	Theodore L.	2/10/69, 24	Army 41st Scout	Lincoln Park	MI
Hales	Raymon D.	7/19/69, 27	Army 58th Scout	Springville	UT
Harding	John H.	10/08/67, 19	Army 557th Tracker	Benton	AR
Harris	Jessie E.	1/31/68, 22	Army 212th MP	Peoria	IL
Hartsock	Robert W.	2/23/69, 24	Army 44th Scout	Cumberland	MD
Hartwick, Jr.	Floyd W.	7/15/67, 20	USMC Scout	St. Charles	MO
Hatcher	David L.	11/12/70, 21	Army 63rd Visual	New York	NY
Henshaw	Patrick L.	12/19/67, 21	Army Scout	Spokane	WA
Hernandez	Victor R.	10/18/68, 24	Army 57th Scout	Fullerton	CA
Hicks	Larry D.	9/24/70, 22	Army Scout	St.Ann	MO
Hilerio-Padilla	Luis	11/13/69, 20	Army Scout	Yonkers	NY
Hilt	Richard M.	2/13/69, 20	Army Scout	Minneapolis	MN
Holland	Wayne B.	10/26/68, 21	Army Scout	Salemburg	NC
Holley	Glynn B.	12/26/69, 20	USAF Sentry	Midland	TX
Holt	Herschel C.	8/03/66, 23	USMC Scout	Nashville	TN
Hoppough	Dennis K.	7/16/69, 22	USMC Scout	Rochester	NY
Howard	James R.1	1/09/67, 20	Army 44th Scout	Detroit	MI
Howard	Mark T.	11/16/67, 21	Army Visual	St. Louis	MO
Huberty	William M.	10/17/66, 21	Army 44th Scout	St. Paul	MN
Hughes III	Edward C.	11/27/67, 19	Army 44th Scout	Garden Grove	CA
Hurksman, Jr.	Wilhelm S.	7/22/68, 20	Army 43rd Scout	Rhinelander	WI
Ilaoa	Faleagafula	5/13/75, 26	USAF 56th SPS	San Francisco	CA

Appendix

Last Name	First Name & Middle Initial	Date of Death & Age	Branch/Unit	Home Town	State
Ireland	Elmer G.	7/01/69, 21	Army 42nd Scout	Star	ID
Jenkins	Steven L.	1/15/69, 21	Army 981st MP	Santa Anna	CA
Jenkins	Clayton D.	6/03/69, 21	USMC Sentry	Pembine	WI
Jenks	Robert J.	3/02/68, 20	Army Scout	Concord	MI
Jesko	Stephen E.	10/16/70, 20	Army Scout	Hereford	TX
Joecken	Richard K.	8/28/69, 22	Army 44th Scout	Columbus	OH
Johnson	Arnold E.	11/16/67, 20	Army Visual	Rochelle	IL
Johnson	Carl I.	6/22/68, 19	Army 34th Scout	Wakefield	MI
Johnson	Herbert B.	7/05/68, 19	Army Scout	Poughkeepsie	NY
Johnson	Larry L.	11/14/68, 19	Army Scout	Anaheim	CA
Johnson	James A.	7/01/69, 22	Army 39th Scout	Jersey City	NJ
Karau	Ronald D.	3/20/71, 21	Army Scout	Lewisville	MN
Kiefhaber	Andrew J.	2/23/69, 20	Army 65th Tracker	New York	NY
Kimbrough	Golsby	7/06/69, 20	Army 35th Scout	Philadelphia	PA
King	Alexander	1/20/69, 21	Army Scout	Woodbine	GA
Kobelin II	John W.	3/06/69, 24	Army 40th Scout	Cheyenne	WY
Koon	George K.	11/16/67, 20	Army Visual	Baltimore	MD
Kuefner	John A.	8/14/69, 20	Army 37th Scout	Duluth	MN
Kuehn	Lloyd M.	3/09/67, 20	Army Scout	Stillwater	MN
Kunz	Anthony, E.	5/04/67, 21	Army Scout	Kerrville	TX
Lagodzinski	Roger T	5/19/70, 22	AR 57th Scout	Buffalo	NY
Land	David A.	6/07/67, 20	USMC Scout	Panama City	Fl
Lawton	Edward L.	9/27/68, 19	Army Scout	Thermopolis	WY
Lebrun	Robert N.	3/22/71, 21	Army Scout	Woonsocket	RI
Lee	Edward G.	5/13/68, 20	Army 44th Scout	Belmont	MA
Levins	Frederick R.	6/16/70, 23	Army Visual	Naples	FL
Lindholm	Dan V.	9/08/68, 20	Army Scout	Lindsborg	KS
Lindsay	Stephen L.	1/24/71, 24	USMC Scout	Shreveport	LA
Lipton	Joseph, P.	5/01/67, 18	USMC Scout	Floral Park	NY
Lockhart	Harlan N.	11/09/66, 23	Army 35th Scout	Fredricktown	OH
Loftis	Joel C.	6/07/69, 23	USAF 35th SPS	La Marque	TX
London	Dennis W.	5/13/75, 26	USAF 56th SPS	Sparks	NV
Magruder	David B.	5/16/70, 21	Army Scout	Monroe City	MO
Mahurin	Elmer W.	10/11/67, 19	Army Tracker 8	Goodman	MO
Mansfield	John, M.	3/09/67, 21	Army Scout	New York	NY
Marchant	Paul L.	10/18/69, 22	Army Scout	Moline	IL
Markey, Jr.	James P.	1/26/71, 23	Army Tracker	Warminster	PA
Marshall	Mark D.	3/29/69, 18	USMC ScoutSouth	Euclid	OH
Marshall	Clifford W.	2/19/71, 21	Army 43rd Scout	Richmond	KY
Martin	Kenneth	3/05/69, 20	Army Scout	Kalamazoo	MI
Martinez	Juan P.	5/05/68, 25	Army 41st Scout	Pueblo	CO

Last Name	First Name & Middle Initial	Date of Death & Age	Branch/Unit	Home Town	State
Mason, Jr.	Benjamin H.	9/04/67, 19	USMC Sentry	Piscataway	NJ
Mattson	Paul E.	4/20/68, 23	Army 59th Scout	Lake Bluff	IL
Maurer	Walter L.	11/01/70, 20	Army Scout	Whittier	CA
May	Robert W.	2/12/68, 20	Army Scout	Buffalo	NY
Mazzone	Joseph M.	9/22/68, 23	Army Scout	Hicksville	NY
McCarty	Glenn W.	2/20/71, 21	Army Scout	Texas City	TX
McFall	Gary R	.9/13/68, 23	Army 34th Scout	Northridge	CA
McGrath	Edward C.	10/06/67, 20	Army 43rd Scout	Crestview	FL
McIntosh	Donald W.	11/08/70, 19	Army 38th Scout	Hutchinson	KS
McLaughlin	James B.	4/16/71, 23	Army Scout	Bangor	ME
Merschel	Lawrence J.	5/01/68, 20	Army Scout	Wayne	PA
Meyer	Leo R.	10/05/68, 20	Army Scout	Fond Du Lack	WI
Michael	James A.	2/13/71, 21	Army Scout	Gainesville	GA
MIller	Timothy L.	11/24/68, 21	USMC Scout	Stockton	KS
Mills	Rodney K.	5/05/70, 22	Army Scout	Alma	MI
Montano	William A.	11/19/70, 19	USMC Scout	Deer Park	NY
Morrison	James J.	2/02/69, 20	Army 39th Scout	Grand Rapids	MI
Munch	Michael R.	5/13/69, 20	Army 57th Scout	Council Bluffs	IA
Muse	Edward G.	1/31/68, 20	USAF Sentry	Tutwiler	MS
Myers	Richard V.	11/13/67, 20	Army 39th Scout	Glenmoore	PA
Newell	Tim E.	9/09/70, 24	Army 47th Scout	Des Moines	IA
Nicolini	Peter J.	5/16/67, 21	Army Scout	Chicago	IL
Norris	Robert N.	12/19/69, 18	Army 42nd Scout	Towanda	PA
Nudenberg	David A.	11/12/70, 24	Army 63rd Tracker	Caldwell	NY
Oaks	Robert L.	11/11/69, 20	Army Scout	Lamesa	TX
Ohm	David J.	7/20/68, 20	Army Scout	Alden	MN
Olmstead	John P.	7/15/67, 20	Army 48th Scout	Warren	IL
Orsua	Charles D.	7/15/69, 19	USAF Sentry	Sunnyvale	CA
Palacio	Gilbert G.	5/06/69, 21	Army 34th Scout	San Antonio	TX
Park	Irving G.	3/06/70, 23	USAF Sentry	Ft. Wayne	IN
Payne	Robert P.	3/18/68, 25	USMC Scout	Hampshire	IL
Payne	Terry J.	8/05/70, 22	Army Scout	La Crosse	WI
Payne III	Howard D.	4/27/71, 24	Army 59th Scout	Doraville	GA
Pearce	Marvin R.	8/25/68, 19	Army 47th Scout	Capitola	CA
Petersen	Harry T.	11/09/70, 21	Army Scout	Salt Lake City	UT
Piasecki	John M.	11/29/69, 22	Army Scout	Chicago	IL
Pierce	Oscar, W.	3/09/67, 23	Army Scout	Pauls Valley	OK
Plambeck, Jr.	Paul W.	11/13/69, 22	Army 39th Scout	Austin	TX
Plattner	Ernest M.	11/08/68, 23	Army Scout	Marathon	NY
Poland, Jr.	Leon, L.	3/26/67, 20	USMC Scout	West Paris	ME
Porter	Richard C.	1/24/71, 21	USMC Mine	Hanover	NH

Last Name	First Name & Middle Initial	Date of Death & Age	Branch/Unit	Home Town	State
Pulaski, Jr.	Peter	1/04/70, 23	Army 42nd Scout	Howard Beach	NY
Quinn	Thomas W.	4/04/69, 21	Army 45th Scout	Minneapolis	MN
Ratliff	Billy H.	9/24/70, 20	Army 76th Visual	Pomeroyton	KY
Ray	William C.	7/04/70, 21	Army Scout	De Mossville	KY
Rhodes	Robert D.	5/27/70, 19	USMC Scout	Scituate	MA
Rivera	James	3/09/68, 20	Army Tracker	New York	NY
Roberts	Virgil J.	1/22/69, 21	Army 557th Tracker	Aztec	NM
Robinson	Charles J.	1/07/69, 21	Army 49th Scout	East Hampton	MA
Rosas	Jose, A.	5/08/67, 28	USMC Scout	Weslaco	TX
Roth	John, H.	3/09/67, 21	Army Scout	River Rouge	MI
Rowe	Michael T.	2/19/69, 20	Army Scout	Statesboro	GA
Sandberg	Charles H.	5/13/68, 29	Army 44th Ascout	Philadelphia	PA
Schachner	David B.	5/14/69, 20	Army 40th Scout	Charlotte	NC
Schossow	Dennis R.	1/22/71, 21	USMC Mine	Sheldon	ND
Schwab	Richard M.	9/06/70, 21	Army 57th Scout	Medord	OR
Schyska	Leroy F.	12/06/67, 18	Army 46th Scout	Moline	IL
Scott	Dave R.	1/24/68, 21	Army 5th SF	Junction City	KS
Segundo	Pete S.	9/05/69, 22	USMC Scout	Oceano	CA
Selix	James M.	10/30/71, 44	Army 47th Scout	Colorado Springs	CO
Severson	Paul R.	8/25/68, 23	Army 5th SF	Glenwood	IL
Sheldon	William C.	5/05/68, 19	Navy Sentry	Chicago	IL
Shepard	Raymond A.	8/03/66, 24	USMC Scout	Chicago	IL
Sheppard	Ronald E.	9/20/68, 22	Army 49th Scout	Webster Groves	MO
Sims	William J.	7/16/69, 21	Army 60th Mine	Compton	AR
Smith	Gary K.	2/27/67, 21	Army 39th Scout	Santa Ana	CA
Smith	Ronald C.	3/03/67, 20	Army 212th Scout	Deerborn	MI
Smith	Michael F.	4/28/68, 19	Army 59th Scout	Omaha	NE
Smith	Winfred L.	6/08/70, 22	Army Scout	Greenville	VA
Smith	Stephen J.W.	6/21/70, 22	Army Scout	Convoy	OH
Smoot	Robert G.	1/05/68, 19	Army Tracker	Sacramento	CA
Southwick	John P.	10/19/69, 19	USMC Scout	Spokane	WA
Spangler	Max R.	1/21/68, 19	Army 45th Scout	Dallas	TX
Spencer, Jr.	Daniel E.	11/12/68, 23	Army Scout	Bend	OR
Steptoe	Raymond	8/15/66, 20	Army 35th Scout	Navasota	TX
Sturdy	Alan M.	7/02/67, 22	Army 41st Scout	Redwood City	CA
Sullivan	Donald S.	1/29/67, 22	Army 40th Scout	Princeton	NC
Sweat, Jr.	Herbert H.	2/21/69, 20	Army Scout	Palatka	FL
Sweatt	Theodore A.	11/27/68, 22	Army 25th Scout	Terre Haute	IN
Taranto	Robert J.	11/29/68, 21	Army 57th Scout	New York	NY
Teresinski	Joseph A.	2/06/71, 20	Army 557th Visual	Oneida	WI
Thibodeaux	Michael L.	7/19/70, 20	Army Scout	Crowley	LA

Tosh III	James C.	8/21/69, 23	Army 25th Scout	Mobile	AL
Triplett	James M.	4/17/69, 22	USMC Scout	Orlando	FL
Truesdell	John L.	3/20/71, 21	Army Scout	Enid	OK
Van Gorder	William J.	6/21/68, 20	Army 57th Scout	Markham	IL
Vancosky	Michael A.	5/04/70, 19	USMC Scout	Scranton	PA
Vogelpohl	Rex A.	1/11/71, 21	Army 57th Scout	Butler	IN
Waddell	Larry, J.	3/09/67, 20	Army Scout	Richmond	OH
Ward	Danny E.	6/01/68, 21	Army 43rd Scout	Downey	CA
Ward	David J.	7/04/68, 20	Army 981st MP	Las Vegas	NV
Webb	Howard L.	6/08/67, 24	Army 42nd Scout	Rehoboth	DE
White	John O.	1/22/68, 21	Army 57th Scout	Saraland	AL
White	Garson F.	2/13/69, 21	USMC Scout	Sontag	MS
Whitehead	Alfred E.	6/16/68, 25	Army 42nd Scout	Harlan	KY
Whitten	Robert E.	5/08/68, 21	Army Scout	Ft. Myers	FL
Wickenberg	Erik B.	7/06/67, 20	Army Scout	Bertha	MN
Winningham	Richard D.	1/07/69, 20	Army 45th Scout	Battle Creek	MI
Wood	Robert H.	4/09/68, 21	USMC Scout	Ft. Benning	GA
Yeager	Michael J.	4/08/70, 19	USMC Mine	Baltimore	MD
Yochum	Lawrence W.	2/13/70, 19	Army 59th Scout	Burney	CA

United States War Dogs Killed in Action (KIA)

Dog's Name	Dog's I.D. No.	Date of Death	Branch/Unit
Ago	0H28	9/20/68	Army 49th Scout
Alex	0K64	9/16/69	Army 47th Scout
Andy	5A48	1/9/70	Army 50th Scout
Anzo	0H79	9/23/68	USMC Sentry
Apache	9M46	1/11/69	USMC Scout
Arko	0K10	7/15/67	USMC Scout
Arko	K094	12/12/68	Army 45th Scout
Arko	0K13	6/5/69	USMC Scout
Arras	K072	1/12/68	Army 45th Scout
Arras	K015	11/27/70	Army 57th Scout
Arry9	12X	1/29/69	USMC Scout
Artus	K012	12/11/70	Army 42nd Scout
Astor	K092	11/10/70	Army 39th Scout
Axel	8X57	4/13/69	USMC Scout
Axel	K059	3/31/70	Army 58th Scout
Axel	84A6	1/29/71	Army 39th Scout
Bark	5A35	6/16/67	Army 42nd Scout
Baron	0X8	12/23/67	Army 25th Scout
Baron	1X33	6/30/68	Scout
Baron	385M	1/30/69	USMC Scout
Baron	53X9	4/7/69	Army 39th Scout
Baron	31A8	4/11/70	Army 58th Scout
Baron	81A3	9/23/70	Army 47th Scout
Bizz16	M6	3/21/69	Army 47th Scout
Black Jack	498M	9/23/71	Army 48th Scout
Blackie	03X7	3/21/69	Army 49th Scout
Blackie	3A33	12/7/69	Scout
Blackie	38A3	9/9/70	Army 47th Scout
Blaze	0B54	2/28/67	12th SPS
Blitz	X239	10/4/67	Army 43rd Scout
Blitz	56A4	5/31/71	Army 59th Scout
Blitzen	07A5		Unknown
Blitzer	5X32	3/17/69	USMC Sentry
Bo Bear	025M	11/12/68	Army 58th Scout
Bo-Bo	7M25	7/24/69	Army 40th Scout
Bobo	66A5	12/26/70	Army 43rd Scout
Bodie	M460	1/16/66	USMC Scout
Bootsy	9X64	9/19/67	Army 48th Scout
Bounce	494A	2/14/71	Army 43rd Scout
Bozo	9X40	9/12/67	377th SPS

Dog's Name	Dog's I.D. No.	Date of Death	Branch/Unit
Brandy	323M	6/25/71	Army 42nd Scout
Britta	0X47	11/27/68	Army 25th Scout
Bruno	26X8	7/16/67	Army 48th Scout
Bruno	8M05	1/30/69	Army 35th Scout
Brutus	2M96		Army 37th Scout
Brutus	44MP98		1st MP
Brutus	46M2	3/17/69	Army 43rd Scout
Buck	61X2	11/24/68	Army 47th Scout
Buck	7X74	6/2/70	Army 42nd Scout
Buck	0108	7/12/70	Unknown
Buckshot	23X9	5/13/68	Army 44th Scout
Buddy	80X5	12/15/68	Army 43rd Scout
Buddy	6M6	19/2/70	Army 59th Scout
Buddy	898M	11/12/70	Army 48th Scout
Bummer	9X58	7/4/67	Unknown
Butch	38M6	4/25/69	Army 33rd Scout
Butch	6M36	11/8/70	Army 38th Scout
Caesar	165A		Scout
Caesar	5X56	3/4/68	Army 39th Scout
Caesar	3A55	5/19/68	Army 38th Scout
Caesar	25A31	0/31/70	Scout
Cap	4K87	6/27/71	Army 34th Scout
Casey	13M7	9/17/71	Army 158th Scout
Ceasar	07A2	4/10/70	Army 50th Scout
Charger	416A	6/2/70	Scout
Chase	98X6	8/20/68	Army 57th Scout
Chief	700M		USMC Scout
Chief	5A67	4/17/69	USMC Sentry
Chief	3M42	12/9/69	Army 57th Scout
Chooch	06M3	4/28/70	Army 48th Scout
Claus	K024	6/18/69	Army 40th Scout
Commander	X482	4/26/69	Army 41st Scout
Cookie	41X5	9/28/68	Army 49th Scout
Cookie	42M2	6/24/69	Army 46th Scout
Country Joe	7K3	11/23/71	USMC Mine
Cracker	60X1	8/19/68	Army 40th Scout
Crypto	8M63	2/23/69	Army 45th Scout
Cubby	612E	12/4/663	77th SPS
Danny	21M2	4/29/70	Army 42nd Scout
Deno	7M28	5/22/69	Army 41st Scout
Diablo	X313	1/31/68	3rd SPS
Dix	M064	2/15/70	Army 57th Scout

Appendix

Dog's Name	Dog's I.D. No.	Date of Death	Branch/Unit
Duchess	55X2	9/13/67	Scout
Dug	112M	6/1/70	Army 47th Scout
Dugan	X322	7/18/69	USMC Scout
Duke	M827		USMC Scout
Duke	9X60	1/15/67	Scout
Duke	5A23	4/7/68	Army 35th Scout
Duke	3A15	6/13/68	Army 25th Scout
Duke	409M	2/23/69	Army 49th Scout
Duke	383M	12/6/69	Army 57th Scout
Duke	230M	3/24/70	Army 57th Scout
Duke	721M	8/4/70	Army 48th Scout
Duke	461A	1/3/71	Army 48th Scout
Duke	84A2	1/21/72	Army 59th Scout
Dusty	724M	7/28/70	Army 37th Scout
Dusty	62M6	4/27/71	Army 58th Scout
Egor	751M	6/23/69	Army 41st Scout
Erik	36X3	11/9/67	Army 44th Scout
Erich	3M92	1/18/70	Army 35th Scout
Fant	K027	10/28/70	Army 47th Scoutq
Feller	03X5	11/8/68	Army 39th Scout
Flare	X272	7/26/69	Army 42nd Scout
Frico	0H57	1/13/67	Army 41st Scout
Fritz	499A		Scout
Fritz	X740	10/18/68	Army 57th Scout
Fritz	2M97	11/7/68	Army 57th Scout
Fritz	999F	2/28/69	12th SPS
Fritz	M275	10/6/69	Army 35th Scout
Fritz	4M69	10/15/69	Army 47th Scout
Fritzie	763F	1/26/69	35th SPS
Gallo	28X5	4/13/67	Unknown
Gar	789M	3/9/70	Army 37th Scout
Gretchen	3M32	11/18/68	Army 44th Scout
Gretchen	40X7	5/29/70	Army 42nd Scout
Gretchen	265A	9/3/70	Army 39th Scout
Gunder	1X07	8/13/67	Army 34th Scout
Hannabel	740M	11/22/69	USMC Scout
Hanno	0H03	2/16/67	Army 33rd Scout
Hasso	0K55	6/18/69	Army 41st Scout
Hector	X459	5/14/69	Army 40th Scout
Heidi	18A6	10/16/68	Army 58th Scout
Heidi	T031	11/12/70	Army 63rd Tracker
Heidi	0030	2/19/71	Army 43rd Scout

Dog's Name	Dog's I.D. No.	Date of Death	Branch/Unit
Heidi	X017	4/23/71	Army 57th Scout
Hunde	M145	2/28/68	3rd SPS
Husky	48X4	11/11/68	USMC Scout
Ikar	X682	7/2/69	Army 40th Scout
Irish	1A56	3/20/68	USMC Sentry
Jack	130M	10/18/68	Army 57th Scout
Jack	7X18	12/17/69	Army 34th Scout
Jack	24M8	9/5/70	USMC Scout
Joe	X134	2/13/70	USMC Scout
Joe	6B54	6/15/70	Army 45th Scout
Kaiser	Unknown	7/6/66	USMC Scout
Kaizer	6M9	11/18/69	USMC Scout
Kat	00M3	4/30/70	Army 48th Scout
Kazan	40A6		Army 57th Scout
Kazan	7X51	6/15/68	Army 57th Scout
Keechie	14X7	12/10/67	Army 34th Scout
Kelly	5M52	7/2/69	Army 39th Scout
Kelly	Unknown	5/18/70	Army 34th Scout
Kelly	55A0	1/23/71	USMC Scout
King	61A0		Army 43rd Scout
King	7M79		Army 34th Scout
King	66X5	1/10/68	Army 43rd Scout
King	334X	2/10/68	981st MP
King	0K87	7/1/68	Army 43rd Scout
King	8X87	9/13/68	Army 34th Scout
King	58X3	12/23/68	Army 41st Scout
King	2A15	2/16/69	Army 48th Scout
King	245M	3/20/69	Army 33rd Scout
King	8M51	5/18/69	Army 49th Scout
King	390M	8/1/69	USMC Scout
King	81M5	8/14/69	Army 37th Scout
King	9A18	11/13/69	Army 39th Scout
King	7A65	2/13/70	Army 59th Scout
King	X200	4/8/70	Army 39th Scout
King	07M6	5/19/70	Army 42nd Scout
King	72M4	6/28/71	Army 47th Scout
King	I32M8	2/20/70	USMC Scout
Krieger	65M8	6/2/71	Army 42nd Scout
Kurt	6A92	6/22/68	Army 34th Scout
Lance	82A6	1/26/71	Army 42nd Scout
Lightning	0M40	5/11/70	981st MP
Little Joe	223M	2/22/70	Army 47th Scout

Appendix

Dog's Name	Dog's I.D. No.	Date of Death	Branch/Unit
Lobo	38X2		Army 34th Scout
Lobo	58AM4	2/15/69	Army 43rd Scout
Lodo	729M	6/25/70	Army 37th Scout
Lucky	2X37	10/17/66	Army 44th Scout
Ludwick	1X74	8/22/66	377th SPS
Lux	0K29	8/19/68	3rd SPS
Mac	X083	11/5/68	Unknown
Machen	2X99	3/31/68	Army 39th Scout
Max	7X72		Scout
Max	8X18	6/4/70	Army 42nd Scout
Mesa	103M	8/24/69	Army 49th Scout
Mike	4X64	7/2/67	Army 41st Scout
Mike	760M	11/10/69	Army 57th Scout
Ming	X528	5/11/68	Army 45th Scout
Mister	3M13		Army 58th Scout
Mitzi	9X43	12/5/67	Scout
Money	32X3	1/24/69	Army 41st Scout
Notzey	X405	4/25/70	Army 33rd Scout
Paper	684M	6/26/69	Army 42nd Scout
Peanuts	3M56	4/13/69	USMC Scout
Penney	9M96	10/5/70	Army 34th Scout
Pepper	94A2		Army 44th Scout
Pirate	8X71	12/2/68	Army 34th Scout
Polo	808M	9/28/68	Army 58th Scout
Prince	0X02		USMC Scout
Prince	7X56		Scout
Prince	8M34		Army 33rd Scout
Prince	182X	12/9/65	3rd SPS
Prince	30X7	3/2/67	Army 48th Scout
Prince	43X3	9/2/67	Army 44th Scout
Prince	0X99	2/20/68	Scout
Prince	3X92	7/10/68	USMC Sentry
Prince	69X7	1/2/69	USMC Scout
Prince	703M	3/15/69	Army 37th Scout
Prince	9A38	7/27/69	USMC Scout
Prince	271M	6/12/70	Army 37th Scout
Prince	288A	10/26/70	Army 59th Scout
Prince	74X1	1/30/71	Army 47th Scout
Princess	45X9	2/2/69	Army 39th Scout
Princess	1MS0	4/13/69	Army 47th Scout
Princess	49A1	8/3/69	Army 39th Scout
Princess	764M	4/19/70	Army 37th Scout

Dog's Name	Dog's I.D. No.	Date of Death	Branch/Unit
Ranger	787M	3/16/69	Army 37th Scout
Reb	21X8	2/23/67	Army 48th Scout
Rebel	Unknown	12/4/66	377th SPS
Rebel	X202	7/19/69	Army 58th Scout
Rebel	94A3	3/8/70	Army 50th Scout
Rebel	X820	5/26/70	USMC Scout
Reggie	3A57	3/10/68	9812st MP
Rennie	7K34		USMC Mine
Renny	A548	1/11/68	35th SPS
Rex	8X60	5/25/67	Army 33rd Scout
Rex	X306	2/7/68	Army 43rd Scout
Rex	0K11	2/7/68	Army 43rd Scout
Rex	4A85	5/4/68	Army 40th Scout
Rex	3X06	1/26/69	USMC Scout
Rex	5A77	2/22/69	35th SPS
Rex	83X4	3/6/70	Army 48th Scout
Rex	93M9	5/29/70	Army 34th Scout
Ringo	X700	2/6/68	Unknown
Rip	2X12	10/16/67	Unknown
Rolf	K086	6/17/70	Army 42nd Scout
Rommel	52X6	6/10/70	Army 50th Scout
Rover	M075	9/7/68	Army 57th Scout
Rover	475A	9/19/70	Army 33rd Scout
Royal	19X8	9/27/70	Army 48th Scout
Rusty	3X22		Army 39th Scout
Rusty	6A97	8/30/69	Army 42nd Scout
Saber	X547	11/30/68	Scout
Sam	80A0		Army 40th Scout
Sam	76X2	4/11/68	USMC Scout
Sam	544M	4/6/70	Army 57th Scout
Sam	5A84	9/24/70	Army 62nd Tracker
Sam	66A7	12/16/70	Army 57th Scout
Sarge	5X94	11/1/66	Scout
Sarge	292M	10/29/69	Army 34th Scout
Sarge	934M	1/12/71	Army 57th Scout
Sargent	6X81	11/27/67	Army 44th Scout
Sargent Bilko	8X00	10/25/68	Army 59th Scout
Satch	M164	1/31/68	212th MP
Savage	M263	9/28/68	Army 49th Scout
Shack	9X28	1/28/69	Army 43rd Scout
Shadow	9X001	1/9/67	Army 44th Scout
Shadow	B387	8/26/68	62nd Army Tracker

Appendix

Dog's Name	Dog's I.D. No.	Date of Death	Branch/Unit
Shadow	X622	5/27/70	Army 40th Scout
Sheba	824M		Army 39th Scout
Sheba	7X54	8/27/71	Army 58th Scout
Shep	48X8	1/24/69	Army 50th Scout
Shep	45X8	1/27/69	Scout
Shep	69A3	1/29/70	Army 47th Scout
Sheps	8X63	1/13/67	Army 41st Scout
Silber	1M57	11/27/68	Army 25th Scout
Silver	X101	7/24/68	Army 59th Scout
Sissy	441A	1/26/71	Army 43rd Scout
Skipper	288M	7/25/70	Army 50th Scout
Smokey	1A82	9/15/66	Scout
Smokey	0X16	5/27/68	Unknown
Smokey	X121	6/1/68	Army 43rd Scout
Smokey	X817	1/27/69	Army 57th Scout
Smokey	36M0	5/13/69	Army 57th Scout
Smokey	7M50	4/26/70	Army 47th Scout
Socks	X889	6/1/69	Army 47th Scout
Spike	M004	3/1/71	MP
Stark	071X	11/16/68	USMC Sentry
Storm	01M3	4/23/69	Army 39th Scout
Stormy	4M33	7/17/70	USMC Sentry
Suesser	0K8	11/21/68	Army 42nd Scout
T-Bone	X564		Army 42nd Scout
Taro	287M	8/30/71	Army 59th Scout
Tasso	0K40	5/26/70	Army 25th Scout
Tech	75A2		Scout
Tempo	50A7	1/19/71	Army 48th Scout
Teneg	T012	3/12/70	Army 62nd Tracker
Thea	5A99	11/8/68	USMC Sentry
Thor	335A	6/3/70	Army 42nd Scout
Thor	326M	4/9/71	Army 63rd Tracker
Thunder	4A45	5/15/68	Army 42nd Scout
Tiger	3A17	8/9/66	Army 25th Scout
Tiger	18A4	9/19/69	Army 38th Scout
Tiger	3M78	8/14/70	Army 57th Scout
Tim	19X2	9/11/68	Army 44th Scout
Tippy	14A7		Army 39th Scout
Toby	Unknown	12/4/66	377th SPS
TobyT	036	1/25/70	Army 63rd Tracker
Toto	52X8	9/12/67	Unkown
Troubles	1X16	12/30/67	Scout

Dog's Name	Dog's I.D. No.	Date of Death	Branch/Unit
Tye	341M	9/29/70	Army 42nd Scout
Unknown	7K25		USMC Mine
Unknown	7K37		USMC Mine
Willie	6M11	7/27/68	Army 59th Scout
Wolf	150X	5/22/68	USMC Scout
Wolf	0K43	1/7/69	Army 49th Scout
Wolf	7X03	2/26/71	Army 57th Scout
Ziggy	2M78	4/10/69	Army 41st Scout

Glossary

Military Acronyms

Acronym	Definition	Acronym	Definition
AK47	Enemy Military Rifle	PFC	Private First Class (E-3)
APC	Armored Personnel Carrier	PSP	Perforated steel plating
CAR 15	American Military Rifle	Punji	Bamboo spear
CG	Commanding General	PX	Post Exchange
Charlie	Enemy	RA	Regular Army
CIB	Combat Infantry Badge	REMF	Rear-Echelon-Mother-Fucker
CO	Commanding Officer	RPG	Enemy Rocket Propelled
C-rations	Canned food		Grenade
FNG	Fucking New Guy	RTO	Radio/telephone operator
IPSD	Infantry Platoon Scout Dogs	RVN	Republic of Vietnam
KIA	Killed in action	S & D	Search and destroy mission
LTC	Lieutenant Colonel	S2	Military intelligence
LZ	Helicopter landing zone	SGM	Sergeant Major (E-9)
M16	American Military Rifle	SOI	Signal Operating Instructions
M60	American machine gun	TET	Chinese Lunar New Year
M79	American Grenade launcher	Top	First Sergeant (E-8)
MOS	Military Occupational Specialty	US	Draftee
MP	Military Police	VC	Viet Cong
NCO	Non-commission officer	VDHA	Vietnam Dog Handlers Associa
NVA	North Vietnamese Army		tion (www.vdhaonline.org)
OCS	Officer Candidate School	WIA	Wounded in action
OD	Olive Drab		
P38	C-Ration can opener		

to marriage licenses to property deeds.

The Parson's case had led Patrick to think long and hard about colonial liberty. From the start, he knew the Stamp Act was wrong and even dangerous. Strangers on the other side of the ocean should not tax colonists without their permission. If money was needed to pay for the recent war, colonists should find their own way to raise it. Now that Patrick was a Burgess, at least he could help decide how Virginia would react to the Stamp Act.

But after Patrick took his oath of office in Williamsburg, he didn't hear much about the Stamp Act. Some Burgesses seemed reluctant to talk of it at all. The spring session of the Assembly was almost over. Many members were already leaving for their homes in other parts of Virginia. Impatiently Patrick turned to a blank page in one of his law books and began to write. In simple but strong language, he explained why he opposed the Stamp Act. He planned to introduce his statements, or resolutions, to the entire Assembly to approve.

One night he met several other representatives at a local tavern. They agreed that the colonists had to send a strong message to Great Britain to show how angry they were at the mere thought of the Stamp Act. Eagerly the men discussed Patrick's new resolutions.

They offered suggestions and made plans. If passed, these resolutions would send a forceful message directly to Parliament and the king.

On Patrick's twenty-ninth birthday, just nine days after he became a Burgess, he rose to face the Assembly. Most of the men were older, more experienced, and better known than he was. But they weren't taking action. Patrick believed he could convince them to stand up to the king.

Carefully he introduced one resolution after another. The first four passed easily. Then Patrick rose to present his Fifth Resolution. Speaking with a powerful voice, he challenged the Burgesses in plain, sometimes shocking, language. Only the Assembly had the power to tax Virginians, Patrick claimed boldly in his Fifth Resolution. Any outside attempt to give its power to other groups threatened British as well as American liberty.

To some Burgesses this was going too far. Patrick's words set off a violent debate. They felt the resolution insulted the king and Parliament. These members exploded in outrage. Despite their bitter opposition, Patrick continued. "Caesar had his Brutus; Charles the First his Cromwell," Patrick declared, reminding his listeners of the overthrow of past rulers. "And George the Third...," he continued.

Horrified, Patrick's rivals drowned out his voice with cries of treason. They thought he was predicting the downfall of King George, too.

Patrick waited until their shouts died down. "And George the Third may profit from their example." His gaze swept the entire Assembly. "If this be treason, make the most of it."

The Burgesses were stunned. Although Patrick proclaimed his loyalty to the king, he had issued a stirring challenge. If the Assembly accepted his defiant resolution, they would be telling the king that he was wrong. No colony had ever done this before.

Anxiously Patrick waited for the Burgesses to cast their votes. He knew the decision could go either way.

4

The Colonists Unite

"By God, I would have given one hundred guineas for a single vote!" an angry Burgess muttered as he left the chamber. Patrick's Fifth Resolution had passed by a count of twenty to nineteen.

In spite of the Burgess's indignation, the Fifth Resolution did not chart a course of action. It simply denied the king's right to tax Americans. Patrick had hoped to push the Burgesses towards further opposition in two final resolutions. He had wanted the Assembly to agree that the colonists didn't have to pay Parliament's taxes. In fact, anyone who even said that Parliament could tax Virginians should be declared an enemy of the colony, according to Patrick. This time, however, his best arguments failed to convince the Assembly. The members voted against the last two resolutions.

Patrick had done everything he could—at least he thought he had. While an unsuspecting Patrick rode home, his opponents called for another vote and canceled the Fifth Resolution. But the force Patrick had unleashed could not be called back. Someone, perhaps Patrick himself, had mailed copies of the Virginia Resolves to other colonies. Soon newspapers as far away as Boston were publishing them all— even the ones the Assembly never passed. Throughout the colonies, people applauded Virginia's bold stance. Other colonial assemblies drafted their own protests, too.

It would take more than words to convince the British Parliament, however. British lawmakers ignored the colonists' wishes and passed the Stamp Act. A special Stamp Act Congress was held in October 1765. Twenty-seven delegates from nine colonies met in New York to hammer out a series of resolutions in protest. They urged colonists not to order goods from Britain until Parliament canceled the Stamp Act. Many colonists and merchants pledged to do just that. Lawyers, including Patrick, avoided legal matters that required stamps, and many courts closed. People even burned straw dummies of stamp collectors, and patriots known as Sons of Liberty held stirring rallies.

35

Few people outside of Virginia knew of Patrick's role in fighting the Stamp Act. But in his own colony, he became a hero. Folks pledged to defend Patrick with their very lives if anyone tried to harm him.

The colonists' uproar shocked Parliament and hurt British merchants who traded with the colonists. Finally, on May 1, 1766, word arrived in Virginia that the Stamp Act had been repealed. Colonists hailed the news as a great victory.

This was an especially happy time for Patrick as he finished work on his new home in Louisa County. The small house overlooking Roundabout Creek was plain and crowded. But Patrick was thrilled to move into the new home. There his fourth child, Anne, was born in 1767.

Patrick continued to move easily between the folksiness of the country and the formality of the courtroom. Although he was only in his early thirties, his reputation as a lawyer was so great that people came to court sessions just to hear him speak.

Blue eyes flashing, Patrick made his listeners forget everything but the points he was making. One observer, sitting in a balcony, became so lost in Patrick's words that he accidentally spit tobacco juice on the people below. Then the man almost toppled over the railing himself!

Patrick knew how to convince others do to the right thing. Unfortunately, he didn't always live up to his own beliefs. He especially struggled with his decision to keep slaves. Owning slaves was a way of life for many white landowners. And many white colonists did not think owning black men and women was wrong. Patrick was different. He knew slavery was wrong, but he continued to own slaves. "I will not, I cannot justify it," he told a friend.

In 1771 Patrick moved his family from Roundabout Creek to a much grander plantation named Scotchtown. Now he had a thousand acres and one of the largest houses in all Virginia. Slaves planted the corn and tobacco. They took care of the animals and cooked in the large kitchen near the main house. But Patrick never doubted that slavery was wrong. "I believe a time will come when an opportunity will be offered to abolish this lamentable Evil," he wrote. If that chance came in his lifetime, Patrick would help. If it didn't, he would teach his children to treat their slaves kindly, as he tried to do.

That same year, Patrick's third daughter, Betsy, was born, followed two years later by his third son, Edward. But Patrick's joy at his new little boy was clouded by worry for Sallie. Sometime after the birth, Sallie became withdrawn and even hostile. Patrick feared she might become dangerous. Little was known about mental illness in those days. If Patrick sent Sallie to the mental hospital in Williamsburg, he couldn't be sure how she would be treated. Since she had to be confined for her own safety, Patrick had two sunny basement rooms prepared for Sallie and the slave woman who attended her.

Patrick may have wanted to spend his time caring for Sallie. But as the colonists' quarrel with Britain heated up, politics claimed more and more of his time and energy. Late one night, in the spring of 1773, Patrick met with Thomas Jefferson and several other men at the Raleigh Tavern in Williamsburg. More and more, Patrick was convinced that all the colonies had to stick together. With his colleagues, he called for a Committee of Correspondence to keep Virginia informed of British threats to American liberty in other colonies.

Patrick and his friends were right about the colonies needing to talk over events. Parliament had recently passed the Tea Act. This new law allowed British tea merchants to sell directly to customers in the colonies and bypass the American merchants. That meant lower prices for the colonists' favorite drink. But colonial traders in tea would be hurt by the arrangement, and people were furious.

Many colonists felt that Parliament and the king did not have the right to control colonial business. They worried that Britain might try to interfere in colonial affairs again in the future if it succeeded this time.

In indignation, some Boston patriots staged a dramatic protest. On December 16, 1773, they dressed up as Mohawk Indians, boarded several ships full of tea from Britain, and threw the entire cargo into the water. Over three hundred chests of tea were ruined in what became known as the Boston Tea Party. An angry Parliament decided to close the port of Boston beginning on June 1, 1774. Much of the colony's power to govern itself was also taken away. British troops were sent to Boston to enforce the harsh measures.

All over America, people reacted to Boston's fate with shock, outrage, and fear. Many believed that a threat to one colony was a threat to all. If British troops could be stationed in Boston, they could be stationed anywhere.

When Patrick arrived in Williamsburg in the spring of 1774, the city was buzzing with talk about Boston. Something had to be done to show the colonists' resentment. But what? Secretly Patrick met with a small group of Virginia Burgesses to work out a plan. They would ask the Assembly to declare June 1 a day of prayer and fasting. All over Virginia, people would pray for the opening of the port and the end of British tyranny.

On June 1, Patrick was already back at his Scotchtown home. Somberly he observed the day, but he was glad to be with his children again. Their mother's condition had not improved, and they needed Patrick more than ever. Throughout their marriage, Patrick's career had kept him away from Sallie a great deal. Now there was little he could do but bring Sallie her meals and sit quietly beside her.

All too soon, Patrick had to say good-bye to Sallie and the children again. In August a special convention in Williamsburg had chosen him, along with several other Virginians, to attend a Continental Congress to be held in Philadelphia. For the first time, representatives from nearly all the colonies would meet together. The fifty-six delegates would decide how to respond to the worsening crisis with Britain.

George Washington, also a delegate, invited Patrick to his home. Patrick stopped at Mount Vernon on his way to the Congress. "I hope you will all stand firm," Martha Washington told her guests at supper that night. "I know George will." Five days later, Patrick, George Washington, and another representative from Virginia, Edmund Pendleton, rode into Philadelphia.

Patrick couldn't wait to grapple with the issues. He believed it was time for the delegates to unite in the cause of liberty. At the convention he declared, "I am not a Virginian, but an American."

Delegates at the convention spent a great deal of time trying to agree on a united response to the closing of Boston's port. Many delegates believed that if the colonists stopped buying British goods, Parliament would have to back down and allow ships to enter Boston. Patrick also felt that trade with Britain should end, but he didn't think that would solve the problem. The king seemed more concerned with proving his power than with ruling fairly. To Patrick's mind, the conclusion was obvious. He told the Congress that Americans would have to fight.

5

Give Me Liberty

Patrick couldn't convince his colleagues that fighting would soon prove necessary. Most delegates still hoped that the colonies could solve their problems with the king peacefully. Few were willing to take up arms against Britain. A very worried Patrick returned home. War was coming. He was sure of it.

Patrick's home life was as unsettled as the colonies' future. Sallie's sickness continued to grow worse. By February 1775 she had died, probably of a fever. For a time, nothing else mattered to Patrick. Weary and grief-stricken, thirty-nine-year-old Patrick called himself a "distraught old man."

But a special Virginia convention was being held the next month to review the work of the Continental Congress. In spite of his great sorrow, Patrick felt he had to attend. Here was another chance to warn people of approaching war. In March Patrick set out for the small town of Richmond, where the Burgesses had decided to meet.

Only one building in Richmond was large enough to hold the seventy-five delegates: Henrico Parish Church. Dark clouds threatened snow as Patrick climbed the hill to the church on March 23. In spite of the chill, a crowd gathered outside to listen through the open windows.

Patrick knew the day's business was likely to turn as stormy as the weather. After the convention voted on routine matters, he rose with a bold resolution. "A well-regulated militia is the natural strength and only security of a free government," he declared. Patrick wanted the colony to recruit and train men to fight.

Patrick faced a situation similar to the one in Philadelphia. Many delegates still hoped the quarrel with Britain could be settled peacefully. They valued their ties to the mother country and feared that Britain would be an impossible enemy to defeat. Its army always won, and its ships sailed all over the world. How could the colonists possibly stand up to such power? They must do everything possible to keep the peace.

Once again, Patrick Henry rose before the packed church. He started speaking calmly but soon roused himself to a mighty pitch of courage. "The war is inevitable—and let it come!!" he exclaimed. "I repeat it, sir, let it come!!!"

Patrick's voice grew louder and louder until it seemed to echo through the church. "Gentlemen may cry peace, peace—but there is no peace. The war is actually begun. The next gale that sweeps from the North will bring to our ears the clash of resounding arms!"

Patrick's whole body was caught up in his words. He slumped and crossed his wrists as if they were fastened by chains. "Is life so dear or peace so sweet, as to be purchased at the price of chains and slavery?" he demanded. Then raising his hands, Patrick gazed at the ceiling. "Forbid it, Almighty God! I know not what course others may take; but as for me, give me liberty or give me death!" With his final words, he pretended to thrust a letter opener into his heart.

For several moments a solemn silence filled the church. No one knew how to reply to such inspired words. But one man listening through a window was so overcome that he threw himself to the ground. "Let me be buried here!" he cried.

Despite Patrick's compelling speech, the tally was close. His resolution passed by five votes, and he was named head of a committee to raise a company of fighting men.

The royal governor, Lord Dunmore, was furious when he learned that Patrick was preparing Virginia to fight. He was also scared. What if the rebels got hold of the gunpowder and ammunition stored in Williamsburg? Secretly he ordered the crew of a British warship to steal the weapons and explosives.

Patrick's temper flared when he heard about Lord Dunmore's order. He summoned armed volunteers from all over Hanover County to an urgent meeting in Newcastle on May 2. He proposed a march to Williamsburg to get the gunpowder back or at least to make the governor pay for it.

The men's anger was further roused by alarming news from Boston. In mid April, British soldiers, called redcoats because of their red uniforms, had tried to capture ammunition stored at Concord, Massachusetts. They were challenged at Lexington by American volunteer fighters. Although both sides had hoped to avoid violence, a shot rang out. Suddenly both sides were firing. When the skirmish was over, ten Americans had been killed and eight wounded. Leaving the casualties, the British marched on to Concord where more fighting broke out.

Patrick's words at Henrico Parish Church had proved true. War had begun in the North. Filled with patriotic anger, Patrick and 150 men prepared to march to Williamsburg.

6

War

As they passed through the countryside, more and more men joined the march, swelling Patrick's ranks to about five thousand. Singing and chanting loudly about liberty, they approached Duncastle, not far from the capital city. Frightened, Lord Dunmore stationed cannons outside his palace, armed his slaves, and ordered British sailors into the town. A clash, like the ones at Lexington and Concord, appeared inevitable. Then, when Patrick was just twelve miles from the city, Lord Dunmore offered to pay for the seized gunpowder if the men would turn back. At first Patrick refused. But later he agreed to the terms and turned his small army towards home.

All over Hanover County, people applauded Patrick's brave action. But the governor was furious at Patrick's victory. He called Patrick a "man in desperate circumstances" and published a proclamation "strictly charging all persons . . . not to aid, abet, or give countenance to the said Patrick Henry. . . ."

Several days later when Patrick headed for Philadelphia and the Second Continental Congress, an armed guard went with him as far as Maryland. Partly this was to honor him. But mostly it was to protect him. Lord Dunmore was eager to get his hands on Patrick!

Events moved swiftly that summer of 1775. Finally the delegates understood they had to fight. It seemed that the king was never going to give the colonists the freedom they wanted. They elected George Washington commander in chief of all the American troops. They also decided to send troops from other colonies to help Boston resist the British troops stationed in that city. In spite of these drastic steps, however, some delegates still hoped to avoid a final split with Britain. Once more, the Congress sent an appeal to King George. It hoped Americans could maintain their ties with Britain.

Returning to Virginia, Patrick couldn't share such hopes. More than ever, he believed America had to make a full break with Britain. On his arrival at another Virginia convention, he learned that he'd been chosen colonel of the First Virginia Regiment and commander in chief of all Virginia forces.

Toward the end of September, Patrick began setting up a soldiers' camp behind the College of William and

Mary in Williamsburg. By this time, Lord Dunmore had left the city for a British warship. On November 7, he announced a state of martial law. That meant that anyone who opposed the king could be branded a traitor and hanged.

In spite of the danger, men continued to join Patrick from all over Virginia. Some brought rifles. Others brought tomahawks, the only weapons they had. The new recruits wore hunting shirts, many of them embroidered with the words "Liberty or Death." One group of men even had animal tails swinging from their hats. Patrick worked hard to turn his ragtag assembly into a real fighting unit.

But some members of the Virginia convention were not happy to see Patrick training soldiers. They felt that he lacked military experience and was more needed in government than on the battlefield. Patrick felt insulted when they didn't discuss campaign strategy and other important matters with him. Finally he felt he had no choice but to quit.

Word of Patrick's decision spread through the encampment. Many disappointed soldiers decided to leave the army too. They trusted Patrick Henry and resented the way he had been treated. Loudly the soldiers declared their "unwillingness to serve under any other commander."

51

Now it was Patrick's turn to feel alarmed. He'd worked too hard warning the colonies of war to allow all those soldiers to quit along with him. Patrick spent an extra night in Williamsburg visiting groups of soldiers and urging them to stay. The soldiers were so inspired by Patrick that the newspaper declared them willing to "spend the last drop of their blood in their country's defense."

As a civilian, Patrick was determined to give all his energy to the cause of freedom. At the Fifth Virginia Convention held in Williamsburg in May 1776, Patrick argued that Americans should end all political ties to Britain. After some debate, a resolution was passed telling Virginia's delegates at the Continental Congress to vote for independence. Celebrations broke out all over Williamsburg. The British flag flying at the capitol was taken down, and a new "Union Flag of the American state" was hoisted.

Even more than a new flag, Virginia needed a new government. Elections had to be held to replace officials who had been appointed by the king. During the convention, Patrick came down with a bad case of malarial fever. Although he could no longer attend the sessions, the Virginia delegates elected him the first American governor to lead a free Virginia. In July 1776, around the time that the Declaration of

Independence was adopted in Philadelphia, a very weak Patrick took the oath of office from his sickbed. He was so ill that witnesses wondered if the new governor would live.

Slowly, however, Patrick began to recover. By September he had moved into the same palace where Lord Dunmore had once ranged cannons against him on the lawn. As governor he attended countless meetings, recruited soldiers, and sent provisions to General George Washington's starving army. "From morning till night I have not a minute from business," he sighed. "There are a thousand things to mend."

In spite of his hectic schedule, Patrick was often lonely. He was used to a lively family life, and he missed his children, who remained at Scotchtown. On one of his trips home, Patrick noticed a lovely dark-haired woman, the daughter of an old friend. Although she was the same age as his own oldest daughter, Patrick felt deeply drawn to her. On October 9, 1777, Patrick and Dorothea Dandridge were married. Returning to Williamsburg after the wedding, they heard that the Americans had defeated the British at Saratoga. Overjoyed, Patrick called for a great celebration.

By 1779 Patrick had served three one-year terms as governor, the most anyone was allowed to serve in a row. Some people wanted to change Virginia's constitution so he could be elected again, but Patrick wouldn't hear of it. He had done everything he could to help the war effort. It was time to let others take over. In May Patrick set off for his new home near the border of North Carolina. Loneliness certainly was not a problem anymore. About fifty people, including his newborn baby daughter, many relatives, and several slave families came with him to the plantation called Leatherwood.

It seemed that Patrick could never stay in one place for long. Soon he accepted a seat in Virginia's General Assembly. In May 1781, Patrick went to Charlottesville to meet with the colony's other lawmakers. It was a desperate time in Virginia, as the redcoats seized military supplies, horses, and food. The Assembly had only begun its work in Charlottesville when an exhausted rider galloped into town. The British were on their way, hoping to capture Governor Thomas Jefferson and the legislators. Not long afterwards, the redcoats themselves arrived.

7

A New Nation

Small groups of Assemblymen scrambled over the Blue Ridge Mountains ahead of the British. Hidden from view, Patrick may even have spied the British troops charging past. Anxiously he and his companions continued their secret escape. Late in the afternoon they reached a small, lonely cabin where they asked a woman for something to eat. When the woman heard that the men had fled from the enemy, she was outraged. "Ride on, you cowardly knaves!" she cried. Then someone pointed out Patrick, and she stared in amazement. "Well then," she said at last, "if that is Patrick Henry, it must be all right." She let the men in and shared her food.

Several months later, in October 1781, George Washington defeated British general Charles Cornwallis at Yorktown, Virginia. Although some fighting would still occur, the tide had turned. America had won the war. At last, Americans could look forward to freedom from Britain. They would be allowed to choose their own government and law-makers. In the midst of his excitement, Patrick had a second reason to celebrate. One month after the victory, Dorothea gave birth to their third little girl.

The year 1783 brought another public and private celebration. The Treaty of Paris officially ended the Revolutionary War, and Dorothea had a little boy that the happy couple named Patrick.

Young Patrick was scarcely two when his forty-nine-year-old father was elected governor again. Packing up the wagons once more, the Henrys moved to Richmond. Patrick served two more terms as governor, then returned to the Assembly as a representative.

All the while, his family continued to grow. His sister once said that the cradle never stopped rocking in Patrick's house. Often when Patrick rode through the streets of Richmond or about his fields, he balanced a toddler on the saddle in front of him and let another child hang on behind. He still loved music, company, and a good joke. As he grew older, he spent more time reading his Bible and occasionally wrote poetry for his children.

The United States was now an independent nation, but there were still many problems to solve. Among other things, the new government did not have the power to form an army, tax citizens, or settle disputes between states. In 1787 leaders from the states met in Philadelphia to make changes to America's first constitution. The convention proposed an entirely new constitution instead. Patrick was suspicious. He worried about the freedom of individual people. The new constitution said nothing about freedom of speech, the press, or religion. Patrick called it "the most fatal plan that could possibly be conceived to enslave a free people."

Nine states had to ratify, or vote to accept, the constitution for it to go into effect. At a state convention held in Richmond, Patrick fought hard to keep Virginia from ratifying. As excited as he was, Patrick couldn't return home until the convention was over. On June 24, 1788, he made a final speech urging the delegates to vote against the constitution. Rain drummed on the roof, and thunder rumbled ominously. Soon even Patrick Henry could not be heard.

In spite of Patrick's best efforts, the Assembly voted to accept the constitution. But no one forgot Patrick's misgivings. Soon the new Congress proposed ten additions to the Constitution, which would guarantee basic rights to American citizens. In December 1791, Virginia became the eleventh state to ratify the amendments, known as the Bill of Rights.

All his life Patrick had worked to promote freedom. Now he had earned the right to some privacy. George Washington offered him several important positions in the new government, but Patrick turned them all down. He was content to practice law and watch over Red Hill, the plantation he bought in 1792. Although he looked older than his fifty-six years, his voice was still so powerful that workers could hear him half a mile away! And he still loved to play the fiddle while his youngest children danced in glee around him.

George Washington didn't give up. Even after he left the presidency, he urged Patrick to run for office. Listening to his friend, Patrick was elected to the Virginia Assembly in 1799. Before he could take office, however, he died on June 6.

Years earlier Patrick had written that great men do not escape disappointments in life. They simply overcome them. Patrick himself had known many setbacks, both in his private and public lives. But he never stopped speaking his mind or fighting for liberty. According to America's third president, Thomas Jefferson, Patrick was exactly what America needed during the stormy years that led to the Revolutionary War. "He was as well suited to the times as any man ever was," recalled Jefferson, "and it is not now easy to say what we would have done without Patrick Henry."

Descriptions of Patrick Henry

Patrick Henry always had plenty to say. Here's what some others had to say about Patrick Henry.

"He is by far the most powerful speaker I ever heard."
  —George Mason, Virginian patriot and politician

"For grand impressions in the defense of liberty, the Western world has not yet been able to exhibit a rival."
  —Edmund Randolph, governor of Virginia, 1786–1788

"By his tones alone it seemed to me that he could make you cry or laugh at pleasure."
  —Judge Spencer Roane, Patrick's son-in-law

"I think he was the best humored man in society I almost ever knew."
  —Thomas Jefferson, third president of the United States

"Patrick Henry has only to say 'let this be law' and it is law."
  —George Washington, first president of the United States

Select Bibliography

Books

Carson, Jane. *Patrick Henry: Prophet of the Revolution.* 1979. Reprint, Williamsburg, VA: Jamestown-Yorktown Foundation, 1992.

Elson, James M., ed. *Patrick Henry and Thomas Jefferson.* Brookneal, VA: The Descendants' Branch of the Patrick Henry Memorial Foundation, 1997.

Elson, James M., ed. *Patrick Henry Essays In Celebration of the Fiftieth Anniversary of the Patrick Henry Memorial Foundation.* Brookneal, VA: The Descendants' Branch of the Patrick Henry Memorial Foundation, 1994.

Hardwick, Kevin R. *Patrick Henry: Economic, Domestic, and Political Life in Eighteenth Century Virginia.* Brookneal, VA: Patrick Henry Memorial Foundation, 1991.

Henry, William Wirt. *Patrick Henry: Life, Correspondences, and Speeches.* New York: Franklin, 1891.

Mayer, Henry. *A Son of Thunder: Patrick Henry and the American Republic.* 1986. Reprint, Charlottesville and London: University of Virginia Press, 1991.

Meade, Robert Douthat. *Patrick Henry: Patriot in the Making.* Philadelphia and New York: J. B. Lippincott Company, 1957.

Meade, Robert Douthat. *Patrick Henry: Practical Revolutionary.* Philadelphia and New York: J. B. Lippincott Company, 1969.

Wirt, William. *Sketches of the Life and Character of Patrick Henry.* Philadelphia: Ayer Company Publications, 1817.

Pamphlets and Articles

The Proceedings of the Virginia Convention in the Town of Richmond on the 23rd of March 1775. 1927. Reprint, Richmond, VA: St. John's Church, 1991.

Fontaine, Edward. *Patrick Henry: Corrections of biographical mistakes, and popular errors in regard to his character...* Scotchtown, VA: 1996.

Mayo, Bernard. "The Enigma of Patrick Henry." *Virginia Quarterly Review* (spring 1959): 176–195.

McCants, David A. "The Authenticity of William Wirt's Version of Patrick Henry's 'Liberty or Death' Speech." *The Virginia Magazine of History and Biography* (October 1979): 387–402.

Robinson, David. "Patrick Henry—An Ornament and an Honor to His Profession." *Colonial Williamsburg* (summer 1990): 21–27.

All quotations in this biography were taken from the above sources.

Patrick Henry didn't write his speeches down, but people remembered his powerful words and style. This book includes the traditionally accepted versions of his most famous speeches. Some historians note that we cannot absolutely prove he said certain phrases.

Index

Graphic Novels Available From PAPERCUTZ™

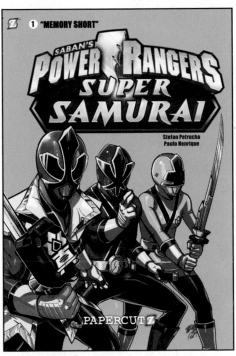
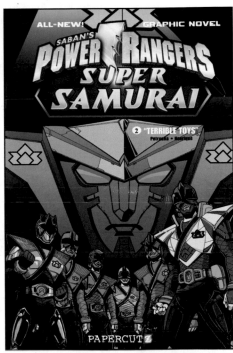

① "MEMORY SHORT"

Stefan Petrucha – Writer
Paulo Henrique – Artist
Laurie E. Smith – Colorist

PAPERCUTZ™
New York

SABAN'S POWER RANGERS SUPER SAMURAI
#1 "MEMORY SHORT"

STEFAN PETRUCHA – Writer
PAULO HENRIQUE – Artist
LAURIE E. SMITH – Colorist
BRYAN SENKA – Letterer

Production by NELSON DESIGN GROUP, LLC
Associate Editor – MICHAEL PETRANEK
JIM SALICRUP
Editor-in-Chief

ISBN: 978-1-59707-331-8 paperback edition
ISBN: 978-1-59707-332-5 hardcover edition

Printed in Canada
May 2012 by Friesens Printing
1 Printers Way
Altona, MB R0G 0B0

Distributed by Macmillan

First Printing

MEET

Saban's **POWER RANGERS**
SUPER SAMURAI

For as long as the Nighlok have existed, there have been Power Rangers sworn to fight them.

The current team of Samurai Power Rangers is a group of teens who grew up knowing that one day they would be summoned to use their uniquely inherited powers and extraordinary skills against evil as the Power Rangers. These skills and powers have been passed down through generation to generation and determine which Ranger they will become.

THE RED RANGER (JAYDEN)

Jayden, the Red Ranger, is the leader of the Samurai Power Rangers. He is a man of few words, but when he speaks he means what he says. He was raised by Mentor Ji after his father died, who was the Red Ranger before him. Jayden has become an excellent warrior and has kept the Moogers at bay on his own for some time. Now, with the help of the other Rangers, Jayden is learning to be a leader and what it is like to have true friends.

Jayden is a kind and caring person but can be firm when action calls. He also carries a secret that he cannot reveal to the other Rangers and at times this knowledge causes him conflict.

His element is fire and his Zord is the Lion.

Weapon:
Spin Sword/Fire Smasher

Signature Move:
Fire Smasher!

Element:
Fire

Zord:
Lion

Notes:
Trained to be a Samurai from a very young age.

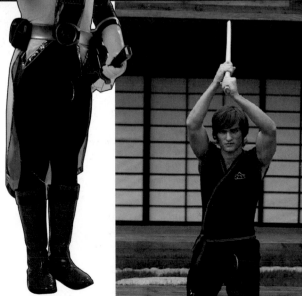

THE PINK RANGER (MIA)

Mia, the Pink Ranger, is the big sister to the group. She is a confident, intuitive, and sensitive person. She is very pragmatic and cares a lot about the well-being of the other Rangers. She trains as hard as the rest of the team, and will jump in to help any Ranger or person in need.

Mia enjoys cooking and often offers up her skills to feed the other Rangers. Problem is that Mia is not a good cook. The humor begins as the other Rangers try their best to act as if her culinary delights are edible.

Mia's element is the sky and her Zord is the Turtle.

Weapon:
Spin Sword/Sky Fan

Signature Move:
Airway!

Element:
Sky

Zord:
Turtle

Notes:
Longs to be a gourmet chef and used to sing

THE BLUE RANGER (KEVIN)

Kevin, the Blue Ranger, has lived his entire life by the code of the Samurai.

Kevin's dream was to be an Olympic swimmer. However, he has placed that dream on hold to become the Blue Ranger. He is a well-trained swordsman and has been raised on the traditions of the Samurai. Kevin is the more sober Ranger who continues his discipline with a daily workout and training. He is honored to be a Samurai and takes his position among the Rangers seriously.

His element is water and his Zord is the Dragon.

Weapon:
  Spin Sword/Hydro Bow

Signature Move:
  Dragon Splash!

Element:
  Water

Zord:
  Dragon

Notes:
  Aside from Jayden,
  Kevin has the best
  technique of all the Rangers.

THE GREEN RANGER (MIKE)

Being a bit of a rebel is truly part of Mike's nature. He is the Green Ranger.

Mike loves to think outside of the box, play video games, and hang with friends. He has a more casual approach to his training but deep down inside takes being a Power Rangers seriously. He is a free spirit and has a great sense of humor. All of his characteristics allow him to come up with new fighting strategies to beat Master Xandred's evil Nighlok. He is a valuable part of the team.

Mike's element is the forest and his Zord is the Bear.

Weapon:
Spin Sword, Forest Spear

Signature Move:
Forest Vortex!

Element:
Forest

Zord:
Bear

Notes:
Mike has a reputation for being creative in battle.

THE YELLOW RANGER (EMILY)

Youngest of the Rangers, Emily is the Yellow Ranger. She is a sweet and kind person who was raised in the country side.

It was actually her sister who was originally to become the Yellow Ranger prior to falling ill. Emily stepped up to the challenge and took her sister's spot on the team. She is determined to make her sister proud and trains harder because of that. She is very musical, and her silliness is infectious. Her wide-eyed optimism often helps the team stay positive when it seems that all the odds are against them.

Emily's element is Earth and her Zord is the Ape.

Weapon:
Spin Sword/Earth Slicer

Signature Move:
Seismic Swing!

Element:
Earth

Zord:
Ape

Notes:
Emily is especially close to Mike the Green Ranger and Mia the Pink Ranger.

THE GOLD RANGER (ANTONIO)

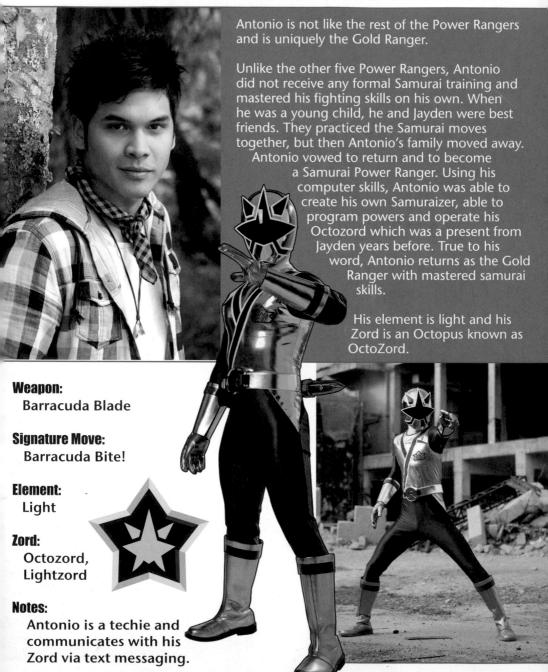

Antonio is not like the rest of the Power Rangers and is uniquely the Gold Ranger.

Unlike the other five Power Rangers, Antonio did not receive any formal Samurai training and mastered his fighting skills on his own. When he was a young child, he and Jayden were best friends. They practiced the Samurai moves together, but then Antonio's family moved away. Antonio vowed to return and to become a Samurai Power Ranger. Using his computer skills, Antonio was able to create his own Samuraizer, able to program powers and operate his Octozord which was a present from Jayden years before. True to his word, Antonio returns as the Gold Ranger with mastered samurai skills.

His element is light and his Zord is an Octopus known as OctoZord.

Weapon:
Barracuda Blade

Signature Move:
Barracuda Bite!

Element:
Light

Zord:
Octozord,
Lightzord

Notes:
Antonio is a techie and communicates with his Zord via text messaging.

MASTER XANDRED

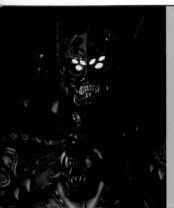

Master Xandred is the leader of the Nighlok Monsters who inhabit the Netherworld.

Jayden's Father, the previous Red Ranger, shattered Master Xandred into a million pieces, vanishing him to the Netherworld forever. Recently Master Xandred awoke and began a reign of terror in an attempt to return to our world. With his trusty advisor, Master Xandred has sent Nighlok to Earth in an attempt to make the humans cry as their tears help raise the Sanzu River. Once the river is high enough, Master Xandred can escape the Netherworld and rule the Earth.

OCTOROO

Octoroo is Master Xandred's trusted advisor. He counsels Master Xandred about the Netherworld and the Nighlok that live there. Often he offers up new plans and tactics to defeat the Rangers. Octoroo is an Octopus-like creature and at times cannot be trusted.

DAYU

Dayu has not always been half human and half Nighlok. She once was a new bride, but she traded her human life centuries ago in an effort to save her husband as a powerful Nighlok promised to spare her husband if she would go with him. The only possession she was allowed to take with her was her guitar which became the "Harmonium." Master Xandred keeps her near because her music soothes him.

ISN'T THAT **WILD**, JAYDEN?

THE BAND'S DEDICATING A SONG TO US AND THEY DON'T EVEN KNOW WE'RE HERE!

SURE, MIA. IT'S NICE.

CLAP CLAP

OR DID YOU WANT TO **FORGET** ABOUT BEING A RANGER FOR ONE NIGHT?

HA! WE'RE **ALWAYS** RANGERS, EMILY.

BESIDES, HE'S TRAINED **ALL** HIS LIFE TO BE A RANGER!

WHAT **ELSE** COULD JAYDEN BE?

WELL, IT MIGHT BE NICE TO LEAD A MORE NORMAL LIFE FOR A CHANGE. LIKE MAYBE AS A...

ROCK STAR!

THE REASON THE RANGERS MUST ALWAYS BE READY LIES IN A PARALLEL DIMENSION, KNOWN AS THE NETHERWORLD.
THERE ON THE SANZU, A RIVER OF MISERY AND SUFFERING, SITS A HORRID SHIP OF ILL INTENT.
HAPPINESS! I HATE IT! IT GIVES ME SUCH A HEADACHE!

AND SO, BACK AT THE CONCERT...

A SMALL *GAP* IN THE WORLD FORMS.

IT'S UNSEEN AT FIRST...

UNTIL IT GROWS....

...*TOO* LARGE TO IGNORE!

AIEEE!

BUT OBLIVITOR HAS AN **UNWELCOME** STOWAWAY!

No matter! On to the mission at hand!

WHAT? A FURRYWORT?

I WON'T HAVE SOME HAIRY **BUMP** REPEATING ALL I SAY!

All I say!

TOP IT! TOP IT NOW!

It now!

SHUT-UP **IMMEDIATELY**, I SAY!

...immediately, I say!

ARGHHHHHH!

MEANWHILE, BACK AT THE SHIBA HOUSE, THE HOME AND HEADQUARTERS OF THE RANGERS, MASTER JI'S MEDITATION IS RUDELY DISTURBED...

THE SENSOR! IT CAN ONLY MEAN ONE THING...

A *NIGHLOK* HAS ENTERED OUR WORLD!

IT'S RIGHT IN THE PARK WHERE THE RANGERS ARE ATTENDING THAT LOUD CONCERT.

GOOD LUCK FOR US, OR IS IT PART OF SOME PLAN?

I HAVE TO WARN THEM TO BE READY FOR AN ATTACK!

IT'S MASTER JI!

BEEP BEEP BEEP

BUT BEFORE JAYDEN CAN ANSWER...

20

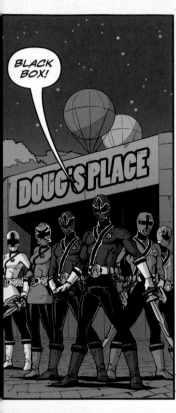

"MAYBE I CAN HELP REMIND YOU, BY EXPLAINING WHO WE ARE AND HOW WE GOT HERE.

"IF YOU DON'T REMEMBER ANYTHING, I SHOULD START AT THE VERY *BEGINNING*!

"CENTURIES AGO, IN JAPAN, NIGHLOK MONSTERS INVADED OUR WORLD.

"BUT SAMURAI WARRIORS DEFEATED THEM USING POWERS PASSED DOWN FROM PARENT TO CHILD!

"AND THEN--

JAYDEN, MAN, GET WITH IT! YOU AND I WERE **BEST BUDDIES** WHEN WE WERE KIDS!

YOU WERE RAISED YOUR ENTIRE **LIFE** AS A SAMURAI!

I WAS? WHAT ABOUT YOU?

ME? NAH. I HAD TO MOVE AWAY. BUT I SWORE I'D RETURN AND I DID!

I'VE NEVER FELT MORE GRATEFUL AND HONORED THAN FIGHTING AT YOUR SIDE!

GRRRRRRRRR!

USUALLY **YOU** GIVE THE ORDERS, BUT THIS TIME, JAYDEN, TRUST ME...

...DON'T MOVE!

KARONGGGGGGG

NICE! I BET THEY'RE HEARING MUSIC NOW!

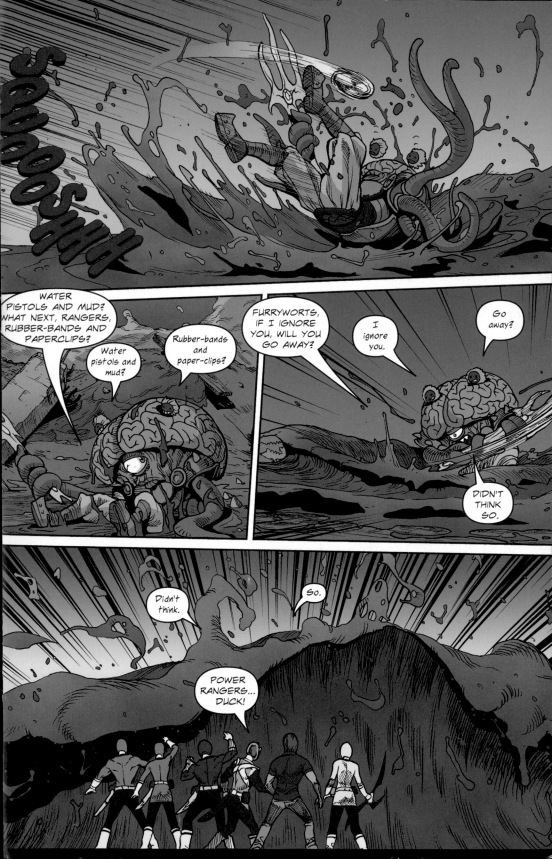

46

Plan to make!

Crowd forget!

THAT... SOUNDED FAMILIAR!

THIS IS SO EASY, I MAY AS WELL FORGET THE PLAN TO MAKE THE CROWD MISERABLE BY FORGETTING YOU AND MAKE THEM MISERABLE BY DESTROYING YOU!

I RE-MEMBER!

SAMURAIZER!

HIS MEMORY RESTORED...

THE RED RANGER RETURNS!

GO... GO. SAMURA

THE **BLACK BOX** ALLOWS A SINGLE RANGER TO CALL UPON THE POWERS OF THE SEVEN ANIMAL ZORDS.

CARE TO DO THE HONORS?

GOT IT!

AND SO, THE RED RANGER MORPHS INTO **SUPER SAMURAI** MODE!

AND NOW I'VE GOT A SUPER SPIN SWORD!

AFTER TAKING OUT THEIR FOLDINGZORDS, THE RANGERS USE THEIR SAMURAIZERS TO WRITE THE KANJI SYMBOL *LARGE!*

ALL SIX RANGERS MORPH INTO MEGA MODE...

AND ENTER THEIR MEGAZORD COCKPIT

ONCE INSIDE, JAYDEN ALSO WRITES THE KANJI SYMBOL *COMBINATION.*

ZORDS *COMBINE!*

IN A DAZZLING DISPLAY, THE FIVE ORIGINAL ZORDS, *APE*, *TURTLE*, *DRAGON*, *LION* AND *BEAR* COMBINE

INTO THE SAMURAI MEGAZORD!

AND THANKS TO THE BLACK BOX, THE GOLD RANGER'S CLAWZORD CAN NOW COMBINE, FORMING THE EVEN MIGHTIER...

CLAW ARMOR MEGAZORD...

OBLIVITOR IS **SHOCKED**, WHEN THE CLAW ARMOR MEGAZORD MAKES THE CATCH!

IT'S TOO **HEAVY!** CAN'T... MANAGE...

STEADY! WE CAN DO IT!

"IF WE JUST FOCUS AND WORK TOGETHER!"

I HAVE AN IDEA!

"WE'LL JUST PUT THE STAGE DOWN..."

"... ON THE *MOOGERS!*"

GRRRGGG

THINK YOU'RE SMART, RANGERS? ONE ZAP FROM MY RAY AND YOU WON'T REMEMBER HOW TO WORK YOUR PRECIOUS...

CLAW ARMOR MEGAZORD...

WHACK

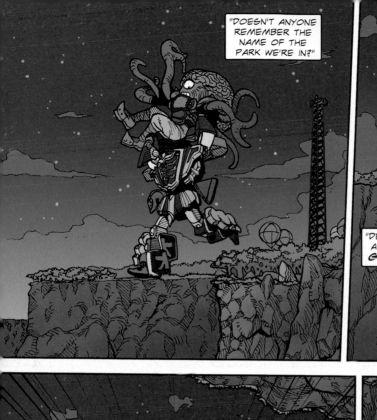

"DOESN'T ANYONE REMEMBER THE NAME OF THE PARK WE'RE IN?"

UH...

"DEEP GORGE PARK! AFTER THE *DEEP GORGE* BEHIND IT!"

OHHHHHHH....

FORGET IT.

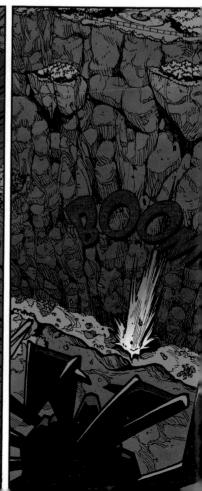

LOOKS LIKE THINGS ARE BACK TO **NORMAL!**

HEY, I REMEMBER MY NAME!

I REMEMBER YOUR NAME, TOO!

WELL, THINGS ARE **ALMOST** NORMAL!

BUT WHO'RE **THOSE** GUYS?

YEAH, I DON'T REMEMBER **THEM** AT ALL!

THIS IS TERRIBLE! NO ONE REMEMBERS THE NAME OF THE BAND GIVING THE CONCERT!

OH, **WE** DON'T MIND.

WE'LL JUST **WIN** THEM BACK WITH OUR MUSIC!

THE END

WATCH OUT FOR PAPERCUTZ™

Welcome to the pulse-pounding premiere of the SABAN'S POWER RANGERS SUPER SAMURAI graphic novel series from Papercutz. I'm Jim Salicrup, the Editor-in-Chief of Papercutz. Papercutz publisher Terry Nantier and I thought the time was right to bring the longest-running TV super-heroes to graphic novels, and fortunately our friends at Saban Brands agreed. To make sure this debut was worthy of the POWER RANGERS we went directly to our top-talents to find the very best writer and artist team—Stefan Petrucha and Paulo Henrique. Here's a brief biography of my ol' pal, Stefan Petrucha...

Born in the Bronx, Stefan Petrucha spent his formative years moving between the big city and the suburbs, both of which made him prefer escapism. A fan of comicbooks, science fiction and horror since learning to read, in high school and college he added a love for all sorts of literary work, eventually learning that the very best fiction always brings you back to reality, so, really, there's no way out.

An obsessive compulsion to create his own stories began at age ten and has since taken many forms, including novels, comics and video productions. At times, the need to pay the bills made him a tech writer, an educational writer, a public relations writer and an editor for trade journals, but fiction, in all its forms, has always been his passion. Every year he's made a living at that, he counts a lucky one. Fortunately, there've been many.

Over the years, I've been fortunate to have the very talented Mr. Petrucha write many comics that I edited; titles such as WEB OF SPIDER-MAN (at Marvel Comics), DUCKMAN, THE X-FILES (at Topps Comics), NANCY DREW, PAPERCUTZ SLICES, and THE THREE STOOGES (at Papercutz). But that's just the tip of the literary iceberg. Stefan's written many other comics, such as MICKEY MOUSE, META-4, SQUALOR, and many more, as well as such prose novels as Ripper (Pholomel), Dead Mann Walking (Ace Books), Blood Prophecy (Grand Central Publishing), Paranormal State: My Journey Into the Unknown (with Ryan Buell; Harper Collins), and many others. Despite knowing Stefan, and being familiar with his work since we were both kids back in the Bronx, he continues to surprise and delight me with every word he writes.

I'm sure there will be lots of surprises, as well as lots of exciting action, and a short biography of Paulo Henrique (who prefers to be known as "PH") in SABAN'S POWER RANGERS SUPER SAMURAI #2 "Terrible Toys" coming soon. Oh, and don't forget to tell us what you thought of this premiere Papercutz POWER RANGERS graphic novel by Papercutz! Send your comments to me at: Jim Salicrup, Papercutz, 160 Broadway, East Wing, New York, NY 10038 or email me at salicrup@papercutz.com. We know there are many loyal POWER RANGERS fans out there, and we'll be eagerly waiting to hear your feedback.

Until then, be sure to check out www.papercutz.com for all the latest news and information on the POWER RANGERS graphic novels, as well as the many other great graphic novels created for all-ages published by Papercutz. And remember, if Master Xandred, Octoroo, or Dayu happen to invite you to a party of any kind, simply say "no," and contact the POWER RANGERS immediately!

Thanks,

JIM

J GRA Petrucha Stefan
Petrucha, Stefan.
Saban's Power Rangers super
 samurai /
22960000561976 IJGF